VCs

OF THE FIRST WORLD WAR

THE FINAL
DAYS 1918

VCs

OF THE FIRST WORLD WAR

THE FINAL
DAYS 1918

GERALD GLIDDON

First published 2000
This edition 2014

The History Press
The Mill, Brimscombe Port
Stroud, Gloucestershire, GL5 2QG
www.thehistorypress.co.uk

British Library Cataloguing in Publication Data.
A catalogue record for this book is available from the British Library.

ISBN 978 0 7509 5368 9

Typesetting and origination by The History Press
Printed in Great Britain

CONTENTS

ACKNOWLEDGEMENTS

I would like to thank the staff of the following institutions for their assistance during the research for this book: the Commonwealth War Graves Commission; the Imperial War Museums; the National Army Museum; and The National Archives. In addition, I would like to thank the archivists and curators of the many regimental museums and libraries who have replied to my requests for information.

Where recently taken photographs have been used, their owners have been acknowledged with the individual illustration.

As with my previous books in the *VCs of the First World War* series, Donald C. Jennings of Florida has been very kind in allowing me to reproduce many pictures of either graves or memorials which appear in this book.

Many of the maps used have been taken from regimental histories or from the *British Official History of the War: Military Operations in France and Belgium, 1914–1918*, edited by J.E. Edmonds, Macmillan/ HMSO, 1922–49.

Maurice Johnson once again spent many hours in The National Archives on my behalf, searching out and reading the appropriate War Diaries. Other individuals who have been of great help in many ways include Peter Batchelor, John Bolton, John Cameron, Jack Cavanagh, Colonel Terry Cave CBE, Barry Conway, D.G. Gage, Ray Grover, Peter Harris, Chris Matson, Dick Rayner and Steve Snelling. Other people who provided additional material but whose names are not mentioned here have been acknowledged in the list of sources at the end of the book.

PREFACE TO THE 2014 EDITION

The History Press have decided to re-issue the *VCs of the First World War* series in new editions and I have taken advantage of this decision by revising and updating the text of the current volume.

Since the initial research for this book was carried out fifteen years ago, there has been an increasing interest in and awareness of the stories and lives of the men who were awarded the nation's and the Commonwealth's highest military honour. Evidence of this can be found in the amount of new books being published on the subject: the reissuing of servicemen's records by The National Archives and the accessibility of other records of family history, which are now available via the magazine *Ancestry*, and from other sources. The Internet has also played a major part, although information received using this method should always be verified by cross-checking. Finally, the founding of the Victoria Cross Society in 2002 by Bran Best has encouraged further research and publication of informative articles on the holders of the Victoria Cross.

While this book was being prepared, the British government announced plans to mark the First World War centenary from 2014 to 2018. One of the ideas is directly linked with the commemoration of men who had won a Victoria Cross during the Great War. For men born in the United Kingdom, a special paving stone will be installed in the town or district most associated with them. It is hoped that those men born overseas will also be commemorated in an appropriate manner. Finally it is hoped that all 628 VC recipients will be named at Heroes Square at the national memorial Arboretum in Staffordshire.

Gerald Gliddon, 2014

INTRODUCTION

This book covers the final days of the war on the Western Front, from when the Allied Armies were poised to capture the Hindenburg Line to the Armistice on 11 November 1918. The last man to win the VC, covered in the previous volume *Road to Victory*, was Temporary Lieutenant (T/Lt) Donald Dean, 24–26 September, and the opening section of this book tells the stories of seven men who received their Vcs for the part they played in the Battle of the Canal du Nord. From then until 6 November, a period of just under six weeks, a further forty-nine VCs were won in the victorious Allied advance. The last period of the war became a sequence of battles to capture a series of river lines; as each one was captured by the Allied armies, the German Army fell back to the next one.

The Third Army, to the right of the First Army, began the Battle of the Canal du Nord on 27 September. At the beginning of the war the canal was still unfinished in places and the Canadian Army's plan was to make use of these dry sections, thus avoiding the hardest parts of the line. Obtaining permission, the Canadian commander, Lieutenant General (Lt Gen.) Sir Arthur Currie, planned to make a crossing on a narrow front to the south, and, once across, to fan out. This turned out to be a great success and, despite the enemy putting up a stiff resistance, the British Third and First Armies advanced 6 miles. This success prepared the ground for the eventual capture of Cambrai.

On 29 September the Fourth Army began the Battle of St Quentin, which ended three days later after the Canal du Nord and St Quentin Canal had been taken. The key part of the operation at the St Quentin Canal was the capture of a section between Bellicourt and

Vendhuille, where it went underground through a tunnel. A preliminary attempt failed, but was followed by a successful assault by the 46th (North Midland) Division. After storming the enemy defences at Bellenglise, the division's Staffordshire Brigade, protected by fog, crossed the canal by footbridges which the enemy had neglected to destroy. Having reached the far bank, the division, together with the 32nd Division, moved to the right and began to outflank the enemy and to take the rear German defences.

On 3 October the Fourth and Third Armies began the Battle of the Beaurevoir Line, a substantial enemy support system which was part of the *Siegfriedstellung* (Siegfried Line). The battle lasted for two days. On 8 October these two armies, together with the French First Army, began an attack south of Cambrai on a 17-mile front. On the following day Canadian patrols entered Cambrai to link up with troops from the Third Army. However, the enemy then made a stand on a line along the River Selle, close to Le Cateau, which lasted two days. On 10 October the Battle of Flanders began, and on 14 October the Battle of Courtrai, lasting for four days. The important town of Lille fell on 17 October, and on the same day the Belgian Army retook the port of Ostend.

To the south, on 17 October, the Fourth Army began the Battle of the Selle, with the target of the Sambre–Oise Canal as far as the prized town of Valenciennes. The battle began on a front of 10 miles to the south of Le Cateau, and the right of the Fourth Army reached the Sambre–Oise Canal after three days. To the north, the Third Army crossed the Selle on 20 October. On 23 October the British Fourth, Third and First Armies combined and advanced a further 6 miles. Overall, the battle lasted eight days. To the north, the Fifth and Second Armies were progressing towards the Scheldt line.

This Allied progress was not achieved without considerable cost; in October, after the fall of the Hindenburg Line, the British suffered 120,000 casualties. The German casualties were also considerable and, in addition, about a quarter of their army surrendered. On 1/2 November the First and Third Armies fought the Battle of Valenciennes, and on 4 November the Battle of the Sambre began. With the support of thirty-seven tanks, the British First, Third and Fourth Armies advanced on a 30-mile front from Valenciennes to the Sambre–Oise Canal, either side of the Forest of Mormal. Early on 11 November the Canadian Corps retook Mons, and after the signing of the Armistice at 11 a.m. the guns finally fell silent.

C.H. FRISBY

Canal du Nord, Near Graincourt,
France 27 September

No fewer than seven VCs were won on 27 September 1918 at the beginning of a four-day campaign to capture the Hindenburg Line with the crossing of the Canal du Nord. The success of the whole operation proved to be of great significance, enabling the Allied armies to make further rapid advances and directly leading to the Armistice six weeks later.

The Guards Division was to seize the high ground between Flesquières and Premy Chapel, half a mile to the west of the town of Marcoing. It was during this fighting that A/Capt. Cyril Frisby of the 1st Coldstream Guards won his VC near Graincourt, together with L. Cpl T.N. Jackson of the same battalion. The Coldstream Guards had No. 3 Company under 2nd Lt Lord Bingham on the right and No. 4 Company under Lt W.H. Gladstone on the left. No. 1 under Lt M.V. Buxton was in reserve and No. 2 under Capt. Frisby himself was in support. Once on the other side of the canal, Frisby's company was to form a defensive flank which would face northwards and also make contact with the 3rd Battalion Grenadier Guards and the 52nd (Lowland) Division.

Frisby's company was ready to move forward at 5 a.m. and, initially, the right column was successful, but in front of the left column an enemy position known as Mouse Post, armed with machine guns and sited in the bed of the dry canal, proved to be much stronger than anticipated. Mouse Post was well protected by iron girders, broken concrete and the debris left from the demolished bridge which carried the Demicourt–Graincourt road. It was earlier thought that these two posts had been deserted, but this proved to be false. In addition, the area was strewn with uncut barbed wire. Attempts by artillery to knock out Mouse Post had been unsuccessful. The story of what happened next was well described in Frisby's citation, gazetted on 27 November 1918:

> For conspicuous bravery, leadership and devotion to duty in action on 27 Sept. 1918, across the Canal Du Nord, near Graincourt, when in command of a company detailed to capture the canal crossing on the Demicourt–Graincourt road. On reaching the canal, the leading platoon came under annihilating machine-gun fire from a strong machine-gun post under the old iron bridge on the far side of the canal, and was unable to advance, despite reinforcing waves. Capt. Frisby realised at once that unless this post was captured the whole advance in this area would fail. Calling for volunteers to follow him, he dashed forward, and with three other ranks, he climbed down into the canal under an intense point-blank machine-gun fire, and succeeded in capturing the post with two machine-guns and twelve men. By his personal valour and initiative he restored the situation and enabled the attacking companies to continue the advance. Having reached and consolidated his objective, he gave timely support to the company on his right, which had lost all its officers and sergeants, organised its defences, and beat off a heavy hostile counter-attack. He was wounded in the leg by a bayonet in the attack on the machine-gun post, but remained at duty throughout, thereby setting a splendid example to all ranks.

On the Allied side of the canal, when about to try and cross the barbed wire and facing heavy machine-gun fire, Frisby called for volunteers, and initially three men put themselves forward to assist him to get through the wire and up the other side of the dry canal. One of these men was Thomas Jackson, whose VC was awarded posthumously. Later, and with the help of twelve more colleagues, they captured the two crucial machine-gun posts.

The 1st Battalion suffered a total of 151 casualties, including nine officers; after the action the survivors marched to billets in the Boursies area.

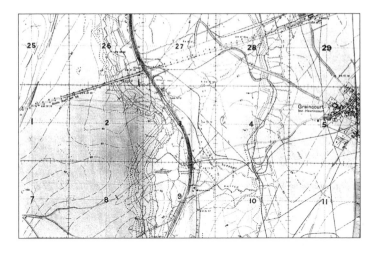

Captain Frisby was presented with his VC in the ballroom of Buckingham Palace on 29 March 1919, at the same investiture that L. Cpl Thomas Norman Jackson's family were presented with their son's award. Also present were Jackson's sister, his aunt, and fiancée Daisy Flatt from Kenley, Surrey. Mr Jackson asked an officer whether they might see Capt. Frisby, who he thought was the last person to see his son alive. The officer said that he would mention this request to the King. When the King was presenting Frisby with his VC, he mentioned to him that Jackson's family were present and that they would very much like to talk to him about their son.

Captain Frisby then conveyed the details of how their son had won his VC and had his photograph taken with the family, agreeing to travel later to Yorkshire in order to unveil a specially commissioned portrait of Jackson.

Cyril Hubert Frisby was the second son of Henry and Zoë Pauline Frisby of Icklesham, Sussex, and was born on 17 September 1885 in New Barnet, Hertfordshire. He was educated at Haileybury College and joined the Army on 26 October 1916 as a private in the Hampshire Regiment. In the following December he attended No. 5 Officer Cadet Battalion in Cambridge and was later given a commission in the

Coldstream Guards on 28 March 1917. Eight months later he was posted to the 1st Battalion in France on 27 November; he was promoted to acting captain on 20 February the following year, and substantive lieutenant on 28 September after winning his VC.

After the war, Frisby relinquished the rank of acting captain on 7 March 1919, and, on 20 April, he resigned his commission and was given the honorary rank of captain.

In 1911 Frisby had married Audrey, daughter of John and Lucy Ogilvie-Grant, at St Andrew's Church, Wells Street, London, W2. The couple had one son, Henry Julian Fellowes, who was born on 20 May 1913. Frisby attended the Royal Garden Party for holders of the VC on 26 June 1920, and in the same year attended the Armistice Day Ceremony at the Cenotaph. In November 1929 he attended the House of Lords Dinner given by the Prince of Wales.

Frisby was one of six winners of the VC in the First World War who are commemorated on a special memorial on the terrace at Haileybury College, and their citations are displayed in the college library. Between the wars he was a prominent member of the British Legion and was made vice-president of the Stoughton and Westborough Branch, before being elected president in March 1940. In 1946 he attended the Victory Parade in London on 8 June.

In 1949 Frisby's father died and left his younger son nothing but six Jubilee Silver cups in his will, as he was already considered to be well provided for. Frisby was certainly comfortably off and was a member of the Stock Exchange. He was keen on sports and, at one time, played rugby for Surrey. He was also a member of the Guards' Club and was a keen golfer, being a member of the Rye and Worplesdon Clubs. In addition, he was a leading British tunny fisherman and, in 1938, off the coast of Scarborough, he made a record-breaking catch, weighing 1¼ tons, using only a rod. He was also a member of the Commonwealth team in international tunny cup matches.

In the 1950s Frisby lived in a house called Glenwoods in Guildford, considered to be one of the best residential properties in the town. It has since been converted into two houses and is set well back from the road, sheltered by trees. In 1956 Frisby took part in the Hyde Park VC Centenary Review and, in 1960, he attended a dinner held by the Victoria Cross and George Cross Association at the Café Royal.

Frisby's wife, Audrey, died on 30 September 1960, and nearly a year later he died at home in Guildford, a week before his seventy-sixth birthday on 10 September 1961. He was buried in Brookwood Cemetery, Reference 220173, St Chad's Avenue, Plot 28, Grave 219662. Audrey was later buried with him. On 27 September a memorial service was held at St Michael-upon- Cornhill, a church which emphasised his links with the City of London. Apart from members of his own family, those who attended included fellow members of the Stock Exchange and representatives of City business houses, as well as members of staff from the Frisby Brothers family firm.

Frisby's brother, Captain (Acting Lieutenant Colonel) Lionel Frisby, who served in the war with the 6th Welsh Regiment and won the Distinguished Service Order (DSO), also worked in the Stock Exchange as a jobber and the two were nicknamed 'The Cowards'.

In addition to his VC, Frisby's decorations included the BWM (British War medal), VM (Victory Medal) with Oak leaf, Defence Medal 1939–45, and Coronation medals for 1937 and 1953. These medals were presented to the Coldsteam Guard's Museum by his son, Julian Frisby, on 4 June 1986. Together with Thomas Jackson's the medals are part of the Regimental Collection at the Coldstream Guards HQ in Wellington Barracks.

VISCOUNT GORT

Canal du Nord, Near Flesquières,
France, 27 September

Acting Lieutenant Colonel Viscount Gort was commanding the 1st Grenadier Guards, the leading battalion of the 3rd Guards Brigade, when he won his VC on 27 September 1918. He was to be one of seven soldiers, three of whom were Guardsmen, to win this honour during the assault on the Hindenburg Line. This part of the action took place during the attack on the section of the heavily fortified line in the advance across the Canal du Nord, near Flesquières. It was dark when the battalion began its march in the small hours of 27 September, led by Gort, accompanied by his adjutant. On reaching the Cambrai–Bapaume road, the Guardsmen paused and waited for zero hour, which was 5.20 a.m., at which time the battalion set off across open country towards the village of Flesquières. The first village they passed through was Demicourt and, until they turned towards the Canal du Nord, they were not troubled by German guns. However, as they drew nearer to the canal, shells rapidly began to fall.

In the attempts to cross the dry canal bed, short ladders were set up against the banks and a crossing effected 100yd to the north of Lock Seven. By this stage casualties had been quite light. Gort left the lock in order to confer with the commander in charge of the supporting tanks, but could find no trace of him. As the battalion was to be in Flesquières by 9.20 a.m., Gort decided to push on with the advance without the promised tank support. Although the ground was very

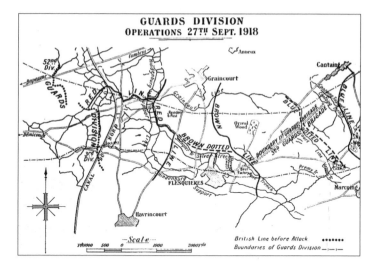

open, Gort, by skillful leadership, managed to make progress without his men suffering too many casualties. However, as they drew close to Flesquières, they quickly realised that the village of Graincourt, to their left rear, was still in German hands. Orival Wood to the north-east of Flesquières should also have been taken, but it hadn't. In addition, two German batteries were still in action in the areas of Beet Trench and at Beetroot Factory, to the north-east of Flesquières. These positions were strongly held and defended by infantry and machine guns.

In order to keep casualties to a minimum, Gort took his men through the northern part of the village, which gave them some protection from the enemy machine guns to the north. At this point, when Gort was trying to establish the exact positions of the enemy, he was slightly wounded above the left eye. The Beetroot Factory was soon captured and its garrison surrendered. Gort's objective was now Premy Chapel Hill to the north of the village of Marcoing. The way towards it was getting easier, although it seemed that neither of Gort's flanks was in British hands. At this point he suddenly saw a tank, which appeared to be some distance from its command. He ran across the open ground to the tank, seemingly oblivious of the enemy. Somehow he escaped being hit and, clambering on to the tank, he shouted instructions to the crew. Seeing the tank rumbling in their direction, the enemy took fright and many of them flung away their weapons before running off. Gort was then hit a second time, being wounded severely in the arm. After losing a lot of blood he had to take to a stretcher, but that did not stop him from issuing instructions. His orderly, Ransom, bound his wounds and, once more, Gort was up and directing the battle. However, he was forced to hand over command after collapsing on reaching Beet Trench and was ordered to leave the field. Some 200 Germans were driven into the sunken road and forced to surrender. Two batteries of field howitzers and six machine guns were also captured. Then enemy artillery began to shell the area of Beet Trench, though the Guardsmen still managed to reach the outskirts of Premy. The success of the Guards' advance was put down to the extraordinary courage and determination of Gort, and his VC was gazetted on 27 November 1918 as follows:

For most conspicuous bravery, skillful leading and devotion to duty during the attack of the Guards Division on 27 Sept. 1918, across the Canal Du Nord, near Flesquières, when in command of the 1st Bn. Grenadier Guards, the leading battalion of the 3rd Guards Brigade. Under heavy artillery and machine-gun fire he led his battalion with great skill and determination to the 'forming-up' ground, where very severe fire from artillery and machine-guns was again encountered. Although wounded, he quickly grasped the situation, directed a platoon to proceed down a sunken road to make a flanking attack, and, under terrific fire, went across open ground to obtain the assistance of a Tank, which he personally led and directed to the best possible advantage. While thus fearlessly exposing himself, he was again severely wounded by a shell. Not withstanding considerable loss of blood, after lying on a stretcher for a while, he insisted on getting up and personally directing the further attack. By his magnificent example of devotion to duty and utter disregard of personal safety, all ranks were inspired to exert themselves to the utmost, and the attack resulted in the capture of over 200 prisoners, two batteries of field guns and numerous machine-guns. Lieut.-Colonel Viscount Gort then proceeded to organise the defence of the captured position until he collapsed; even then he refused to leave the field until he had seen 'the success signal' go up on the final objective. The successful advance of the battalion was mainly due to the valour, devotion and leadership of this very gallant officer.

He received his decoration from the King at an investiture in the ballroom of Buckingham Palace on 13 December 1918.

John Standish Surtees Prendergast Vereker (known as Jack), who later became the 6th Viscount Gort and Baron Kiltarton, was born on 10 July 1886 at 1 Portman Square, London. He was the eldest son of the Anglo-Irish 5th Viscount Gort and his wife, Eleanor, who was the daughter of the writer R.S. Surtees. He grew up in County Durham in the main family home at East Cowes Castle and its beautifully wooded grounds. Queen Victoria used to be a regular visitor to the family when calling on his mother. Gort attended Malvern Link Preparatory School before moving to Harrow School. It was while a student there in 1902 that his father died and he succeeded to the Irish title; the family motto was 'Truth conquers'. In 1908 his mother, the Dowager Lady Gort, married Colonel S.M. Benson. Gort is a county town in western Ireland.

From Harrow, Gort passed into Sandhurst, beginning his Army career by entering the Royal Military Academy (RMA), Woolwich in January 1904. After leaving as an ensign, he became a second lieutenant in the Grenadier Guards on 16 August 1905, then a full lieutenant on 1 April 1907. He spent much recreation time in horse riding. In 1911 he took an active role in the funeral arrangements for King Edward VII. On 23 February of the same year, he married a third cousin, Corinna Katherine Vereker, daughter of Capt. George Medlicott Vereker. The ceremony took place in the Guards' Chapel. Later the couple had two sons: Charles, born on 23 February 1912, and Jocelyn, born on 27 July 1913. Sadly, the latter only lived twenty months. A daughter, Jacqueline, was born on 20 October 1914. Gort was created a Member of the Royal Victorian Order (MVO) in 1910. He was made Aide-de-Camp (ADC) to the General Officer Commanding (GOC), London District, from 3 September 1913 to 4 August 1914, and immediately afterwards was promoted to captain.

At the outbreak of war, Gort was ADC to the GOC, 2nd Division, Major General (Maj. Gen.) C.C. Monro, and was in France as early as mid-August, in time for the retreat from Mons and the advance to the Aisne. On 30 August he had been badly wounded in the groin. When Monro was promoted to GOC 1 Corps on 26 December 1914, Gort went with him as ADC. On 22 February 1915 he was on the staff as General Staff Officer (Grade 3) (GSO 3) at 1 Corps and, at the end of March, was appointed brigade major, 4th (Guards) Brigade, 2nd Division. On 18 May the brigade took part in the attacks against Festubert, but the action was later called off.

Gort still had his post as brigade major when the Guards Division was formed in August 1915 and the 4th Guards Brigade was renumbered as the 1st. He was awarded the Military Cross (MC), which was gazetted on 23 June 1915. In August, when the Guards Division was set up, he went with the 1st Guards Brigade to prepare for the Battle of Loos under Maj. Gen. the Earl of Cavan. Gort was made brevet major in June 1916 and, on 30 June was appointed GSO 2 (Ops) General Headquarters (GHQ). In early 1917 he was involved in planning a landing on the Belgian coast, but this was subsequently cancelled. In April 1917, probably to his relief, he returned to regimental duty as acting lieutenant colonel in command of the 4th Grenadier Guards. The unit's first task was to assist in building a railway line over ground destroyed by the enemy in their retreat to the Hindenburg Line in the spring.

In the June 1917 Birthday Honours he was awarded the DSO for earlier staff work and, on 26 September, was awarded a bar to his DSO for gallantry at the Battle of Pilkem Ridge on 31 July, during which he was wounded in the arm. The details were published in the *London Gazette* on 9 January 1918 as follows:

For conspicuous gallantry and devotion to duty. Although hit in two places in the shoulder by the bursting of a shell early in the day, and in great pain, he refused to leave his battalion, and personally superintended the consolidation subsequent to a successful attack. He remained with them until 5 p.m. on the following day, when he was ordered to come out and have his wounds dressed. His conduct set a very fine example of self-sacrifice, and was of great value in maintaining the high morale and offensive spirit of his battalion.

By October 1917 Gort was back with his battalion during the Battle of Passchendaele, until again being wounded during the attack on Gonnelieu (Battle of Cambrai) on 1 December 1917. He later returned to duty and remained until the action that won him the VC. On 8 March 1918 Gort was given a great honour when appointed to be commanding officer of the 1st Grenadier Guards, the oldest Regular infantry battalion. In the German Spring Offensive, his regiment became part of the British Third Army and helped to repel enemy attacks in the Arras sector. In August the Grenadiers were sent southwards to join General Rawlinson's Fourth Army in the battle for Amiens and helped it to push the enemy back to the Hindenburg Line. It is for his role on this occasion that he was awarded a second bar to his DSO and the citation was published in the *London Gazette* on 11 January 1919 as follows:

> For conspicuous gallantry and devotion to duty in command of his battalion he led his men up by night to relieve a battalion which had attacked and failed to reach its objective. Regardless of danger he personally reconnoitered the line ahead of his troops, and got them onto the objective before dawn. During the three following days he again made forward reconnaissances, and leading his battalion gradually on, advanced the line 800 yards and gained a canal bank. It is impossible to speak too highly of this officer's initiative.

After the war, during which Gort was Mentioned in Despatches (MiD) no fewer than eight times, as well as being wounded several times, Gort spoke warmly of his former orderly, Private (Pte) Ransom. Speaking during a smoking concert that took place near his home at East Cowes in May 1919, he paid a glowing tribute to Ransom, who was with him during the Canal du Nord crossing and was subsequently killed. Soon after the war, Gort attended the first post-war Staff Course at Camberley, and was chief instructor at the Senior Officers' School in Sheerness.

In 1925 a whiff of scandal attached itself to Gort after he divorced his wife; the judge granted a *decree nisi* with custody of the children, who were then aged 13 and 11. The grounds for the divorce proceedings were his wife's relationship with a member of the

Spanish Embassy staff in London, Luis de Silva. The pair had met during a visit to Spain and, on her return, the official had made many visits to the Gort family home, details of which were later found in a diary kept by Lady Gort. During the proceedings the Gort marriage was described as being fairly happy. They had various homes, the most recent being in Belgrave Square. During the war Lady Gort had run a millinery business in Grosvenor Street, and any profit had been given to the Red Cross.

On 16 October 1926 Gort took an active part in the unveiling of the Guards Memorial by the Duke of Connaught in Horse Guards, London. Gort led the Grenadier Guards section during the parade, and six other winners of the VC took part. During the proceedings the Duke of Connaught was assisted by General (Gen.) Sir George Higginson, who was then 100 years old. In the late 1920s Gort was GSO 1 at Colchester and lived at 1 Ypres Road, Reed Hall. On occasions he took part in public functions that were held in the town. At the end of 1929 he left the garrison town to take over command of the Grenadier Guards. He served in China and, later, India as Director of Military Training between 1932 and 1936.

In 1934, 75 acres of the East Cowes Estate were put up for sale, including the castellated mansion and lodges, the park and farm, together with five detached houses. As war clouds gathered once again in Europe during the late 1930s, Gort was made a major general in 1935 and, in the following year, he returned to Camberley as commandant. In September 1937 he went to the War Office as Military Secretary to the Secretary of State for War for three months. At the end of the year he was appointed Chief of the Imperial General Staff (CIGS) by Hore-Belisha, Secretary for War: a decision which was greeted with considerable surprise, as Gort had leapfrogged ninety more senior officers in his promotion. A few days after this he was made a full general.

War broke out on 3 September 1939, and Gen. Sir W.E. Ironside took over as CIGS when Gort was appointed commander-in-chief (C-in-C) of the British Expeditionary Force (BEF) on 4 September. During what turned out to be a short period in northern France, he received several important visitors, including the King and Winston Churchill in his role of First Lord of the Admiralty. In 1940, at a special ceremony close to Gort's HQ in a French château,

Gort, together with Gen. Ironside (CIGS), was presented with the *Légion d'Honneur* by Gen. Gamelin, C-in-C of the Allied Forces in the field. In the German invasion of France during May 1940, Gort had to make the momentous decision whether the British should stay and fight with the French or fall back on Dunkirk. Eventually, when Germany had let the British Army 'off the hook', the great evacuation of Dunkirk was organised with considerable help from the Royal and Merchant navies, along with a fleet of 'little ships'. Aerial protection from the Royal Air Force (RAF) was not too much in evidence. Gort returned home with his defeated troops and the *Sunday Times* on 2 June 1940 described the situation in France in the following words:

> From the beginning of the German offensive in the West until now the British Army in France has had an incredibly difficult and thankless part to play, and has played it to perfection. It has had to execute first a rapid advance, accompanied with a precision and a degree of immunity to loss that testified abundantly to the organisation of the force, and then a series of strategic withdrawals imposed upon it, not by any reverses on its own front, but by events elsewhere ... In spite of all a succession of rearward and wheeling movements, some of them, as after King Leopold's surrender, exacted at the shortest notice and demanding an equally sudden switch of communications, was so conducted as to maintain the B.E.F. to the last almost intact in power and cohesion as a fighting body. No commander could have brought off such an achievement without troops of the highest training and discipline and, above all, of superb fighting spirit ...

On reaching London, Gort went straight to the War Office on 3 July, where he spoke to Gen. Sir John Dill, who had taken over from Ironside as CIGS, a position which at that time in the war could be compared with a game of musical chairs. After that, Gort met Anthony Eden, now the Secretary for War.

To what extent Gort was responsible for the defeat of the BEF cannot be discussed in great detail here, but it is obviously clear that he *was* blamed and his Army career never recovered from what was considered at the time to be a major military defeat. From that point until his premature death in the early months of peace, Gort was finished.

With no wife to turn to in his time of trouble, he must have become an exceedingly lonely and disillusioned man.

However, 'the show must go on' and he was given various positions, none of which was any more than a diversion for an active and very much 'hands on' general. His first post after Dunkirk was Inspector-General to the Forces for Training and Inspector-General Home Guard, 1940–1. Despite his disappointment at being given this non-active job, Gort still had some important work to do, but one feels that the jobs could have been carried out easily by less qualified men. In October 1942 Gort's Despatches were released, in which he summarised the main causes of the defeat: 'Failure of Allied support on either flank. A "Weygand Plan" based on thin air; insufficient equipment; and inadequate reserves … '.

Between 1940 and 1944 Gort was ADC General to the King. Between 1941 and 1942 he was made C-in-C, Gibraltar, and was Governor and C-in-C, Malta, from 1942 to 1944. While in Malta he suffered burns during an air raid in January 1943 when a drum of petrol burst at his feet. In the 1943 New Year Honours list Gort was made a field marshal, together with Sir Archibald Wavell. After Malta Gort was appointed High Commissioner and C-in-C, Palestine, and later High Commissioner for Trans-Jordan from 1944 until 1945. He left his position as High Commissioner in Palestine at the end of 1945 when he became unwell. He was seriously ill for five months before dying of inoperable cancer on 31 March 1946 in Guy's Hospital, London. During his stay in hospital the King conferred on him a British viscountancy and he became Viscount Gort of Hamsterly in the County of Durham. He was buried in the family vault of St John the Baptist Church, Penshurst, Kent. Penshurst Place became the home of his son-in-law, Maj. W.P. Sidney, Lord De L'Isle, who also won a VC, at Anzio in 1944.

Gort's recreational interests included hunting and sailing, as well as flying his own aeroplane. Tragically, his son and heir, the Hon. Charles Standish Vereker, a second lieutenant in the Grenadier Guards, died in 1941 after suffering concussion in an accident. Therefore, on Gort's death the title was inherited by his brother.

Gort was a very highly decorated soldier and his decorations and honours are in private hands. In addition to the VC, DSO and two bars, and MC, he was made a Knight Grand Cross, Order of the Bath (GCB), Commander, Order of the British Empire (CBE), Knight of Justice, Order of St John of Jerusalem (KStJ), and Member of the Royal Victorian Order (MVO).

For service in the First World War he was also presented with a 1914 Star & Clasp '5 Aug–22 Nov 1914', BWM (1914–20) and VM (1914–19, plus Mentioned in Despatches. His other decorations included the 1939–45 Star, Africa Star, Defence Medal (1939–45), War Medal (1939–45), General Service Medal (1918–62) with one clasp, 'Palestine 1945–48', King George V Coronation Medal (1911), King George V Silver Jubilee Medal (1935), King George VI Coronation Medal (1937), and French Grand Cross of the *Légion d'Honneur*.

He was later commemorated with a plaque in St Paul's Cathedral and in the King's Chapel, Gibraltar, where a new north chancel window was installed in 1952, which showed the arms of many of the Rock's governors, including Monro and Gort. He is also remembered in the Garrison Church, Portsea.

In 1954, when the *British Official History of the War in France and Flanders, 1939–1940* was published, Gort was described as not 'an intellectual man nor had he the mind of an administrator; by temperament and training he was a fighting soldier'. It was hardly fair to blame him for the defeat of the BEF in May 1940, as a result of facing superior German forces, but for Gort it was his last fighting command in the field. The stigma of being associated with this 'defeat' altered the shape of the rest of his career, and probably shortened his life by several years.

S.L. HONEY

Bourlon Wood, France, 27 September

Three members of the Canadian Army won VCs during the capture of Bourlon Wood on 27 September 1918. The wood was a vital part of the strongly defended German Hindenburg Line and, in the past, had proved a major stumbling block for the Allies. General Currie, the Canadian Army Corps Commander, planned to carry out the tasks allotted to him in two parts. First would come the crossing of the Canal du Nord and the capture of Bourlon Wood, together with the high ground close to the Arras–Cambrai road; then, in the second part of the action, the Canadian Corps would capture the bridges over the Canal de l'Escaut, to the north-east of the German-held town of Cambrai. This would lead to a firm line being established as far as the Canal de la Sensée.

Zero hour on 27 September was 5.20 a.m., and the Allied armies opened a heavy barrage against the enemy positions. To the right of the line, the 10th Canadian Brigade quickly crossed the canal, meeting little opposition; but the 11th and 12th Brigades, who were leading the 4th Division on the right and left respectively, soon met trouble from the south of their position. In tough fighting the 87th Canadian Battalion reached the southern part of Bourlon village by 9.45 a.m., and the 54th Battalion, passing through, then went around the north of the wood in order to reach the far side. The relative slowness of the British attack to the south led to the plan for encircling the wood being abandoned. The 54th Battalion then found itself in a salient, but did manage to reach the village of Fontaine-Notre-Dame to the east of Bourlon Wood. The 75th and 87th Battalions came up on their left. To the north, the 12th Brigade fought all day, and their 85th and 38th Battalions were severely hit in their attempts to capture part of the Marquion trench system. However, their work allowed the 78th and 72nd Battalions to reach most of their objectives, with the final resistance in the wood overcome by 8.00 p.m. The day had turned out to be a complete triumph for the Canadian Corps and a disaster for the German 188th Infantry Regiment, who lost very heavily. Lieutenant Samuel Honey, of the 78th Battalion, performed outstandingly. He was heavily involved in clearing German strongpoints, leading to the eventual capture of Bourlon Wood, and was awarded the VC, gazetted in the *London Gazette* on 6 January 1919 as follows:

On 27 Sept., when his company commander and all other officers of his company became casualties, Lieut. Honey took command and skillfully reorganised under most severe enemy shelling and machine-gun fire. He continued the advance with great dash and gained the objective, but finding his company was suffering casualties from enfilade machine-gun fire, he made a personal reconnaissance and, locating the machine-gun nest, he rushed it single-handed, capturing the guns and ten prisoners. Having organised his position, he repelled four enemy counter-attacks, and when darkness fell he again went out himself alone, and having located an enemy post, he led out a party and captured the post of three guns by stealth. He immediately advanced his line, and his new position proved of great value in the jump off the following morning. On 29 Sept., he led his company against a strong enemy position with great initiative and daring, and continued on the succeeding days of the battle to display the same wonderful example of leadership and bravery.

Sadly, Honey died on 30 September of wounds received during the last stages of the attack by his battalion, and was buried at Quéant Communal Cemetery, British Extension, Row C, Grave 36. The cemetery is quite some distance from where he fell and is 12 miles south-east of Arras, roughly midway between the Arras–Cambrai

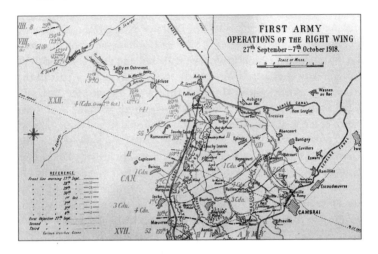

and Bapaume–Cambrai main roads. His posthumous VC was sent by the War Office to Canada, then by post from the Governor General on 27 March 1919 to his father. No presentation ceremony took place.

Samuel Lewis Honey was the son of the Reverend George H. and Metta Honey (née Blaisdell), who came from Boston, Massachusetts, USA. Samuel was born on 9 February 1894 at Conn, near Mount Forest, Wellington County, Ontario. His father was a Methodist Minister of the Hamilton Conference, a calling which involved the family in continuous moves, reflected by the number of schools and colleges the boy attended. He went to the Continuation Schools of Drayton and Princeton, then he attended Normal School in London, Ontario, and when only 17 years of age he obtained a teaching permit and taught at the Six Nations Indian Reserve, near Brantford, Ontario, after which he taught in Huron County. He then continued his education at Walkerton High School, where he won a scholarship and passed the Honour Matriculation examinations with first-class honours in English and French, and second-class honours in Latin and German. After his graduation in June 1914 he resumed teaching in York County.

Honey planned to enrol at Victoria College, but the outbreak of war intervened and, a few months later, he joined the Army on 22 January 1915 as a private in the 34th (Ontario) Battalion. He left Canada for Britain as a sergeant in October and, in the same year, he was appointed an instructor in physical training and bayonet fighting, having taken a course at Aldershot. In August 1916 he left for France with the 78th Battalion of the 4th Division, and won a Military Medal (MM) in a trench raid on 10 January 1917 (*London Gazette*, 26 April 1917).

He later earned a Distinguished Conduct Medal (DCM) for his deeds in the 1917 Arras battles at Vimy Ridge (*London Gazette*, 16 August 1917):

... when his platoon commander was wounded he assumed command, leading his men forward in the face of terrific fire, until compelled by casualties to dig in. He held the position for three days, encouraging his men by splendid example.

Honey was subsequently recommended for a commission in the 78th Battalion, Manitoba Regiment at about the same time (9 April) he returned to England for officer training. Afterwrads he rejoined his battalion in France in October, where he was soon promoted to lieutenant.

Nearly fifty years after the war began, on 26 July 1964, a plaque commemorating Honey's life was unveiled by his sister beside the Westcott United Church, Conn. The plaque was one of several to be erected in the province by the Department of Tourism and Information. The ceremony, attended by several local dignitaries, was sponsored by the Mount Forest Branch (134) of the Royal Canadian Legion, and the township of West Luther. The inscription on the plaque is virtually a retelling of the original VC citation. A similar plaque is to be found in Valour Place, Cambridge, Ontario, and in the Galt Armoury. Honey was survived by two brothers, George B. Honey and C.S. Honey, who lived in Fort Erie. His decorations which, apart from the VC and DCM, included the MM, BWM and VM are in the collection of the Canadian War Museum.

If one visits Bourlon Wood today, it becomes very clear how important it would have been to hold on to, as it is on high ground and offers a spectacular view over a wide area. A section of the wood, which still contains many trench lines, was later presented to the

Canadian people as a memorial to their fighting troops for their efforts in September 1918. A Canadian memorial, similar to the one at Maple Copse, is in the centre and the local villagers use the wood as a recreational park. A more recent commemorative gesture is to be found close by, in the form of a memorial to local members of the Free French who were killed by the Gestapo in June 1944.

T.N. JACKSON
*Near Graincourt, France,
27 September*

On 27 September, No. 31034 Pte (L. Cpl) Thomas Jackson of the 1st Coldstream Guards worked closely with Captain Frisby of the same battalion in the attack against the German defences close to the Canal du Nord on the Demicourt–Graincourt bridge between Locks Six and Seven. The two men each won a Victoria Cross, but sadly Jackson's was to be a posthumous award. Gazetted on 27 November 1918, the same day as Frisby's, it read as follows:

For most conspicuous bravery and self-sacrifice in the attack across the Canal Du Nord, near Graincourt. On the morning of the 27th Sept. 1918 L.-Corpl. Jackson was the first to volunteer to follow Capt. C.H. Frisby, Coldstream Guards, across the Canal Du Nord in his rush against an enemy machine-gun post. With two comrades he followed his officer across the canal, rushed the post, captured the two machine-guns, and so enabled the companies to advance. Later in the morning, L.-Corpl. Jackson was the first to jump into a German trench which his platoon had to clear, and after doing further excellent work he was unfortunately killed. Throughout the whole day until he was killed this young N.C.O. showed the greatest valour and devotion to duty, and set an inspiring example to all.

Jackson was buried 7 miles west of Cambrai in Plot II, Row D, in the Sanders Keep Military Cemetery, named after a German fortification which stood between the Hermies and Havrincourt roads. The grave inscription has a quotation from St Luke's gospel: 'Father forgive them, for they know not what they do'. Sanders Keep had been captured by the Scots Guards on the same day that Jackson earned his decoration; he was one of many Guardsmen buried there and it is fitting that the site overlooks the place where he won his VC.

The award was presented by the King to Jackson's parents in the ballroom of Buckingham Palace on 29 March 1919, when they were able to meet and talk to Capt. Frisby, who was presented with his VC on the same day. Frisby was probably the last man to see Jackson alive.

Thomas Norman Jackson was born at 3 Market Street, Swinton, Rotherham, South Yorkshire, on 11 February 1897. He was the son of Thomas Edwin and Emma Jackson. Before enlisting, Thomas was employed for a short period by Messrs Ward and Sons, mineral water manufacturers. His father also worked for the same firm. Later, Thomas Jackson worked as an engine cleaner at the Great Central Railway Locomotive Depot at Mexborough.

On 22 November 1915 he enlisted at Mexborough, joining the 1st Battalion Coldstream Guards in France in October 1917. He took part in the Battle of Cambrai in the following month. A local Sheffield newspaper, published in November 1918, stated that Jackson was a member of the Primitive Methodist Church and Bible class in Swinton. He was said to be robust and athletic in physique, and particularly fond of swimming, boxing and wrestling.

On 28 November 1918, two months after Jackson's death, the same newspaper published an article about their local hero under the heading 'Stories of Heroes Crossing the Canal Du Nord':

> The Crossing of the Canal du Nord by the Territorials of Notts and Derbyshire and the Guards Division, and their subsequent smash through the Hindenburg Line, was one of the most glorious exploits of the war, and had a great deal to do with bringing about the armistice. The list of V.C. heroes published last night includes an account of individual deeds of daring during the crossing, and the posthumous award to a former Swinton

G.C.R. engine cleaner, Lance Corporal Thomas Norman Jackson, aged 21 years, of the Coldstream Guards.

When the troops of a whole area were being held up, and the operation was in danger of being a failure, it was young Jackson, his officer (Capt. Frisby) and two other brave men that dashed into the canal, crossed it under heavy point-blank fire, and swept away the machine-guns barring the passage. Soon after Jackson had the distinction of being the first man to reach a trench of the Hindenburg Line, where he was killed.

After Jackson's death, Capt. Frisby wrote to his grieving parents: 'Your son's heroism was of the very highest order, and I have had pleasure in recommending him for the highest honour.' Another witness, Lt Moore, wrote: 'Your son was magnificent; his example made a difference to the whole battle. He has been recommended for a posthumous VC and I pray with all my heart that he may get it. No man ever deserved it more.'

On 30 July 1919 Capt. Frisby, who had already met Jackson's family at Buckingham Palace, travelled to Jackson's home in Swinton to unveil a painting of him by Mr J.H. Bentley the following day. The portrait had been commissioned by the Swinton Special Constables. It was later displayed in the Swinton Library in Station Street. While in the town Frisby retold the story of how Jackson won his VC:

Cpl Jackson had distinguished himself in the attack on the Canal du Nord. The official story in the *London Gazette* does not really tell you what he did on that day on the 27 September. A big attack was to take place on the Hindenburg Line. Our jumping-off place was about 50 yards from the Canal du Nord. The canal had no water in it. It was about 50ft across and 15ft deep. Its walls were nearly vertical, and were made of brick, faced here and there with concrete. The Germans had festooned these walls with barbed wire, so that it was impossible to slide down them; one of my platoons was detached to capture the crossing and hold it, and enable the rest of the battalion to cross. There was nowhere else to cross. I sent two sections of Lewis-gunners and bombers, sixteen men in all, and Cpl Jackson was of that number of sixteen men. Only two returned, Cpl Jackson and Sgt Smith, another Yorkshireman. The rest became casualties as soon as they got into the wire. The Germans were bombarding us with trench mortars. Cpl Jackson actually got into the bed of the canal, and located the German strong-post underneath the iron bridge. When volunteers were called for, to make another effort, someone said, 'Here we are, sir.' 'Come on,' I said. 'Who is it?' 'Cpl Jackson, sir.' That small party got across; the post was taken, and the battalion were enabled to get across and carry on the attack. Later on Cpl Jackson's platoon was detailed to go to a certain German trench. I was told by one of the officers that as soon as they got into the trench Cpl Jackson called out, 'Come on, boys.' He was first in the trench. I am told that he killed the two Boches and was then killed.

Apart from the VC, Jackson's other decorations included the BWM and VM. These, together with his VC, were presented to the Coldstream Guards Regimental Headquarters (RHQ) by Jackson's brother, Bernard, on 12 June 1969.

G.F. KERR
Bourlon Wood, France, 27 September

To the left of the Canadian 4th Division's attack on 27 September 1918, against the Canal du Nord and Bourlon Wood, the 1st Division was also successful. Guns of the 1st Canadian Field Artillery allowed the 1st Brigade to move quickly into the village of Inchy-en-Artois on the west side of the Canal du Nord. The dry bed of the canal was quickly negotiated and the 4th Battalion, moving north-easterly, managed to capture its allotted section of the Marquion Line. The 1st Battalion then moved on, but the 2nd and 3rd Battalions were delayed by heavy fire coming from a railway embankment to the north of Bourlon Wood. With the timely assistance of the 72nd Battalion, the enemy resistance was overcome and the advance continued. The role played by Lt George Fraser Kerr, commander of the 3rd Battalion's left support company, in dealing with a German strongpoint close to the Arras–Cambrai road at Raillencourt was crucial. As a result, four machine guns and thirty-one prisoners were captured. His almost inevitable VC was gazetted on 6 January 1919 as follows:

> For most conspicuous bravery and leadership during the Bourlon Wood operations on 27 Sept. 1918, when in command of the left support company in attack. He handled his company with great skill, and gave timely support by outflanking a machine-gun which was impeding the advance. Later, near the Arras–Cambrai road, the advance was again held up by a strongpoint. Lieut. Kerr, far in advance of his company, rushed

this strongpoint single-handed and captured four machine-guns and thirty-one prisoners. His valour throughout this engagement was an inspiring example to all.

Lieutenant Kerr was decorated at an investiture with the VC, together with an MC and bar, on 20 May 1919 in the Quadrangle of Buckingham Palace.

George Fraser Kerr was born in Deseronto, Ontario, Canada, on 8 June 1895. He was the son of John James Kerr, who ran a dry goods store in the town, and Isabell Fraser. He was educated in local schools and, later, in Toronto after the family moved there in about 1903. When the war began in 1914, Kerr, who was working in a bank, joined up as a private in the 3rd Battalion (Toronto Regiment) at Valcartier on 22 September. He sailed for Britain in early October and, after training, arrived in France on 11 February 1915. Two days earlier he had been promoted to corporal, with his leadership qualities having been noted. On 13 June 1916 he won the MM at Mount Sorrel in the Ypres Salient. This was an important position, which allowed the Canadian troops good observation over enemy positions. It had been captured by the Germans on 2 June, but following a huge artillery bombardment on 13 June it was recaptured by the Canadians. The Canadians remained in the Salient for three more months. During this time, the enemy made several attempts to recapture Mount Sorrel, but these attacks were repulsed. Towards the end of July, Kerr was seriously wounded and, on 31 July, he was sent back to England for medical treatment.

Approximately a year later, Kerr was judged fit enough to return to active service. By this time he had been commissioned in the 12th Reserve Battalion, although once in France he rejoined his former unit, the 3rd Battalion.

In 1918 his military record was outstanding, demonstrating his courage and initiative. As a consequence, he won the MC during the Allied offensive at Amiens on 8 August 1918. During the fighting he discovered a gap opening up in the Allied lines and, together with his platoon, he quickly filled this gap and subsequently put an enemy machine gun out of action. Thirty of the enemy were killed and a battery of 77mm guns were captured in the process. Later he filled a further gap in the line and went forward with the advancing troops. This time he was wounded, but continued to the final objective. On the way, a nest of two machine guns was accounted for. Despite his wounds, Kerr continued to serve for another couple of days.

While he was recovering from his wounds, he learnt about the impending attack against the Canal du Nord and Bourlon Wood. His unit was to take part in this assault and Kerr was determined not to miss out. Despite being ruled unfit by his doctors, he discharged himself from the hospital and promptly rejoined his unit at the front. It was during the subsequent fighting that he won a bar to his MC at Quéant. The *London Gazette* announced his MC on 2 December 1918, and the bar was added on 1 February 1919. The citation was as follows:

> For conspicuous gallantry, initiative and skill during the Drocourt–Quéant attack on the 2nd and 3rd September 1918, when he led his company forward with great dash. Later he led two platoons to the assistance of one of the attacking companies, which was held up by heavy machine-gun fire, surprising the hostile machine-gun crews, and personally accounting for several of the enemy. His splendid courage afforded a most inspiring example at a critical time.

Kerr's military career ended on 16 July 1919 when he was discharged as medically unfit. He arrived back in Canada as one of the country's most decorated soldiers.

Kerr became a manager of a firm of metal suppliers called Lewis, Lazarus and Sons in Toronto. He was still active in the militia and, on 1 March 1921, was promoted to captain in the Toronto Regiment. He travelled to England for the House of Lords Dinner on 9 November 1929, but during the voyage broke his arm. Because of this he suffered a great deal of pain and had to consult a specialist once his ship had docked in port. He requested that his injury should not be reported in order to prevent his wife becoming alarmed about his health. However, much worse was to follow, for within a month he died after a tragic accident. His body was found sitting in his car. Apparently, while waiting for the engine to warm up, he had been poisoned by carbon monoxide fumes and asphyxiated. The accident, which was described in a local newspaper as a 'Peacetime Tragedy', happened on 8 December 1929 at his home at 38 Cheltenham Avenue, Lawrence Park, Toronto.

Kerr was buried in Mount Pleasant Cemetery in Toronto, Plot 14, Section 36, Lot 6-E 1/2, with full military honours. Representatives from the government and numerous organisations attended. Kerr's coffin, draped with a Union Jack, was followed by a soldier carrying his decorations on a cushion. Other holders of the VC also attended; men who only a few weeks ago had attended the House of Lords Dinner in London with Kerr. At the gates of the cemetery on Yonge Street, a guard of honour was drawn up, comprising members of the 3rd Canadian Infantry Battalion. The coffin was then transferred to a gun carriage and the procession moved slowly towards the Kerr family plot. At the graveside, a short burial service was conducted, while a biting cold wind blew snow across the ground. Rifle volleys rang out over the grave and the 'Last Post' and 'Reveille' were then played. The Canadian Governor General sent a cable to Kerr's family in which he commiserated with them for their loss.

Kerr's wife, Mary Beeman (1886–1952), shares the family grave, together with their daughter, Mary Louise Kerr (1925–77).

A Heritage Foundation plaque to his memory has been erected in Valour Place, Cambridge, Ontario, formerly named Galt. Frederick Hobson and Samuel Honey are also commemorated there.

Forty-four years later, on 2 November 1973, a plaque commemorating the life and career of Capt. George Kerr was unveiled in Centennial Park, between Main Street and the waterfront in Deseronto, his birthplace, one of a series erected throughout the province. It was arranged and sponsored by the Earle J. Brant Memorial Branch, Royal Canadian Legion. The unveiling ceremony was performed by Capt. Kerr's grandchildren, David, Carol and Allison Ross. His decorations, which also included the MM, 1914–15 Star, BWM and VM, are in the collection of the Canadian War Museum in Ottawa.

G.T. LYALL

North of Cambrai, France,
27 September

Lieutenant Graham Lyall was an officer in the 102nd (Central Ontario) Battalion, and won his VC during the operations of the 4th Division at Bourlon Wood on 27 September, together with another VC winner, Lt S.L. Honey. They both had to deal with German strongpoints during the capture of the Wood. Lyall's VC was gazetted on 14 December 1918 as follows:

For most conspicuous bravery and skillful leading during the operation north of Cambrai. On 27 Sept. 1918, whilst leading his platoon against Bourlon Wood, he rendered invaluable support to the leading company, which was held up by a strongpoint, which he captured by a flank movement, together with thirteen prisoners, one field-gun and four machine-guns. Later, his platoon, now much weakened by casualties, was held up by machine-guns at the southern end of Bourlon Wood. Collecting any men available, he led them towards a strongpoint, and, springing forward alone, rushed the position single-handed and killed the officer in charge, subsequently capturing at this point forty-five prisoners and five machine-guns. Having made good his final objective, with a further capture of forty-seven prisoners, he consolidated his position and thus protected the remainder of the company. On 1 Oct., in the neighbourhood of Blecourt, when in command of a weak company, by skillful dispositions he captured a strongly defended position, which yielded sixty prisoners and seventeen machine-guns. During two days of operations Lieut. Lyall captured in all three officers, 182 other ranks, twenty-six machine-guns, and one field-gun, exclusive of heavy casualties inflicted. He showed throughout the utmost valour and high powers of command.

A Canadian newspaper described Lyall's actions in the following way:

This most remarkable record is probably unexcelled in all the annals of war. His feat required not only courage and resource, but also the very highest type of military intelligence; a thorough understanding of military technique, and a personality of the most inspiring character.

Lyall received his VC from the King on 15 March 1919.

Graham Thomson Lyall was the only son of the Revd R.H. Lyall, and was born in Chorlton, north of Manchester, on 8 March 1892. His father was vicar of St John's, Farnworth, from 1894 to 1900, and the family then moved to Nelson, Lancashire, where Lyall's father became vicar of St John's, Darwen. The family home was in Turncroft Lane, Darwen. Lyall was educated at Nelson Municipal Secondary School and, later, at a naval engineering college. He was a keen sportsman throughout his life: an expert swimmer, he also excelled at tennis, cricket and hockey, as well as going in for shooting, canoeing and rowing.

In 1912, after he had left college, he emigrated to Welland in Ontario, Canada, where he completed his education at Toronto University, qualifying as a mechanical engineer. He acquired a job with the Canadian Steel Foundries at Welland, then later worked for the Canadian Niagara Power Company at Niagara Falls, Ontario. He was also a member of the British Institute of Engineers.

Lyall enlisted on 23 October 1914 in the 19th ('Lincoln') Regiment in St Catherines, Ontario. He was placed on active duty and served with the Welland Canal Force as Canal Guard in Niagra and, after serving for several months on Lock Seven, he joined the

Canadian Expeditionary Force (CEF). He left for England in September 1915 and joined the 81st Canadian Infantry Battalion in October, becoming an acting corporal on the first of the month. After further training, he left for France in 1916 with the 4th Canadian Mounted Rifles. He took part in the Battle of the Somme and the Battle of Vimy Ridge. During this period, he had been promoted through the ranks for conspicuous bravery and was granted a commission on 28 April 1917, after a short course at the Canadian Officers' Training School in Bexhill, Sussex. He then joined the 102nd Battalion, 2nd Central Ontario Regiment.

After the war, Lyall returned to his former home at Darwen, where the local inhabitants presented him with a French bronze clock, together with other ornaments. He was married on 24 April 1919 in the High United Free Church, Airdrie, Lanarkshire, to Elizabeth Moffat, eldest daughter of Alexander Frew, the Provost of Airdrie, and Elizabeth Moffat Frew. Lyall's father took part in the marriage ceremony. Lyall became a manager of Drumbathie Brickworks (Alexander Frew & Co.), and the couple lived at Forrest Park, Drumgelloch, Airdrie. He later became managing director of Aerocrete (Scotland) Ltd, Victoria Works, Airdrie. On 26 June 1920 he attended the Garden Party for VC winners and their families in the grounds of Buckingham Palace, and was also a guest at the House of Lords Dinner on 9 November 1929.

Lyall joined up again in the Second World War, having been called up in the Territorial Army (TA) Reserve of Officers, and was promoted to major (Ordnance Mechanical Engineer, 2nd Class), temporary lieutenant colonel (Ordnance Mechanical Engineer, 1st Class) and acting colonel, Royal Army Ordnance Corps (RAMC). Sadly he died of heart failure in his sleep on 28 November 1941 at Mersa Matruh in Egypt, and is buried in Halfaya Sollum War Cemetery, Plot XIX, Row B, Grave 2. On 5 June 2005 the Countess of Wessex, Colonel-in-Chief of The Lincoln and Welland Regiment, which developed out of the 19th Regiment, unveiled a plaque to his memory in St Catherine's City, Niagra. It was set up on the north-west corner of Lake Street and Welland Avenue. In Remembrance week of 2006, Lyall's decorations, together with those of Cpl Fred Fisher, were placed on display in St Catherine's Historical Museum. They had been on loan from 2002 to the REME Museum in Aborfield, England.

His decorations still belong to his family and apart from the VC, they include the BWM, VM, 1939–45 Star, Africa Star, WM (1939–45), King George V Silver Jubilee (1935) and, finally, a Coronation Medal for King George VI of 1937.

T. NEELY

Flesquières, France, 27 September

The Guards Division and the 3rd Division were both heavily involved in capturing part of the strongly defended Hindenburg Line and its support line in the area of the Canal du Nord and the village of Flesquières on 27 September 1918. It was the last real German line of defence and the area had already seen heavy fighting in November 1917, and again in the spring of 1918 when it was retaken by the enemy. The 3rd Division was to the right of the Guards Division and had already crossed the dry bed of the Canal du Nord that morning. Corporal Thomas Neely was a member of the 15th Platoon of D Company of the 8th King's Own Royal Lancaster Regiment, 76th Brigade. On 27 September the battalion was on the outskirts of the village of Flesquières, preparing to attack at zero hour, 5.20 a.m. The left-flank attack was to be the heaviest, in order to capture the heights of Bourlon Wood, and the subsequent advance would then lead on to the River Sensée.

The 8th King's Own was one of the leading battalions of the 76th Brigade, which began in support before passing through the lines of the 8th Brigade. During the attack, the King's Own came up against a line of numerous concrete machine-gun posts that ran through the village as part of the enemy support line. As a result, most of the officers of the leading companies became casualties, and the whole advance was held up by heavy fire from the left flank. It was then that Neely and two men dashed out and saved the day, with the non-commissioned officer (NCO) gaining a Victoria Cross. His citation, published in the *London Gazette* on 14 December 1918, tells the story of the action as follows:

For most conspicuous bravery during operations at Flesquières on 27 Sept. 1918. His company was held up during the advance by heavy machine-gun fire from a flank. Corpl. Neeley [*sic*], realising the seriousness of the situation, at once, under point-blank fire, dashed out with two men and rushed the positions, disposing of the garrisons and capturing three machine-guns. Subsequently, on two successive occasions, he rushed concrete strongpoints, killing or capturing the occupants. The splendid initiative and fighting spirit displayed by this gallant non-commissioned officer in dealing with a series of posts, in some cases single-handed, was largely responsible for the taking and clearing of a heavily fortified and strongly garrisoned position, and enabled his company to advance 3,000 yards along the Hindenburg support line.

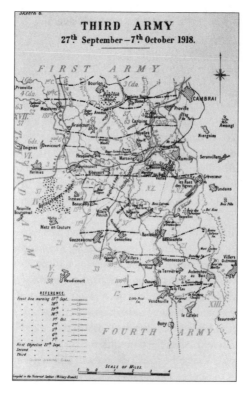

The 62nd (2nd West Riding) Division (VI Corps), who were then to advance to the third objective, was unable to progress until Allied artillery enabled them to do so. It was shortly before 11 a.m. that the advance resumed. To the right, the village of Ribécourt was taken, as was the Bourlon Ridge on the left flank. During the operation the 8th King's Own captured 800 prisoners and more than 200 machine guns. By nightfall, when the battalion was relieved, the British had advanced an incredible 4 miles. Neely was immediately promoted in the field, after his heroism at Flesquières, to lance sergeant, but was tragically killed during another attack three days later at Rumilly, to the east of Marcoing. He is buried 4 miles south-west of Cambrai in Masnières British Cemetery, Marcoing, Plot II, Row B, Grave 21. The cemetery had been establsihed by the 3rd Divisional Burial Officer in October 1918. Flesquières has two British war cemeteries and they are an all too vivid reminder of the importance of this section of the Hindenburg Line during the war.

Neely's posthumous VC was presented to his parents in a private investiture in the ballroom of Buckingham Palace on 27 February 1920. At the same investiture, a posthumous VC was also presented to the parents of Cpl John McNamara of the 9th East Surreys. Only one travel warrant had been issued for the Neely family, which was in Mrs Neely's name. Her husband was unemployed at the time, so was unable to afford the cost of train travel to London. Fortunately, funds were found, together with an assurance of employment.

Thomas Neely was the son of James Herbert Neely and Mary Agnes Neely (née Egan), and was born at 13 Tabor Street, Poulton-cum-Seacombe, Wallasey, Cheshire, on 26 August 1897. He was one of a family of five girls and two boys. His birth certificate shows his name to be spelt Neely, but most records list him as Neeley. His father was a gas fitter, but found employment hard to come by and had to work as a casual labourer for several years. While Thomas was still a small child, the family moved to the other side of the Mersey, settling at 91 Claudia Street, City Road, Walton, Liverpool. Thomas attended St Francis de Sales School, Hale Road, Walton.

Before enlisting, he worked at Bibby's Mills, based in Great Howard Street, which specialised in seed-crushers and cattle fEEd manufacture. Neely was small and stocky, and it came as no surprise to his friends and colleagues that, in September 1914, he joined the Cheshire Regiment Bantam Battalion. Later he transferred to the King's Own Royal Lancaster Regiment. On 16 July 1918 the *London Gazette* published details of his MM, and soon after he was sent home on leave. On 26 August he returned to the frontline and was made a corporal. Although his company commander suggested that he apply for a commission, Neely was quite content to stay an NCO. His VC and MM were sold at auction by Messrs Spink on 25 November 2010 for £110,000. Apart from the VC and MM, they should have included the BWM and VM, but it appears the family never received them. Thomas Neely is commemorated with a memorial plaque in The Priory at Lancaster. His name was also remembered in Birkenhead Town Hall on a Memorial Board to seven winners of the VC from the area of the Wirrall, which was unveiled by Ian Fraser VC on 29 March 1984. This board was later updated and moved to Wallasey Town Hall and was unveiled by its instigator, Mr Denis Rose, and Melba Fraser, widow of Ian Fraser VC, on 22 February 2012. The names of five more local VC winners had been added and this Wirrall board covered the Ellesmere Port and Neston districts. The names of the same twelve men are also included on a plaque at the Birkenhead Cenotaph Memorial. In 2014 it is hoped that a Victoria Cross/George Cross (VC/GC) Association display will be set up in the ground floor stairwell of Birkenhead Town Hall.

After his death in 1977, the ashes of Sergeant (Sgt) Henry Tandey VC, DCM and MM were placed in the Masnières British Cemetery, close to Lance Sergeant (L. Sgt) Thomas Neely's grave.

M.F. GREGG
Near Cambrai, France,
27 September–1 October

In the Marcoing section of the Hindenburg Line, Germany's famous 'impregnable' defensive system, Lt Milton Gregg of the Royal Canadian Regiment (RCR) won the VC for gallantry during the period between 27 September–1 October 1918. The aim of the Canadian 3rd Division was to take the village of Fontaine-Notre-Dame, to the east of Bourlon Wood, and then force the Marcoing Line, which would then open the way to the very important town of Cambrai.

Led by the Royal Canadian Regiment, the 7th Brigade began well and by 8.50 a.m. on 28 September had captured the Marcoing Line But then strong enemy resistance from the Marcoing support line slowed the advance down. The Germans were out to delay the fall of Cambrai and the crossings of the Canal de l'Escaut for as long as they possibly could. By mid-morning the RCR were pinned down under heavy fire from the front, and from Sailly on the left flank. The Princess Patricia's Canadian Light Infantry (PPCLI) then joined the action and, by early afternoon, the two battalions had secured the Marcoing position between the Arras and Bapaume roads. Many of Gregg's achievements were carried out during this period of the advance, and the VC citation, published on 6 January 1919, takes up the story:

For most conspicuous bravery and initiative during operations near Cambrai, 27 Sept. to 1 Oct. 1918. On 28 Sept., when the advance of the brigade was held up by fire from both flanks and by thick uncut wire, he crawled forward alone and explored the wire until he found a small gap, through which he subsequently led his men, and forced an entry into the enemy trench. The enemy counter-attacked in force, and through lack of bombs the situation became critical. Although wounded, Lieut. Gregg returned alone under terrific fire and collected a further supply. Then, rejoining his party, which by this time was much reduced in numbers, and, in spite of a second wound, he reorganised his men and led them with the greatest determination against the enemy trenches, which he finally cleared. He personally killed or wounded 11 of the enemy, and took 25 prisoners, in addition to 12 machine-guns captured in this trench. Remaining with his company in spite of wounds, he again on 30th Sept. led his men in attack until severely wounded. The outstanding valour of this officer saved many casualties and enabled the advance to continue.

Gregg was decorated with his VC by the King at an investiture in the ballroom of Buckingham Palace on 26 February 1919.

Milton Fowler Gregg was born in Mountain Dale, King's County, New Brunswick, Canada, on 10 April 1892. He grew up on a farm owned by his father, George Lord Gregg, who had previously been a successful farmer in Devon; his mother, Elizabeth Celia Myles, came from Ireland. Gregg was educated at the local public school, and at the Provincial Normal School in Fredericton. He went on to Acadia University and then to Dalhousie University, graduating in 1916. After leaving university, he became a schoolteacher in Carleton County, New Brunswick.

The first step in his military career was as a trooper in the 8th Princess Louise's New Brunswick Hussars in 1910. He enlisted as a private in the CEF in November 1914 and served with the 13th Canadian Infantry Battalion (Royal Highlanders), who wore the Black Watch tartan, and then left for training in England, where he found himself, alongside many of his countrymen, training on Salisbury Plain. When he sailed to France in February 1915, he remained with the 13th Battalion and took part in the Second Battle of Ypres, being wounded in the fighting at Festubert on 31 May. While recovering from his wounds in England, he attended an Imperial Officers' Training Course in Cambridge between May and August. He was commissioned on 1 November 1916. His service papers at this time suffered from a mix-up, which resulted in him becoming briefly an officer serving in the British Army and a member of the King's Own Royal Lancaster Regiment. However, this was not for long as he soon transferred to the 40th Canadian Battalion. On 25 April 1917 he was transferred to the Royal Canadian Regiment from 26th Reserve Battalion.

Gregg was wounded at Lens, near Vimy, on 9 June 1917, and was also awarded the MC when leading a trench raid. The citation of 25 August read as follows:

> For conspicuous gallantry and devotion to duty in leading a bombing attack against a hostile machine-gun which he out-flanked and annihilated the crew, thus permitting the advance of his party to continue unchecked. His prompt action greatly assisted the success of a much larger operation. Later, although himself wounded, he carried a seriously wounded officer out of action to a place of safety.

Four days later he was invalided and detached to the Nova Scotia Regimental Depot. He returned to France on 22 November and rejoined the RCR on the 27th. In August 1918, during fighting in the Arras battles, he won a bar to his MC (*London Gazette* 8 October):

> During an attack on the Bois de Sart on 26th August 1918 he became detached from his company with his platoon, and being subjected to withering machine-gun fire, he led a bombing party forward and rushed two machine-gun crews, killing them. Pushing on with his platoon he found his position isolated and dug in, and by a personal reconnaissance connected up with the left flank, and by skillfully dispersing his men enabled an enemy counter-attack to be repulsed ...

He returned to England for a fortnight's leave at the end of August. After winning his VC, Gregg was wounded again on the 30 September, having been made adjutant of the RCR the day before. He rejoined on 11 October and, at the end of the year, was granted another two weeks' leave. He returned to England on 6 February 1919 and left with his unit for Canada on 1 March. On his return to Canada he married Dorothy Alward of Havelock, New Brunswick, and the couple later had a daughter. Gregg was then transferred to the Canadian Militia. After the war he went into private business, trying his hand at advertising, then became a company secretary in the mining industry, and later worked as a motorcar dealer. On 9 November 1929 he attended the House of Lords Dinner. In 1934 he was invited to become the Sergeant-at-Arms at the House of Commons in Ottawa, a post which he held from 1934 to 1939, when he was given a leave of absence. His job was no sinecure and his duties on Parliament Hill included the traditional one of mace-bearer; he was also responsible to the Speaker of the House for the smooth running of the administration of the buildings and for supervision of the large staff. Gregg was Dominion Treasurer of the Canadian Legion, (1934–9), and took part in the ceremonies connected with the unveiling of the Vimy Ridge Memorial in France in 1936.

On the outbreak of the Second World War Gregg rejoined the Canadian Army. Posted as second-in-command of the RCR, he proceeded to England with the unit in 1939. In the following year he was made lieutenant colonel commanding the West Nova Scotia Regiment, and in April 1940 his unit was inspected by the King. In 1941 he became commandant of the Canadian OTCU in England, until it was abolished. He returned to Canada in 1942, where he took charge of the Officers' Training Centre in Brockville, Ontario. In the following year he was made brigadier and commandant of the Canadian School of Infantry in Vernon, British Columbia, a position that he held until the middle of 1945. He then retired from the Army.

Although Gregg had not had much academic experience, he had been invited to become Chancellor of the University of Brunswick in 1944. He was later elected to Parliament (1947–57), serving in Prime Minister Mackenzie King's Liberal Cabinet, in which he was Minister of Fisheries (1947–8), Minister of Veterans' Affairs (1948–50) and Minister of Labour (1950–7). In 1957 he was defeated by a Conservative in the general election held in June. Between 1952 and 1958 he was the Royal Canadian Regiment's honorary colonel, and he was a member of the Canadian contingent at the 1956 Hyde Park VC review in London. In the late 1950s he served with the UN's Children's Fund in Iraq for a year before occupying a similar post in Indonesia from 1960 until 1963. In 1964 he became the Canadian High Commissioner to Guyana, holding this position for three years. Gregg retained a home in Ottawa, in addition to his home at Fredericton. In 1977, when in his eighties, he attended the 60th anniversary commemorations of the Canadian capture of Vimy Ridge.

Gregg listed his recreations in *Who's Who* as rugby, football, hunting, motoring and fishing. It is surprising that a man with such an active life had any time for recreations. He died in New Brunswick on 13 March 1978 at the age of 85, and was buried near his home in Snider Mountain (formerly Mountain Dale) Baptist Church Cemetery, Fredericton. He was survived by his second wife, Erica Deichmann. Later, the names of both of his wives were inscribed on his headstone.

His medals were stolen on Christmas Eve in 1978 from the Royal Canadian Regimental Museum in London, Ontario and have never been found. However, a replacement set has been cobbled together for display purposes. The length of the list of his awards underlines his very considerable service to Canadian life: he had been a soldier, politician, administrator and diplomat.

The award list for the First World War, apart from the VC, MC and bar, included the 1914–15 Star, BWM and VM. His other awards included Officer of the Order of Canada (OC), Defence Medal 1939–45, Canadian Volunteer Service Medal (1939–45) with 'Maple Leaf' clasp, War Medal 1939–45, King George V Silver Jubilee Medal (1935), King George VI Coronation Medal (1937), CBE, Queen Elizabeth II Coronation Medal (1953), Canadian Centennial Medal (1967), Queen Elizabeth II Silver Jubilee Medal (1977), Colonial Auxiliary Forces Long Service Medal, Efficiency Decoration (ED) with 'Canada' clasp, Canadian Forces DFC (1949), and Commissionaires Long Service Medal. Also on display in the museum is his Officers' Service Dress and a bust depicting him. The University of New Brunswick also has a Gregg Centre in Fredericton, which was set up for the study of war and society. An Annual Student Bursary is also in operation in Gregg's name, as is a trophy called the 'Mons Box', an award for officer trainees who have displayed good leadership skills.

The Hon. Milton Gregg is also remembered in a number of other ways, including having a mountain named after him in Jasper National Park, Alberta. He also had a barracks named after him, which carries the following inscription:

So named in this centennial year of the Royal Canadian Regiment to honour the memory of a gallant soldier, states- man and scholar. A native of New Brunswick, Brigadier the Honourable Milton F. Gregg, VC, OC, CBE, MC, ED won the Victoria Cross in 1917 [*sic*] while serving as a Lieutenant with the Regiment. He died in March 1978 at the age of 85.

L. McGuffie
Wytschaete, Belgium, 28 September

On 28 September, to the north of the Cambrai sector, the Allied aim was to renew the battle for Ypres and regain Wytschaete Ridge. The offensive was planned to begin at 5.30 a.m., and the 103rd Brigade of the 34th Division was destined to play a prominent part in the battle. The artillery barrage began five minutes before zero hour, when the 1/5th Battalion King's Own Scottish Borderers attacked a strongpoint known as Piccadilly Farm. Prisoners were taken and parties from the 14th Division joined the Borderers. The battalion then took up positions to the south-east of the farm on the Messines–Ypres road. Another platoon was in a position to the north-east of Quarante Wood. Things were going well for the attackers until a long-range barrage of machine-gun fire from 'Damm Strasse' began to cause problems. Sergeant L. McGuffie had been in action from the start of the attack on Piccadilly Farm, where, owing to officer casualties, he had taken charge of a platoon. He was subsequently responsible for the capture of more than a dozen prisoners and of several dug-outs, earning him a VC. The award was gazetted on 14 December 1918 as follows:

> For most conspicuous bravery and resourceful leadership under heavy fire near Wytschaete on 28 Sept. 1918. During the advance to Piccadilly Farm, he, single-handed, entered several enemy dug-outs and took many prisoners, and during subsequent operations dealt similarly with dug-out after dug-out,

forcing one officer and 25 other ranks to surrender. During the consolidation of the first objective he pursued and brought back several of the enemy who were slipping away, and he was also instrumental in rescuing some British soldiers who were being led off as prisoners. Later in the day, when in command of a platoon, he led it with the utmost dash and resource, capturing many prisoners. This very gallant soldier was subsequently killed by a shell.

Wytschaete fell at 6.30 a.m. the following day, and the way across the Ypres–Commines Canal was now clear. Tragically, McGuffie never knew that he had won a VC, as he was killed a few days later on 4 October 1918. He was buried in Zantvoorde British Cemetery in Belgium, Plot I, Row D, Grave 12. The cemetery is 6 miles to the south-east of Ypres. The village of Zantvoorde was in German hands

for almost the entire war, until being captured by the British on 28 September 1918. McGuffie's posthumous VC was presented to his mother by the King in a private ceremony at Buckingham Palace on 17 May 1919.

Louis McGuffie was the third of four sons of Edward McGuffie, a general labourer, and his wife, Catherine McGuffie (née Gilmour), of 1 North Main Street, Wigtown, Galloway, Scotland, where he was born on 15 March 1893. Louis was educated at Wigtown Public School, then enlisted in the 1/5th King's Own Scottish Borderers with the service number of 240693. His three brothers also enlisted. Louis was posted to Gallipoli in 1915, prior to being transferred to France and the Western Front.

Two days after being given her son's VC at Buckingham Palace on 17 May 1919, Catherine McGuffie returned to Wigtown from London to be greeted at the station by the Provost and other local dignitaries. She was escorted home in a procession, preceded by a local band, which later played a selection of Scottish airs in front of her house. In the evening, the Right Hon. the Earl of Stair, Provost Dyer of Stranraer and several other local dignitaries called on Mrs McGuffie to express their high appreciation of her son's bravery and of their deep regret that he had not survived the war.

At the end of the year, a beautifully designed bronze tablet on a granite background to McGuffie's memory was unveiled at Wigtown on the inside wall of the County Buildings. It was paid for by Sir Peter McLelland and placed at the entrance to the first flight of steps, where it would be seen by everyone entering the building. The tablet was unveiled by the Lord-Lieutenant of the County, Sir Herbert Maxwell. At some point, the residents of Wigtown had subscribed to the Mrs McGuffie Fund, and subscribers were publicly thanked at this ceremony. McGuffie's name is also included on the Wigtown War Memorial, which looks out over Wigtown Bay. On 19 August 1971, Robert McGuffie, one of Louis' surviving brothers, presented his decorations to the Museum of the King's Own Scottish Borders at The Barracks, Berwick-on-Tweed. Apart from the VC they included the 1914–15 Star, VM, BWM and VM.

H. TANDEY

Marcoing, France, 28 September

On 28 September the battle plan for VI Corps was for the 187th Brigade to take part in a major attack, led by the 2nd and 62nd (2nd West Riding) Divisions. The start time was to be 6.30 a.m., with a planned advance against the village of Masnières on the Scheldt Canal. The 186th Brigade was to pass through the lines of the 185th Brigade, then take the village of Marcoing and capture the crossing to the east of the village where a small bridgehead was to be formed.

Initially the attack was successful against an uneven opposition, and the right of the 187th Brigade was able to reach the Marcoing Line, while the 186th Brigade reached a trench to the west of the village. After sporadic fighting the village was duly cleared and the western bank of the 50yd-wide canal was reached. A small group from the 2/4th Hampshires used the lock gates to cross, and the 5th Duke of Wellington's crossed in single file via a destroyed railway bridge. At this point the enemy began to stiffen its opposition and fierce fire checked the advance of both brigades. However, artillery barrages in the late afternoon allowed the advance to move forward once more.

Private Henry Tandey, who on 26 July had been transferred from the Green Howards to the 5th Duke of Wellington's Regiment of 186th Brigade, was at Marcoing, where he won his third gallantry medal within a period of five weeks. On this occasion it was the Victoria Cross, which was gazetted on 14 December 1918, but a fuller account taken from the Special Order by the GOC 62nd (West Riding) Division is more descriptive and detailed:

For desperate bravery and great initiative during the capture of the village and the crossings at Marcoing and the later counter-attack on September 28th 1918. During the advance on Marcoing this soldier's platoon was held up by machine-gun fire and stopped. He at once crawled forward under heavy fire, located the machine-gun position, led a Lewis-gun team into a neighbouring house from which they were able to knock out the gun, and his platoon continued the advance.

On arrival at the crossings the plank bridge was broken, and under heavy fire and seemingly impassable, he crawled forward, putting the planks into position and making the bridge passable under a hail of bullets, thus enabling the first crossing to be made at this vital spot. He must have seen that the chances of losing his life amounted to almost a certainty.

Later in the evening, during an attack by his company to enlarge the bridgehead and capture Marcoing support trench, he, with eight comrades, was surrounded by an overwhelming number of Germans, and though the position was apparently hopeless, he led a bayonet charge through them, fighting so fiercely that 37 of the enemy were driven into the hands of the remainder of his company in the rear and taken prisoner, the party winning clear though he was twice wounded. Even then he refused to leave, leading parties into dug-outs and capturing over 20 of the enemy, and though faint from loss of blood, stayed till the fight was won.

This was the third time Tandey had been wounded, and he was sent home for medical treatment. On his recovery, he was decorated by the King at Buckingham Palace on 17 December 1919.

Henry John Tandey was the son of James Tandey, a soldier and stonemason, and Catherine, and was born in Swains Buildings, Kenilworth Street, Leamington, Warwickshire, on 30 August 1891. James had served in the 16th Lancers and in the South African War. He later became a journeyman stonemason. Henry, often known in later life by the nickname 'Napper', spent part of his childhood in an orphanage and was educated at St Peter's School. At the age of 18, he took a job as stoker/assistant engineer at the Regent Hotel in Leamington, owned by the Cridlan family, before deciding to join the Green Howards (Alexandra, Princess of Wales's Own Yorkshire Regiment) in Richmond, York, in August 1910. Tandey was not a big man, being under 5½ft tall and weighing only 119lb. He was posted to the 2nd Green Howards, with the service number 9545. He served with the 2nd Battalion from 23 January 1911 to 24 October 1916, which included pre-war service in South Africa and Guernsey. Two months after the war began he was with them at Zeebrugge, as part of the BEF's attempt to prevent Belgium being overrun by the German Army, and he also took part in the First Battle of Ypres. During the same month, he rescued a wounded comrade and carried him back to the first aid post (FAP) from the position known as the Menin Crossroads, or Krulseeke Crossroads, close to Ypres. In 1923 the Green Howards commissioned a painting of this incident by Fortunino Matania, the journalist-illustrator, which was later to contribute to a great historical controversy.

In March 1915 Tandey took part in the Battle of Neuve Chappelle. Eighteen months later, in October 1916, Tandey was sent home after being wounded in the leg during the Battle of the Somme. According to the Ministry of Defence, he was later transferred to the 3rd Battalion in Richmond, where he was later cleared for active service, and he served from 5 May 1917 until 10 June 1917. He was sent to Flanders to join the 9th Battalion from 11 June 1917 to 27 November 1917 and, during this period, was wounded again. He was back with the 3rd Battalion from 23 January 1918 to 14 March 1918, then with the 12th Battalion in France from 15 March 1918 to 25 July 1918. Just why Tandey changed battalions so often is not clear, although he did refer to his later changes of unit, when he was transferred from the Green Howards to the 5th Battalion Duke of Wellington's (West Riding) Regiment (62rd West Riding Division), in a letter to Canon Lummis, dated 16 August 1957: 'Attached to 5th Huddersfield Territorials, West Riding Regt. My division had both March & April retreats in 1918, instead of being reinforced, were disbanded & the remnants attached to other units, hence to 5th West Riding.'

Tandey was transferred from 26 July 1918 until 4 October 1918 and, because of his heroic achievements during a period of only six weeks, a tug-of-war began between the two regiments with which he served. However, it must be pointed out that Tandey always considered himself to be a Green Howards man. In September, Tandey earned a DCM and the citation of 5 December 1918 described what happened at Vaux Vraucourt:

> For most determined bravery and initiative during operations from August 25th to September 2nd 1918, particularly during the attack on a system of trenches on August 28th. He was in charge of a reserve bombing party, and finding the parties in front temporarily held up he called on the two other men of his party and worked across the open in the rear of the enemy and rushed the post, coming back with 20 prisoners, after having killed several of the enemy. His daring action and initiative largely contributed to the capture of the Northern Trench. He was an example of daring courage throughout the whole of the operations.

About ten days later, he won a MM at Havrincourt and the citation of 13 March 1919 was as follows:

> During an attack at Havrincourt on September 12th 1918 this man exhibited great heroism and devotion to duty. He went out under most heavy shell fire and carried a badly wounded man on his back. He then went out again and found three more wounded men and put them under cover and fetched a party of men to bring them in.
>
> During a bombing attack on the Hindenburg Line on September 13th he volunteered to be leading bomber and then led the party over the open ground. He made himself responsible for holding the bombing block in the trench and whilst doing this the post was attacked by the enemy in strength. The German officer shot at him point-blank and missed. Pte Tandey, quite regardless of danger, then led his party against the enemy and drove them away in confusion. This soldier's conduct was throughout of the highest order and for gallantry and determined leadership beyond all praise.

After winning his VC and badly wounded in the leg and arm, Tandey returned to England and, according to Ministry of Defence records, was in hospital until the end of the war. He was discharged on 1 March 1919 and then re-enlisted with the 3rd Duke of Wellington's in Halifax. He was later employed on recruiting duties and was made a lance corporal. In the same year, the Freedom of Leamington was conferred upon him on 21 January, and he was presented with a gold plated casket and decorated scroll. A few weeks later, on 27 February, the local council organised a fundraising ball for Tandey. In the following year, he took part in the service for the burial of the Unknown Warrior in Westminster Abbey, where he was one of fifty holders of the VC who were selected to line the aisle of the abbey as the guard of honour. On 4 February 1921 he was posted to the 2nd Battalion, serving in Ireland, and four days later, at his own request, he reverted to private. Between the end of the war and his discharge, Tandey moved around considerably, serving in Gibraltar, Turkey and Egypt. He later became a recruiting sergeant until his discharge from the Army on 5 January 1926.

After he was discharged, Tandey returned to Warwickshire, settling down in Coventry, where he was to spend the rest of his life. He had married Edith ('Edie') Warwick and began work with the Standard Motor Company where he was a commissionaire for thirty-eight years.

Not only was there a controversy about which regiment Tandey belonged to when he won his three gallantry medals, but a further controversy began in the late 1930s, arising from the incident at the Menin Crossroads in October 1914. In 1938 a rumour began to circulate in the British press that, on 28 September 1918, Private Tandey had had a German soldier, one Adolf Hitler, in his sights, but because the man was wounded at the time Tandey refrained from pulling the trigger. This story 'ran and ran' and was only laid to rest as impossible nearly sixty years later in 1997. A report in the *Sunday Graphic* of 1 December 1940 described a conversation that Hitler had at Berchtesgaden in 1938 with the British prime minister, Neville Chamberlain. Hitler had pointed to a figure in a picture displayed on his study wall. Produced by Fortunino Matania, it showed a group of men from the 2nd Battalion, Green Howards, in retreat at Petit Kruiseek on the Ypres–Menin road in October 1914. Hitler had apparently requested a copy of the picture from the Green Howards, which was duly sent. In the picture, entitled 'Menin Crossroads', Tandey was portrayed carrying a wounded soldier. Of this incident, Hitler said to Chamberlain: 'That man came so near to killing me that I thought that I should never see Germany again'.

When Chamberlain returned from meeting Hitler, he telephoned Tandey to tell him what Hitler had said. In the writer's view, it was purely Hitler's fantasy: Hitler was always a great admirer of the British Tommy or private soldier, and also possibly wanted to stress this admiration for a former foe in order to cajole the British prime minister into seeing his territorial demands as legitimate. Somehow, intentionally or not, Hitler transposed the 1914 portrait of Tandey for that of another British soldier who might well have failed 'to pull the trigger'. I don't want to spoil a good story, but Hitler and Tandey could not have been in opposition on 28 September 1918 because Hitler's unit, the 16th Bavarian Reserve Regiment, was not close to Marcoing at the time and, furthermore, Hitler himself was on the point of returning from leave.

As previously mentioned, Tandey was working for Standard Motors and, in the late 1930s, he was working in an office in Priory Street, just around the corner from Coventry Cathedral. He had a home close by, in what was then No. 22 Cope Street. Just over a year after the Second World War broke out, Tandey's home was bombed during the great enemy raid on 14 November 1940. This was the night that the cathedral was destroyed, although the enemy targets were mainly the many aircraft factories scattered across the city. The aerial and anti-aircraft (ack-ack) defences were hopelessly inadequate as protection, and the resulting loss of life was considerable, with a total of 568 people killed and more than a thousand injured.

Tandey once more displayed his heroic qualities, helping people who had been bombed out of their homes. By a stroke of fate, Tandey's wife was staying with her sister in Leamington at the time. From their home he was able to rescue only a clock, which had been presented to him by the Duke of Wellington's Old Contemptibles Association in April 1920. Tandey continued to work for Standard Motors, where he was described as a 'quiet chap, unassuming and deferential'. During his long career, he worked in several buildings occupied by the firm. It was said that wherever Capt. Black, later Sir John Black and head of the company, was working, there Tandey could be found on the door.

After the Second World War, Tandey attended the Victory Parade in London on 8 June 1946, as well as most of the Victoria Cross/George Cross functions in the subsequent years. In 1958 Edith died of a stroke and Tandey was remarried in 1963 to Annie Whateley. In the same year, the Green Howards Old Comrades' Association put on a special show in honour of Tandey on some wasteland at Queen Elizabeth Barracks in Strensall, near York, and an authentic Western Front trench was dug, with survivors of the First World War being invited to take part in a sort of re-enactment. Beer and 'bangers' were provided, along with mouth-organ music and much else intended to appeal to the Old Comrades. Also that year, the *Coventry Standard* of 4 October mentioned in an article about Tandey's life that he had by then worked for the Standard factory for thirty-eight years and had been a member of the original Triumph Company in Priory Street, which later became Standard. On 1 July 1976 Tandey took the salute at a special parade at Leamington Town Hall to mark the 60th anniversary of the first day of the Battle of the Somme, and the Royal Regiment of Fusiliers exercised their right to march through the town. On the saluting dais with him was the Mayor of Leamington and other dignitaries. Tandey's verdict on the modern soldiers' turnout was complimentary: 'The parade was very good'. Following the parade, a regimental display was staged in the Pump Room Gardens, with the band playing.

Having been in declining health for several years, Tandey died of cancer at the age of 86 at 7 Loundon Avenue, Coventry, on 20 December 1977 after a short illness. He left instructions for his funeral to be a private affair, rather than the official military one to which he was entitled. It took place at the Church of Christ the King, Barker Butts Lane, Coventry, followed by cremation at Canley on 23 December 1977. Although it was a private occasion, the mayors of Coventry and Leamington both attended and the Royal British Legion provided a guard of honour drawn from their branch at the Standard Motor Company. Later, Tandey's final wish was carried out in May 1978 when his ashes were buried by his nephew in Masnières British Cemetery, Marcoing, close to the grave of Thomas Neely VC.

A maple tree was planted in his memory at Jephson Gardens in Leamington, as his former home in Cope Street is now under the Coventry Sports Centre. Three years later, in 1981, an exhibition was arranged in the art gallery in Leamington when medals and memorabilia of the town's Victoria Cross winners were displayed. The four men around whom the display was arranged were Charles Goodfellow, John Cridlan Barrett, Henry Tandey and William Amey.

Further links with the Victoria Cross were to be found at Tandey's former place of work, the Regent Hotel, Leamington. Here a Victoria Cross Lounge was created in 1984, designed to commemorate the two local men who won the VC in the autumn of 1918. Colonel John Cridlan Barrett was a member of the family who used to own the hotel. Reproductions of pictures depicting the deeds of the two men were displayed: Barrett's 1/5th Leicesters was by Terence Cuneo; Tandey's was, of course, the one by Matania. The two paintings were unveiled by Earl Spencer and the ceremony marked the 80th anniversary of the Cridlan/Barrett family connection with the hotel. The Regent Hotel closed in May 1998 and later became a Travel Lodge. Tandey's name is also remembered with Tandey Court in Union Road, Leamington

On 26 November 1980, Sir Ernest Harrison OBE purchased the nine medals belonging to Henry Tandey for £27,000 from Annie Tandey, although his bid was anonymous at the time; it is now known that he was bidding against the town of Leamington. In 1982 Harrison also purchased the medals of CSM Stanley Hollis for £32,000, with the intention of bequeathing them to the Green Howards Regimental Museum in Richmond, Yorkshire. However, after a visit to the museum he decided to present them in person, so they could be placed with the thirteen other VCs owned by the museum. They had been handed over at a special ceremony on 11 November 1997 at the Tower of London. Sir Ernest had been closely involved with a project to commemorate the role of the Green Howards in Normandy during the Second World War, and was a Trustee of the Green Howards Normandy Memorial Trust. In 2006 Tandey's two regiments were amalgamated as part of the new Yorkshire Regiment, together with the Prince of Wales's Own Regiment. At a special service held in Lichfield Cathedral on 10 June 2007, Tandey was one of the VC holders who had connections to Staffordshire and Warwickshire to be honoured. The occasion also marked the 150th anniversary of the first VC to be presented. Family members were present at the service. In 2011 it was mooted locally that a Blue Plaque would be erected outside the Angel Hotel in Regent Street, Leamington. The area was close to where he was born and attended school at St Peter's, and the plaque was unveiled on 28 September 2012.

With his VC, DCM and MM, Henry Tandey must have been one of the most highly decorated private soldiers in the First World War. In addition, he had qualified for a 1914 Star with clasp, BWM and VM. For the Second World War he was awarded the Defence Medal 1939–45. He also qualified for Coronation medals for 1937 and 1953, and the Queen Elizabeth II Silver Jubilee Medal (1977). He was also Mentioned in Despatches on five occasions.

E. SEAMAN
Terhand, Belgium, 29 September

At the end of September 1918, three divisions of the British Army were placed under the command of the King of the Belgians. One of these was the 36th (Ulster) Division, and it was with considerable secrecy that this division moved from its position at Messines Ridge, transferring to a position between the 9th and 29th Divisions in the Ypres Salient. The 109th Brigade was in the van of the 36th Division and, at 9.30 a.m. on 29 September, it moved forward to capture Terhand, north of the Menin road. The 2nd Royal Inniskilling Fusiliers were to the right, the 9th Inniskillings on the left and the 1st Inniskillings in support. The attack made rapid progress over relatively unspoilt country. The 2nd Battalion had the hardest task, and in the early afternoon were held up by machine-gun fire; but by 3.45 p.m., Terhand had been captured. By then the 9th Battalion had reached the southern outskirts of Dadizeele to the north-east, which was quickly taken and consolidated by the 9th (Scottish) Division.

Lance Corporal Ernest Seaman was in A Company, 2nd Inniskillings when he won a posthumous VC, gazetted on 15 November 1918 as follows:

> For most conspicuous bravery and devotion to duty. When the right flank of his company was held up by a nest of enemy machine-guns, he, with great courage and initiative, rushed forward under heavy fire with his Lewis-gun, and engaged

the position single-handed, capturing two machine-guns and twelve prisoners, and killing one officer and two men. Later in the day he again rushed another enemy machine-gun post, capturing the gun under heavy fire. He was killed immediately after. His courage and dash were beyond all praise, and it was entirely due to the very gallant conduct of L.-Corpl. Seaman that his company was enabled to push forward to its objective and capture many prisoners.

On the night of 29 September the 109th Brigade held the line that it had won, enabling the 108th Brigade to pass through and renew the attack. The captain in command of A Company later wrote of Seaman:

He was one of the best soldiers whom I had ever met, an excellent soldier in every sense of the word, and very keen in his duties. He always volunteered to help in any extra work that had to be done, no matter how dangerous and difficult, and for his constant devotion to duty and gallantry in voluntarily attending his wounded comrades under heavy fire, I recommended his being awarded the Military Medal.

His VC was presented to his mother, Mrs Sarah Palmer, in the ballroom of Buckingham Palace on 13 February 1919.

Ernest Seaman, the son of Henry Seaman and Sarah Elizabeth Seaman, was born on 16 August 1893 at 9 Derby Street, Heigham, Norwich. Seaman's father died when Ernest was still quite young, leaving him and an elder sister, Ethel. His mother later married Mr S. Palmer and they had one son, Reggie. The Palmers ran the King's Inn public house in Bungay Road, Scole, on the Norfolk/Suffolk border. Seaman attended Scole Council School, which had been founded in 1853 and which is now Scole Primary School. While at school, Seaman was known as 'Peddler Palmer'. In addition to helping run the King's Head, Mr Palmer also ran a pony-and-trap service, as well as a taxi service for passengers from Diss station. Seaman, who as a boy was described as short, plumpish and reserved, moved from Scole to Trimley, near Felixstowe in Suffolk, where he lived with an aunt and worked at the Grand Hotel, Felixstowe, for three years. In 1912 he decided to seek his fortune elsewhere and, like many of his generation, emigrated to Canada. However, he returned to England after the war broke out, joining the Army in 1915. He was of relatively poor physique, being judged not strong enough for regular service, so he became a member of the Expeditionary Force Canteens (Army Service Corps) on 16 December 1915. Later owing to the increasing casualty rate, grades of medical fitness were lowered and, at some point, Seaman was 'combed out' from catering for active service and transferred to the Royal Inniskilling Fusiliers, where his service number was 42364. It is this connection which explains why his name is included on the memorial for men from disbanded Ulster regiments who had been awarded the VC, which is displayed in St Anne's Cathedral, Belfast.

During his Army service he spent much of the time in the Ypres Salient, in particular around the Passchendaele Ridge. He was killed on 29 September 1918 in the action that gained him a posthumous VC at Terhard in Belgium. He was reported missing and his name is commemorated on Panel 70–72 at Tyne Cot. At St Andrew's Church, Scole, a copy of his VC citation is displayed as part of the roll of honour of men from the village who served in both world wars. Seaman's name is also one of the thirteen commemorated on the Scole war memorial and his name appears on the war memorial at Felixstowe. Originally, the letters VC were not recorded there, but this oversight was rectified by a stonemason at a special ceremony, attended by about a dozen of Seaman's relatives, who also laid a wreath at the memorial. As Seaman served with the 36th (Ulster) Division, his name is also listed on the Victoria Cross memorial in front of the Ulster Tower in Thiepval, France.

Seaman's home at the King's Head in Bungay Road, Scole, no longer exists, having been replaced by a modern housing development. Further along the road, towards Bungay, is the village of Billingford, where another VC winner, Gordon Flowerdew, grew up (one can see his home from the main road). It is amazing that two winners of the VC should live in neighbouring Norfolk villages, that both men should emigrate to Canada, and that both should return to England and win Victoria Crosses posthumously on the Western Front. Seaman's VC is in the collection of the Royal Logistic Corps, successor of the old Army Service Corps and whose origins go back to the Army School of Catering before the First World War. Apart from the VC, he was entitled to the 1914–15 Star, BWM and VM.

B.W. VANN
*Bellenglise and Lehaucourt,
France, 29 September*

During the battle for a section of the St-Quentin Canal, north-west of St-Quentin, between 29 September and 2 October, Capt. Bernard William Vann, A/Lt Col of the 1/8th Sherwood Foresters, won the VC when in command of the 1/6th Sherwood Foresters, 139th Brigade, 46th (1st North Midland) Division.

The 46th Division, on the left of the IX Corps, was instructed to cross the canal and capture the first objective, while the 32nd Division was to pass through their lines and capture the second objective. The 1st Division to the south would then follow up on the right of the 46th Division. The Midland Division had the advantage of being able to look down on the canal and its German defences. On a small rise to the west of the canal was a line of strong defences, complete with strongpoints and machine-gun posts. The 35ft-wide bed of the canal was a mixture of water, mud and very strong belts of barbed wire, but the very heavy artillery was to deal with these, virtually destroying them immediately prior to the launch of the assault at 5.50am. on what was a foggy morning.

The 137th (South Staffordshire) Brigade, also of the 46th Division, was to advance from the lines of the 8th Sherwood Foresters at the same time as the 1st Division was to advance on the right as far as Bellenglise Bridge. The chief feature of the village was a great tunnel or dug-out, which had been built by the Germans for shelter. The main enemy trenches ran along the eastern side of the

St Quentin Canal, which meant that the attacking troops would have to descend the steep canal bank in full view of the enemy. Despite this situation, the 1/6th South Staffordshires did succeed in crossing the canal and entering the village, and before the enemy could escape from the Bellenglise tunnel they were quickly captured by a small party of men. The village was then mopped up and the 1/6th Sherwood Foresters passed through on their way to the village of Lehaucourt to the east.

Vann's battalion came under heavy artillery and machine-gun fire, and his gallantry is described in the following citation in the *London Gazette* of 14 December 1918:

> For most conspicuous bravery, devotion to duty and fine leadership during the attack at Bellenglise and Lehaucourt on 29 Sept. 1918. He led his battalion with great skill across the St Quentin Canal through a very thick fog and under heavy fire from field and machine-guns. On reaching the high ground above Bellenglise, the whole attack was held up by fire of all descriptions from the front and right flank. Realising that everything depended on the advance going forward with the barrage, Lieut.-Colonel Vann rushed up to the firing line, and with the greatest gallantry led the line forward. By his prompt action and absolute contempt for danger the whole situation was changed, the men were encouraged and the line swept forward. Later, he rushed a field-gun single-handed, and knocked out three of the detachment. The success of the day was in no small degree due to the splendid gallantry and fine leadership displayed by this officer. Lieut.-Colonel Vann, who had on all occasions set the highest example of valour, was killed near Ramicourt on 3 Oct., when leading his battalion in attack.

During the attack and capture of Ramicourt–Montbrehain on 29 September, 1,500 prisoners were captured. Of the 1/6th Sherwood Foresters, four officers and twenty-five other ranks were killed, with 109 wounded and eight men missing. Four days later, on 3 October, Lt Col Vann was leading his men from the front when he was shot through the head by a sniper, soon after his battalion had crossed the Beaurevoir–Fonsomme Line, which consisted of a strong barbed wire entanglement with a double line of shallow trenches. Concrete machine-gun emplacements were every 50yd. Vann, who had been known to some of his friends as 'Vasi' was buried south-west of Bellicourt. However, in 1920, his body was exhumed and re-buried 12 miles east of Peronne in Bellicourt British Cemetery, in a field across the canal, where forty-eight men – almost all from the 46th (North Midland) Division – are interred. The cemetery was designed by Charles Holden and William Harrison Cowlishaw. The inscription on Vann's headstone in Plot II, Row 0, Grave 1 reads: 'A Great Priest Who In His Days Pleased God'. The inscription was written by the Bishop of Peterborough, who had ordained Vann in 1911.

Vann's posthumous VC was presented to his widow, Mrs Doris V. Vann, by the King on 26 November 1919 at the same ceremony at which the Mannock family received Major (Maj.) Edward Mannock's VC, DSO and two bars, MC and bar. Mrs Vann was also sent her husband's plaque and scroll. He left £527 7s 1d gross in his will.

Bernard William Vann was the son of Alfred George Collins Vann MA, headmaster of Chichele College, Higham Ferrers, Northamptonshire, and of Hannah Elizabeth Vann. He was the fourth of five sons and born on 9 July 1887 at 46 High Street in nearby Rushden. He attended the school that his father ran, before going up to Jesus College, Cambridge in 1907. He became a keen sportsman and, while at university, won a Hockey Blue in his final year. He was also a sergeant in the Officers' Training Corps (OTC).

From Cambridge he took up a position as a schoolmaster at Ashby de la Zouch Grammar School. At some point, he assisted Northampton Town as a centre forward, turned out a dozen times for Burton United, and played three times for Derby County.

After deciding to enter the Church, Bernard Vann was ordained as a deacon on 22 September 1911 at St Barnabas, New Humbertstone, by the Bishop of Peterborough. This post was followed by serving for two years as a curate at St Saviour's, Leicester. He later took up a position at Wellingborough School (January 1913 to August 1914) as chaplain and assistant master.

When the war began in August 1914, Vann attempted to enter the Army as a chaplain, but, unwilling to wait a long time for a vacancy, he decided to join an infantry regiment as a private instead. After being discharged from the OTC, he enlisted on the 31 August in the 1/28th Battalion (County of London Regiment) (Artists' Rifles), and he was appointed to the 1/8th Sherwood Foresters (The Notts & Derby Regiment), 139th Brigade, 46th (North Midland) Division) the following day. He gave his height as 5ft 11in.

In February 1915 Vann arrived in France for the first time in his military service, and in May he was buried alive and badly bruised by the explosion of a trench mortar. On 6 June he was made temporary captain, then, on 15 August July, he was awarded the MC and took part in the Battle of Loos. In October he received severe gunshot wounds in an assault on the Hohenzollern Redoubt, but continued to throw grenades until told to come away by the brigade commander. He returned to recover in England in mid-October. He was promoted to captain on 1 June 1916 and on 20 June to acting major.

After Vann's death, an officer colleague wrote in *The Times*: '... although suffering continuous agony for days before hand from neuritis, caused by one of his many wounds, he insisted on leading his company on a raid, and himself killed or captured several Germans. He was so bad that the next day he had to be taken away, and was ill in England for several months.'

Two months later, Vann won a bar to his MC at Blairville, when leading his company in a raid on an enemy trench called Italy Sap (citation in the *London Gazette* of 14 November). In the same month he had a mental breakdown and returned to England for several months to recover from neuritis in the back of his neck. In February 1917 he was awarded the *Croix-de-Guerre* with Palm and was declared fit on 15 March when a patient in Connaught Hospital, Aldershot. He attended the Adjutant Command School until July and, on 23 September, was sent to command the 2/6th Battalion Sherwood Foresters and was promoted to acting lieutenant colonel on 6 October.

On 21 October he proceeded to England on 'special leave', returning to France six days later. He returned to England for two weeks, from 3 to 17 December, then on 27 December he married Doris Strange-Beck, a Canadian nurse, daughter of Geoffrey Strange-Beck of Port Arthur, at St Paul's, Knightsbridge. Doris had travelled from Canada in order to work at St Dunstan's. On 18 March 1918 Vann was on leave again, then returned to his battalion on 3 April. On 23 May he was admitted to hospital and on 10 June he rejoined the 1/6th Battalion 'from rest station'.

At the end of August, Vann arranged for his wife to travel to France, and the couple spent ten days' leave in Paris. During this time Mrs Vann conceived, and the couple's son, named Bernard Geoffrey, was born on 2 June 1919.

During the war, Vann became an excellent example of a soldier-priest. He was of fine physique and had a great zest for life. He was clearly loved by his men, not only as a fearless leader but also as a spiritual father. During the war he was wounded no fewer than eleven times, perhaps even more. A brother officer wrote an account of him which was printed in *The Times* after he was killed:

> I remember an occasion when as a subaltern his outspoken expressions led to something like a heated argument with his Army Commander, General Allenby, who however, never forgot him, and always inquired kindly about him.
>
> It was his extraordinary courage and tenacity which will be remembered by all who knew him; where danger was Bernard Vann must inevitably be. Buried and badly bruised by a trench-mortar in May 1915, he just dug himself out, and set to work to organise the defence, and help to dig out others. He was in bed for days afterwards, but refused to go down the line. When, shortly afterwards, a neighbouring unit recently arrived in France was temporarily confused and out of hand under a first experience of liquid fire, it was Vann who, revolver in hand, saved a serious situation, and, by pure personal example, restored confidence at a critical moment. Wounded severely at the Hohenzollern Redoubt in October 1915, he continued to carry on an incessant bombing fight for several hours until ordered by the brigadier to come away.

Vann's name is commemorated on the Higham Ferrer's Memorial in the town's main square. He is also commemorated with a plaque in the 8th Sherwood Foresters' Memorial in St Mary Magdalen's Church, Newark. Vann's home address was Coates Rectory,

Cirencester, Gloucestershire, where he spent much of his childhood. After his father's death in 1906, his mother, Hannah Elizabeth, kept house for her brother and Vann's uncle, the Revd D.C. Simpson, and the sons often visited the rectory. The house where the family lived is now called the Old Rectory and is adjacent to St Matthews Church, where Vann's name is listed on a roll of honour, together with a photograph and a brief account of his life. His brother, Capt. A.H.A. Vann of the 12th West Yorks, was killed at Loos on 25 September 1915 and his name is listed on both the Loos Memorial and the roll of honour. The names of the two of the three Vann brothers are also listed on the war memorial in Coates, which is opposite the former National School built in 1859. The memorial has been restored, so that the names of the dead from both world wars are now clearly legible.

Bernard Vann junior, who never knew his father, later became a naval lieutenant commander and died in 1994; his wife survived him. Bernard Vann senior's medals of VC, MC and bar, 1914–15 Star, BWM and VM, as well as Croix de Guerre were in the hands of the family, but in May 2011 they were acquired by Lord Ashcroft and are displayed in the Imperial War Museum. They are minus Vann's First World War Trio medals.

In his role as a priest, Vann always carried a portable altar, together with the Eucharistic vestments, and 'his greatest joy was to be able to say Mass for the men he loved so well and to give them Communion'. After his death, the by then battered chalice that he used, together with his Bible, was returned to his widow in a small leather case which is still in the care of the family. The chalice was later presented by his family to the rector of Coates, the Revd Canon Andrew Bowden, who used it occasionally in services.

In 2006 a Blue Plaque was unveiled at Vann's birthplace at 46 High Street, Rushden. It was unveiled by Bernard's grandson, who wore his relative's decorations at the ceremony. The arrangement for the plaque had been made by the Rushden and District History Society.

B.A. WARK

Bellicourt, Nauroy, Étricourt,
Magny La Fosse and Joncourt,
France, 29 September–1 October

Bellicourt was a village between St Quentin and Cambrai; it was served by a light railway and the St Quentin Canal passed under it through a 3-mile tunnel. The Hindenburg Line ran west of the village and the barges in the tunnel sheltered German reserves. About 3 miles to the south of Bellicourt, where the canal was once again open, lay the village of Bellenglise. The 5th Australian Division was instructed to attack the Hindenburg Line at Bellicourt, then to advance through several villages and on to Joncourt, thus reaching the Beaurevoir Line, the last bastion of the Hindenburg Line.

One of the Australian battalions due to take part in the attack was the 32nd, under Maj. Blair Wark. The battalion was to form the right flank of the Australian advance on 29 September: their jumping-off point was to the front of Bellicourt, and the start time was set at 9 a.m. Owing to heavy mist, together with the smoke from the artillery barrage, visibility was very poor. The first check came from two enemy machine guns, which Wark disposed of with the assistance of a tank whose noise he had heard in the fog. On reaching the southern end of the canal tunnel, he came across some 200 troops of the 117th American Regiment who appeared to be without any sort of leader. Apparently they should have passed to the east of the tunnel and then moved southwards. He quickly commandeered these men, attaching them to his own force.

A short time later, when it was still foggy, he arranged for further tank support. His men, preceded by the tanks, moved towards the village of Nauroy, mopping up as they went. They were between Bellicourt and the tunnel mouth when the fog began to lift and Wark organised his troops to attack Nauroy from a southerly direction. By 11.30 a.m. his men were in the village, sweeping all before them, and capturing forty Germans in the process. Behind them, with the assistance of two more tanks, the area was mopped up along with part of the Le Catelet Line beyond. Wark moved on and many more machine guns, field guns and Germans were quickly captured. On the second ridge beyond Nauroy, he linked up with men from the 4th Leicesters of the 46th (North Midland) Division, which had been part of the 137th Brigade's successful crossing of the canal. Bridges had been seized so quickly that the enemy had no time to destroy them, and Wark began to move against his final objective, via Magny-la-Fosse, from which there was only weak machine-gun fire. The advance then headed north-eastwards towards the village of Joncourt, with little opposition.

By mid-afternoon Wark's troops were understandably very tired, so he decided to halt on a spur to the south-west of the village. Patrols were then sent out, which established that, surprisingly, Joncourt was not occupied by the enemy, though fire came from the direction of the village, affecting the left flank and rear of Wark's position. The line was withdrawn slightly and also strengthened; an attack from the enemy was repulsed with the assistance of the 31st Battalion, together with some men from the 46th (North Midland) Division, at 5.30 p.m. At 7 a.m. the next day the 32nd Battalion moved forward once more, reaching the village from a position just north of Étricourt. Heavy shelling and machine-gun fire began, but a line was established between Joncourt and Étricourt. On 1 October at 6 a.m. the battalion, with a company from the 30th Battalion, attacked what turned out to be strong opposition, despite being assisted by an accurate artillery barrage. Joncourt and the ground beyond it was eventually reached. Thus the 5th Australian Division had reached its objective of the Beaurevoir Line. Major Blair Wark was awarded the VC for his work over three days from 29 September to 1 October, which was gazetted on 26 December 1918 as follows:

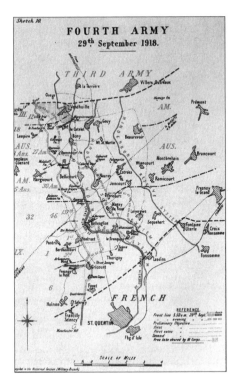

For most conspicuous bravery, initiative and control during the period 29 Sept. to 1 Oct. 1918, in the operations against the Hindenburg Line at Bellicourt, and the advance through Nauroy, Étricourt, Magny La Fosse and Joncourt. On 29 Sept., after personal reconnaissance under heavy fire, he led his command forward at a critical period and restored the situation. Moving fearlessly at the head of, and at times far in advance of, his troops, he cheered his men on through Nauroy, thence towards Étricourt. Still leading his assaulting companies, he observed a battery of 77mm guns firing on his rear companies and causing heavy casualties. Collecting a few of his men, he rushed the battery, capturing four guns and ten of the crew. Then, moving rapidly forward with only two N.C.O.s, he surprised and captured 50 Germans near Magny La Fosse. On 1 Oct. 1918, he again showed fearless leading and gallantry in attack, and without hesitation, and regardless of personal risk, dashed forward and silenced machine-guns which were causing heavy casualties. Throughout he displayed the greatest courage, skillful leading and devotion to duty, and his work was invaluable.

General Rawlinson, commander of the Fourth Army, issued the following order concerning Wark's actions: '... shows that the gallant deeds for which he won his V.C. extended over a period of twelve days ... It is beyond doubt that the success achieved by the brigade during the heavy fighting was due to this officer's gallantry, determination, skill and great courage.' Wark was presented with his VC in the ballroom of Buckingham Palace on 13 February 1919.

Blair Anderson Wark was born at Bathurst in New South Wales on 27 July 1894. He was the fourth child of Alexander and Blanche Adelaide Wark (née Forde) and attended the Fairleigh Grammar School in the town. On moving to Sydney he studied to be a quantity surveyor at St Leonards Superior Public School (North Sydney) and later at Sydney Technical College. At the age of 18 he served as a senior cadet, rising to the rank of sergeant, before joining the 18th (North Sydney) Infantry. In August 1913 he was promoted to second lieutenant and, for the next year, until the war broke out, he was involved in full-time defence duties at the port of Sydney. Two of his brothers also served in the Australian Imperial Force (AIF).

A year after the war began, Wark was appointed to the AIF on 5 August 1915, and was posted as a lieutenant and company commander to the 30th Battalion. He proceeded to Liverpool, a suburb of Sydney, where he attended an infantry school. He then completed another course, this time at the Royal Military College in Duntroon. On 9 November he embarked for Egypt with the 30th Battalion, where he served with the Suez Canal defences until June 1916, when he left for France, arriving in Marseilles on the 23rd. He had been promoted to captain on 20 February and also made company commander.

The first major battle he took part in was the disastrous Fromelles operation in the summer of 1916, in which he was wounded on 19 July. He was then taken to No. 7 Stationary Hospital with gun-shot wounds to his leg, and on the 22nd he was transferred to England and to the 3rd General London Hospital. Later, on 7 August, he was moved to 5th Australian Auxiliary Hospital, Digwell House, Welwyn. After finally recovering from leg wounds in September, and after a short leave, he returned to France on the 30th. About ten days later he was transferred to the 32nd (South Australian and Western Australia) Battalion and was to remain with them until the end of the war.

On 2 January 1917 Wark attended Army Infantry School and, in February, returned to the 32nd Battalion. He had been recommended for the DSO for his conduct at Fromelles and action at Sunray Trench in March 1917, but this wasn't confirmed.

On 27 April he was awarded his majority, remaining as com-pany commander. On 29 July 1917 at Polygon Wood, during the Third Battle of Ypres, he won the DSO (gazetted on 3 June 1918). On several occasions the enemy attempted a counter-attack against Wark's company's position, but Wark's men managed to smash their leading waves, with the remainder of the counter-attack dealt with by the artillery. After Wark had sent out patrols, he was able to ascertain that the enemy was contemplating a further counter-attack, which, when it came, was promptly broken up. He was in command of the battalion in June, but still managed to spend six days' leave in Paris. In January of the following year, he went to Aldershot for a senior officers' course, returning to France in the summer of 1918. In June he was Mentioned in Despatches and, at some point, he was granted sixteen more days of leave, which he spent in England.

Before Blair Wark was demobilised on 28 September 1919, he got married to Phyllis Marquiss Munro at St George's Parish Church in Worthing on 31 May. The couple then returned to Australia on 10 June, when Wark resumed his job as a quantity surveyor in Sydney. In June 1920, during a visit to Australia, the Prince of Wales was introduced to a group of eleven Australian holders of the VC, and Maj. Wark was in charge of the group in the grounds of Government House. A number of scouts and nurses were also introduced to the Prince. Wark's AIF appointment was terminated three months later.

Blair Wark became a respected member of Australian society, holding various honorary positions, including director of the Royal North Shore Hospital, Life Governor of the New South Wales

Benevolent Society, and councillor of the National Roads and Motorists' Association of New South Wales. He also joined the committee of the Hawkesbury Race Club. In addition, he held directorships of various insurance and petrol companies.

Five years after he and Phyllis were divorced in 1922, Wark married Katherine ('Kit') Mary Davis at St Stephen's Presbyterian Church, Sydney on 10 December 1927, and the couple were to have two daughters and one son. On 23 November 1934, Prince Henry, Duke of Gloucester, met Wark and some of his colleagues during a visit to Australia.

In 1940 Wark returned to active service during the Second World War, being appointed to the 1st Battalion (City of Sydney's Own Regiment) as a major on 17 April. A few weeks later, on 26 July, he was made temporary lieutenant colonel when he assumed command. Sadly, on 13 June 1941, he died very suddenly while bivouacked at Puckapunyal Military Camp, Victoria, and his body was taken to Melbourne and then to Sydney. He was later cremated at Eastern Suburbs Crematorium, Sydney, after a full military funeral had taken place on 16 June. His ashes were then interred in Worongra Crematorium Columbarium, Shelf D-30.

Wark is commemorated in a number of ways and in New South Wales his name is remembered on a Garden of Remembrance wall, with a plaque at Columbarium and a memorial at Rookwood Cemetery, New South Wales. In 1956 his widow, Kit, attended the Victoria Cross centenary celebrations in London and she was to live for another twenty years, dying in May 1976. After the Great War, one of Wark's captured 77mm guns was sent back to Australia, where it became part of the collection of the Australian War Memorial in Canberra. His decorations are also normally held here, but at the present time they are on loan to the Queensland Museum in Brisbane. Apart from his VC and DSO, his medals included the BWM (1914–20), VM and MiD Oakleaf (1914–1919), WM (1939–45), Australian Service Medal (1939–45) and King George VI Coronation Medal (1937).

Also in Canberra, Wark is commemorated in the Victora Cross Park Memorial. Finally, he is listed as one of the Australian VC holders in the Queen Victoria Building, Sydney.

J. MacGregor
Near Cambrai, France, 29 September–3 October

The operations to capture the Hindenburg Line were well advanced by 29 September 1918, with the attempt to cross the dry Canal du Nord having begun on 27 September. The Canadian Corps' involvement was very successful in the initial assault and, in addition to crossing the canal, the Canadians captured two heavily defended wired trench systems: the Marquion Line and the Marcoing Line. At the end of operations on 29 September, the Canadians were close to the walls of the enemy held city of Cambrai.

During the actions of 30 September, the 3rd and 4th Canadian Divisions managed to advance 2 miles to Ramillies, Eswars and Cuvillers, while the 8th Brigade, which was part of the 3rd Division, covered Cambrai. Capt. John MacGregor, was a member of the 2nd Canadian Mounted Rifles (CMR) and they, together with their sister unit, the 1st Canadian Mounted Rifles, were ordered to capture bridgeheads in the Canal de l'Escaut area of the northern part of the city. However, they were delayed by fierce fire from the direction of Ste-Olle, a village that had not yet been taken, and the regimental historian of the 2nd CMR describes the fighting on that day 'as the most desperately fought engagement of the war for our battalion'. However, once Ste-Olle had fallen, the two Canadian battalions were able to move forward into the outskirts of the suburbs of Cambrai in the area of Neuvilly-St-Rémy. On their left flank, two battalions of the 7th Brigade were held up opposite Tilloy.

On 1 October the four Canadian divisions took part in an early attack, which began at 5 a.m., and they advanced for about a mile, capturing the high ground to the east of Tilloy. During the advance they coped with intense fire and several counter-attacks. On the following day, the Canadians, expecting a German attack, brought their artillery down heavily on the German frontline. This barrage was designed to catch any planned enemy counter-attack, but the foe had already withdrawn. Captain John MacGregor had been deeply involved in the fighting and was awarded a VC, which was gazetted on 6 January 1919 as follows:

> For most conspicuous bravery, leadership and self-sacrificing devotion to duty near Cambrai from 29 Sept. to 3 Oct. 1918. He led his company under intense fire, and when the advance was checked by machine-guns, although wounded, pushed on and located the enemy's guns. He then ran forward in broad daylight, in face of heavy fire from all directions, and, with rifle and bayonet, single-handed put the enemy's crew out of action, killing four and taking eight prisoners. His prompt action saved many casualties and enabled the advance to continue. After reorganising his command under heavy fire he rendered most useful support to neighbouring troops. When the enemy were showing stubborn resistance he went along the line, regardless of danger, organised platoons, took command of the leading waves and continued the advance. Later, after a personal daylight reconnaissance under heavy fire, he established his company in Neuvilly St Rémy, thereby greatly assisting the advance into Tilloy. Throughout the operations Capt. MacGregor displayed bravery and heroic leadership.

He was presented with his VC in the ballroom of Buckingham Palace on 26 February 1919. James MacGregor, one of John's two brothers, was killed in 1918 while serving as a corporal in the Cameron Highlanders.

John ('Jock') MacGregor was born in Cawdor, Nairn, Scotland, on 11 February 1889, one of five children of William, a farmer, and his wife, Jessie (or Hannah) Mackay. He was educated first at Clunas School, then at either Cawdor Public School or Nairn Academy. In 1908, at the age of 19, he emigrated to Canada, where he trained as a mason and carpenter.

When the First World War broke out he was working in British Columbia, but in March 1915 he enlisted as a trooper in the Canadian Army, after travelling 120 miles on snowshoes in order to reach the recruiting office at Prince Rupert. He became a private in the 11th Canadian Mounted Rifles and, after training, served in France from 22 September 1915 with the 2nd CMR. In June 1916 the battalion was part of 8th Brigade, 3rd Canadian Division, and lost much of its strength during the fighting around Sanctuary Wood, near Zillebeke. In September, MacGregor was promoted to sergeant, and in April 1917 he won a DCM at Vimy Ridge. On 12 May he was commissioned in the field as a lieutenant and, two months later, the citation for his DCM was published in the *London Gazette* of 26 July 1917 as follows:

> For conspicuous gallantry and devotion to duty. He single-handed captured an enemy machine-gun and shot the crew, thereby undoubtedly saving his company from many casualties.

He was also awarded the MC, which was gazetted on 16 August 1918 as follows:

> For most conspicuous gallantry and devotion to duty. Whilst he was assembling his men prior to a raid the enemy bombed the trench. He, however, changing his point of attack, led his men over the wire into the enemy's trench, and successfully dealt with the garrison of the trench and three concrete dug-outs, himself capturing one prisoner. He then withdrew his party and his prisoner successfully to our trenches. Before the raid he, together with a sergeant, had made several skillful and daring reconnaissances along the enemy wire, which materially assisted in the success of the enterprise.

On 5 February 1918 he was promoted to temporary captain and subsequently won a bar to his MC. The citation was published in the *London Gazette* on 10 December 1919:

For conspicuous gallantry and leadership from 5th to 8th November, 1918, at Quievrain and Quièvrechain. Through his initiative the bridges over the Hounelle River were secured. His personal reconnaissances and the information he derived from them were of great use to his commanding officer. His prompt action in seizing the crossings over the river did much towards the final rout of the enemy.

He was confirmed in his rank of captain and, on demobilisation in 1919, was gazetted as a major in the Canadian Militia. He returned to his home in British Columbia, moving to Powell River in 1925, at which time he was working with construction crews. On the occasion of an announcement of a forthcoming House of Lords Dinner in 1929 for holders of the VC, MacGregor was tracked down by a friend, who wished to inform him of the impending event. At the time MacGregor was working in the mountains of British Columbia on a hydroelectric plant, and he told the story of what then happened:

> I was in my cabin one night, when suddenly a friend burst open the door. He told me that several wireless stations were asking if anybody knew where I lived, for the authorities wished me to attend the Prince's banquet.
>
> My friend had motored 100 miles to tell me, and he simply rushed me into his car and off to the nearest railway station at Salmon Arm. There we caught the Toronto Express with only ten minutes to spare. I was not even able to let my wife and family know that I had caught the train.
>
> There was a two hours' stop at Toronto where I bought some spare gear, and we got to New York only two hours before the *Olympic* sailed. The presence of the Canadian contingent at the House of Lords Dinner was partly subsidized by the Canadian National and Canadian Pacific Railways, Cunard and White Star Steamship Lines, in addition to several Canadian provinces.

MacGregor said at the time:

> I have not been home since 1919, when I was demobilized. My old mother, who is nearly eighty, does not know I am here. I did

not have the chance to send her a cable before leaving, and my visit will be a big surprise to her.

During the visit to his mother in Nairn, the local citizens presented him with a clock, together with a silver tea service.

In 1933 MacGregor was persuaded by friends to stand in the provincial elections as an independent candidate, but he was unsuccessful. Six years later, in 1939, when the King and Queen visited Vancouver, MacGregor was presented to them. At the outset of the Second World War, MacGregor again joined the Army, this time as a private in the Canadian Scottish Regiment, where he was soon promoted to captain. In 1941 he was made second-in-command of the 2nd Battalion and promoted to major. In early 1942 he became commander of the 2nd Battalion. In 1943 he proceeded overseas, returning a year later to command the Kent (Canadian) Regiment. He then served as acting brigadier while commanding the 2nd Battalion during its training at Wainwright, Alberta. After the Second World War, MacGregor was awarded the Efficiency Decoration (ED) which he received for his services in both world wars.

At some point he married Ethel, who had nursed him when he had a hand injury. They returned to British Columbia, where he established a concrete plant at Cranberry Lake, which was later sold to his son, Don. Powell River is a 'company town' about 73 miles to the north of Vancouver, and on a day when Viscount Alexander of Tunis, then Governor General of Canada, visited the town, 'Jock' MacGregor was appointed to be his aide for the day.

After a long illness MacGregor died at Powell River Hospital on 9 June 1952, having suffered from cancer for six years. Three holders of the VC attended his funeral, including C.W. Peck, Charles Train and G.R. Pearkes. 'Jock' was survived by his wife, two sons, James and Donald, two sisters and a brother. His ashes were buried in Cranberry Lake Cemetery, Powell River. Fifty-four years later, the Commonwealth War Grave Commission (CWGC) considered the grave was in need of a better stone and a standard Commission headstone replaced the original plaque. His two eldest sons attended the ceremony; both were in wheelchairs and both were to die shortly afterward. Seven years before, James had published a biography of his father, *MacGregor VC*.

MacGregor had always been a very shy man and one who was impatient of inactivity; he was at his best as a frontline soldier. His career as one of Canada's most decorated soldiers was summed up by Sir Arthur Currie, onetime C-in-C of the Canadian Army:

> MacGregor ... combines good judgement with sound military knowledge and wide experience. Good power of command and leadership; he inspires men. Excellent character, good appearance, strong personality; tactful, resourceful, and co-operative.

MacGregor was to become one of Canada's most highly decorated soldiers of the First World War. Apart from his VC, MC and bar, and DCM, he was also eligible for the following medals and decorations: 1914–15 Star, BWM and VM. For the Second World War he received a 1939–45 Star, Voluntary Service Medal (Canada) and clasp, 1939–45 War Medal, Coronation Medal 1937 and the Efficiency Decoration. His VC and Efficiency Decoration were the two decorations that most pleased him.

In mid-November 1996 MacGregor's decorations were put up for sale at Messrs Spink in London. His younger son, Donald, was very keen to get them back to Canada where they belonged. They had probably left the MacGregor family in the early 1980s. However, on the eve of the sale the medals were suddenly withdrawn: owing to the lack of an export licence they should never have been allowed out of Canada in the first place. By that time Donald had endeavoured to raise at least $100,000 in assurances, as he wished to present the medals to Powell River or a suitable museum where they could be seen by the public. The story ended happily, with the medals being duly presented to the Canadian War Museum on 11 August 1997 by Don MacGregor: $40,000 were raised by private sources; $35,000 came from the Canadian government; and $100,000 from Canadian Heritage.

During his life 'Jock' MacGregor was described as a man of action, who became extremely impatient with the 'paperwork' which was part and parcel of his military seniority. He was described by one journalist as being big, blunt and burr-voiced. He was obviously a great character.

J. CRICHTON
Near Crêvecoeur, France, 30 September

At the end of September 1918, the British 5th Division and the New Zealand division were ordered to capture the village of Lavacquerie, followed by the Bonavas Ridge, which ran to the south-west of the

village of the same name. They were then to cross the St Quentin Canal and seize the crossings over the Canal de L'Escaut/River Scheldt between Vaucelles and Crêvecoeur. They were also to capture Crêvecoeur and then move out into the high ground in front of Lesdain to the south-east, on to the mill at Esnes and then to the village of La Targette. This would enable them to capture a 'triangle' of ground.

The 15th Brigade of the 5th Division set off at 4 a.m. and had to travel 2½ miles before reaching the St Quentin Canal. They had little difficulty in reaching their first objective, a line about 1500yd from the canal, but were held up in front of the village of Banteux on the western bank. Meanwhile, the New Zealand division sent out a patrol from its 2nd Brigade at 3 a.m. and found the western bank of the canal evacuated in their section, with the Vaucelles bridge destroyed. All approaches to the bridge were swept by fire, so it was impossible to make a crossing of what was only 40yd of water. Other patrols found bridges to the south, towards Banteux, that were passable. For his role in the fighting at Crêvecoeur, Pte James Crichton, a member of the 2nd Battalion, Auckland Infantry Regiment, New Zealand Expeditionary Force (NZEF), was awarded the VC, which was gazetted on 15 November 1918 as follows:

> For most conspicuous bravery and devotion to duty [near Crêvecoeur], when although wounded in the foot, he continued with the advancing troops, despite difficult canal and river

obstacles. When his platoon was subsequently forced back by a counter-attack he succeeded in carrying a message which involved swimming a river and crossing an area swept by machine-gun fire, subsequently rejoining his platoon. Later he undertook on his own initiative to save a bridge which had been mined, and though under close fire of machine-guns and snipers, he succeeded in removing the charges, returning with the fuses and detonators. Though suffering from a painful wound, he displayed the highest degree of valour and devotion to duty.

In Col H. Stewart's *History of the New Zealand Division in France*, the author tells the story of Crichton's extraordinary adventures, which is worth quoting in full:

In front of Crêvecoeur the Scheldt River bends eastwards of the canal, forming a flat large marshy island connected with the village by a stone bridge. A branch of the river also cuts the island and in the attack the 2nd Aucklands had to cross the canal and the two branches of the river. One company (15th) was detailed to seize the canal and river crossings and Crêvecoeur itself. Two other [companies] were to continue the attack beyond. The 15th crossed the canal and established themselves on the island and one platoon crossed the branch of the river and made for the stone bridge. Until they had almost reached it they were not fired upon, but then they were stopped by a terrible fire and had to take shelter in a ditch in an angle between the two branches. The other sections of the battalion had been checked before getting to the first river crossing and a private of the platoon now volunteered to let the company commander know of their position. He had to swim the river, as passage by the footbridge they had stormed was now impossible, being under heavy fire from the enemy. He had already been badly wounded but had said nothing about it and took the hastily written message from his NCO.

He removed his respirator and helmet, swam over and then the Cpl threw his helmet and respirator over to him. He then ran across the open marsh to his company HQ under a hail of machine-gun bullets but was unhit when he delivered the note. He also reported that there were mines under the stone bridge leading into the village. His OC asked him to tell his Cpl to hold his ground and try to destroy the mines at nightfall. Crichton got back safely although again under heavy fire and reported to Cpl Steward. The Cpl meanwhile had found that some of his men were missing, but he did not know if they were dead, and Crichton undertook to try and find them. He went nearer the bridge but found only dead men. Then finding a hedge that ran towards the bridge with a shallow ditch on one side of it, he worked up to the bridge, fired on every time he showed himself. Then suddenly jumping up he got to the river bank and then jumped again into the river and got under the arch. Here he took out two fuses of the mine and sank the latter in the river.

He took back the fuses and detonators to Cpl Steward and then went over that terrible journey to HQ again with them. This time Capt Evans would not let him go back to his platoon but detailed him as a stretcher-bearer to carry wounded to the dressing station behind the canal. Here his own wound was at last detected and he was sent back to hospital. His chaplain said it was a wound that most men would have gone out with at once, but his perseverance and pluck in spite of his disability earned him a VC.

Many years after the war, Crichton added the following footnote to the published account:

I shifted the mine as promised to help Steward all I could. So when I was wet I thought I would have a look at the bridge. So I got under it and found seven mines, one cwt each. I put all the mines in deep water. It took me several hours to get the mines loose. They were lashed down with wire and wedged to the top of each arch with wood. I knew that Steward and the boys would have no chance if the bridge went up, as they were hemmed in a corner. Steward got a commission in the Second World War and became a major. He died just after the war.

Crichton was decorated by the King in the ballroom of Buckingham Palace on 26 February 1919.

James Crichton was born in Carrickfergus, County Antrim, Northern Ireland, on 15 July 1879, the son of Irish/Scottish parents. His family soon moved to Northrigg by Blackridge, West Lothian, Scotland, and at the age of 10 James worked in the local coalmines. Known throughout his life as 'Scotty', he enlisted in the Royal Scots in 1897 and, two years later, transferred to the Cameron Highlanders in order to take part in the South African War. He was awarded the South African Medal with five clasps.

A short time before the Great War broke out, he emigrated to New Zealand in 1914, enlisting in the NZEF. His civilian occupation had been a cable splicer with the Post Office and Telegraph Department in Auckland. Physically he was of small stature, being only 5ft 5in tall. He also had dark brown hair with grey eyes. In October he was made a corporal with the New Zealand Army Service Corps (NZASC) and then, in the same month, he embarked for Egypt with the NZEF on the 16th. Six months after training, he sailed to Gallipoli on 19 April 1915, landing at Anzac Cove on 25 April.

On the Gallipoli Peninsula he was promoted to quarter-master sergeant (QMS) in January 1916, and warrant officer 2nd class (WO2) on 23 March. He left Egypt for France with his unit on 9 April and took up duties as a baker on the 18th.

Crichton continued to serve with the 1st Field Bakery, NZASC for another two years, but, having grown tired of baking bread, he transferred to the 3rd Entrenching Battalion on 19 May 1918. On 27 August he transferred to the 2nd Battalion, Auckland Infantry Regiment, as a private, considering this the last chance in which he would see some action – he was not to be disappointed. The story that Crichton told about this decision was as follows:

> Towards the end of the war, as a sergeant-major he was selected to train for a commission. He was practising bombing in a training trench when he met a senior officer of the Auckland infantry, who were up in the line. The officer said he would take him up if Crichton could get permission.
>
> 'You will lose your present rank and the chance to be an officer if you do,' he was told when he sought the necessary authority.

On 30 September Crichton not only saw some fighting, but excelled in action and was to win a Victoria Cross. He was wounded in the right foot at the same time, which led him being evacuated to England. After a spell in hospital he returned to New Zealand on 23 June 1919, before being discharged owing to his wounds received in action. He married a short time later.

In 1937, the year of the coronation of King George VI, Crichton was recalled to the Army and asked to serve between February and July. He travelled to England as part of the New Zealand contingent for the coronation, arriving at Tilbury Docks about three weeks before the ceremony, which was to take place on 12 May. Crichton was one of a party of fifty officers and men, including ten veterans, among them three holders of the VC: Crichton (then a sergeant), Samuel Frickleton and Leslie Andrew. The small group was chosen to represent the New Zealand Mounted Rifles, Artillery, Infantry and Engineers, and they camped at Pirbright under the command of Maj. N.W. McD. Weir. On the day of their arrival, they were inspected at St Pancras by the Australian High Commissioner and by members of the War Office staff. While in London Crichton's wristwatch was badly damaged, so he took it to a jeweller's for repair. On returning to collect it a few days later, he was about to pay when he was told to 'accept [the cost of the repair] as a small token of our appreciation'.

Nineteen years later he attended the VC review in London in 1956, and in the following year was presented to the Queen and the Duke of Edinburgh during their visit to New Zealand in early May. His job in later years was as a foreman cable-joiner with the Post Office in Auckland.

James Crichton died at Auckland Hospital, Takapuna, on 22 September 1961 at the age of 82, and was buried three days later at the Waikumete Memorial Park Soldiers' Cemetery, near Auckland, in the Protestant Section, Block L, Section 4, Plot 9. He was survived by his wife and daughter.

James Crichton is commemorated in a number of ways, but the local council in the town where he was born had always been against the idea of putting up any sort of memorial. However, a few years ago, in a new century and with the co-operation of the Ulster History Society and members of Crichton's family, justice was finally done. He is now remembered with a blue plaque on the building at

75 Woodburn Road, Carrickfergus, a site once occupied by his birthplace. The plaque was unveiled on 24 April 2006 in the presence of members of his family. The ceremony was followed by the unveiling of plaques to him and Daniel Cambridge (VC recipient during the Crimean War) at the town's Museum and Civic Centre. In Scotland, Crichton's name is listed on the Armadale & District Roll of Honour, which also covered Blackridge.

In addition, two paintings of him exist: one at the National Collection of War Art in Auckland, painted by Francis McCracken (1920–1921); and an earlier one, painted by John Wheatley in 1919, held in the collection of the Imperial War Museum in London. Crichton's name was also remembered at the Dunedin RSA War Memorial Building until the mid-1980s, when the plaque was transferred to the VC Winners' Queens Gardens Cenotaph in the town.

His decorations, apart from the VC and South African Medals, include the 1914–15 Star, BWM (1914–20), VM (1914–19), War Medal (1939–45), New Zealand War Service Medal (1939–45), and Coronation Medals for 1937 and 1953. They were donated to the Auckland War Memorial on 30 June 2001.

J. RYAN

Near Bellicourt, France, 30 September

By mid-September the outer defences of the German-held Hindenburg Line had been reached and, on 18 September, the line was attacked by the 1st and 4th Australian Divisions of the Australian Corps. This attack was a total success and, by 29 September, the next phase of the planned advance was ready, with the 27th and 30th American Divisions now earmarked to take part. However, despite fighting with extreme gallantry, the Americans were unable to capture their objectives, which in turn had been planned as jumping-off positions for men of the Australian Corps. As a result, the Australians had to fight their way forward without adequate artillery support, but by 1 October they had managed to capture the ground which had been the objective of the Americans. In the next few days the Australians forced their way through the last defences of the Hindenburg Line, and once they had achieved this triumph they were not used again before the Armistice.

During the attack of the 14th Brigade (5th Australian Division), the 55th Battalion was in action close to Bellicourt, supporting the 53rd, the leading battalion, in the final stages of the advance. The Australians were to cover the right flank and then move in an easterly direction, together with the 15th Battalion (4th Australian Division). At 6 a.m. on 30 September the Australian battalions moved forward, but, owing to a weak artillery barrage, they found that the enemy machine-gunners, who were scattered around the area, began to cause havoc.

In fact, the enemy fought so ferociously that their counter-attacks pushed the Australians back into the Le Catelet trench system, which faced Cabaret Wood to the north of Bellicourt. The fighting grew even more intense and, soon after midday, the enemy launched such a strong counter-attack that it pushed the Australians back even further; in particular, a bombing party to the rear put the Australians in a very dangerous position. It was at this point that Pte John Ryan took a very active role in the battle when he took command of a group of men and led the party to attack the enemy with bayonet and bomb. He was faced with the enemy in a trench to the north of him and with another party established on a bank in the open. Under Ryan's gallant leadership, his men took the Germans in the flank, causing sufficient casualties and confusion to result in their speedy withdrawal. The Germans were pursued by bombs and Lewis gun fire; with their line now broken, the Australians were able to retake the lost trench.

By this time, however, Ryan had been wounded in the shoulder and had to withdraw from the fight. At about 4.30 p.m. another enemy counter-attack appeared to be imminent, although this time it didn't materialise. The 119th American Regiment had assisted by bringing ammunition and bombs to the line, and American troops had also taken over a captured section of the Le Catelet Line.

Private John Ryan's well-deserved VC award was gazetted on 26 December 1918 as follows:

For most conspicuous bravery and devotion to duty during an attack against the Hindenburg defences on 30 Sept. 1918. In the initial assault on the enemy's positions Private Ryan went forward with great dash and determination, and was one of the first to reach the enemy trench. His exceptional skill and daring inspired his comrades, and despite heavy fire, the hostile garrison was soon overcome and the trench occupied. The enemy then counter-attacked, and succeeded in establishing a bombing party in the rear of the position. Under fire from front and rear, the position was critical, and necessitated prompt action. Quickly appreciating the situation, he organised and led the men near him with bomb and bayonet against the enemy bombers, finally reaching the position with only three men. By skillful bayonet work, his small party succeeded in killing the first three Germans on the enemy's flank, then, moving along the embankment, Private Ryan alone rushed the remainder with bombs. He was wounded after he had driven back the enemy, who suffered heavily as they retired across No Man's Land. A particularly dangerous situation had been saved by this gallant soldier, whose example of determined bravery and initiative was an inspiration to all.

Five months after he had rejoined his battalion in December, Pte Ryan was presented with his VC during an investiture by the King in the Quadrangle of Buckingham Palace on 22 May 1919.

Edward John Francis Ryan, known as John, was the second son of Michael and Eugenia (née Newman) Ryan, and was born in Tumut, New South Wales, on 9 February 1890. His father worked as a labourer. John was educated locally before also becoming a labourer. When the war in Europe broke out, John enlisted on 1 December 1915 at Wagga Wagga, in the district of Riverina. He marched 300 miles to Sydney with a group known as the Kangaroos, collecting recruits on the way. He was posted to the 2nd Reinforcements of the 55th Battalion (NSW) of the AEF and his service number was 1717. Ryan left Sydney on 14 April 1916 and sailed for France, spending two months in Egypt en route. He joined his unit on 23 September at Fleurbaix.

He served with the 55th Battalion for the rest of the war, apart from the period from January to July 1917 when he was detached to the Anzac Light Railways Unit. After he was wounded on 30 September 1918 during his VC action, he was to spend much of the following year in hospital before being finally sent home to Sydney on 24 October 1919, though his wounds had still not fully recovered. An article in the *Sydney Morning Herald* described him at this time as being 'a thin little man with a smiling face that has been burned a deep mahogany brown'.

Like so many servicemen briefly famous for winning the VC, he was to find it very difficult to adjust to civilian life and, even when he was employed, he found it difficult to keep his job. Things didn't get better either and ten years after the war, when the world was suffering from a global economic depression, he found the going even tougher and decided to take to the road, which he did for about four years. In August 1935 he was completely destitute and he walked from Balranald, New South Wales, to Mildura in Victoria. Here he was given a temporary job by the local council, and later found employment in an insurance office in Melbourne for a few years.

However, by May 1941, once more in poor health, he was again without employment. Then, on the day that he was supposed to start another job, he was so unwell that he was taken to the Royal Melbourne Hospital where he died of pneumonia on 3 June.

Despite Ryan's seemingly tragic life after the war, he was at least given a great send-off by the State of Victoria. Eight holders of the Victoria Cross attended his funeral and he was buried with full military honours in the Catholic Section of the Springvale Cemetery, Melbourne. His gravestone was erected by the State Government of Victoria to the 'memory of a gallant soldier'. Not surprisingly, in his circumstances, Ryan never married, but he was survived by two brothers and a sister, Mrs P.G. Grant of Yas, New South Wales. It was she who presented her brother's VC to the Australian War Memorial in Canberra in November 1967. His other decorations were the BWM, VM and King George VI Coronation medal. One of Ryan's brothers, Malcolm, had been a trooper with the Australian Light Horse.

Ryan's name is also remembered with a wall plaque in Springvale Cemetery, a Ryan Street in Canberra, the Victoria Cross Park Memorial in the same city, and in the Victoria Cross Memorial in the Queen Victoria Memorial, Sydney.

R.V. GORLE
Ledegem, Belgium, 1 October

On 1 October, during the fourth and last Battle of Ypres, 'A' Battery, 50th Brigade, Royal Field Artillery supported an attack at Ledegem, between Ypres and Kortrijk to the east. The attack began at 6.15 a.m. with a barrage that lasted half an hour. Neither the 36th (Ulster) Division to the right nor the Belgian troops to the left had been able to advance, so British troops had been forced to retreat from ground to the north of the village. However, they did remain in control of a position at Ledegem Station. 'A' Battery did wonderful work in firing over open sights on to Hill 41 on the right and came into action three times in front of the infantry, which helped the 36th (Ulster) Division to regain the ground that had been lost. The Allied advance continued the following day. One of the members of the battery was T/Lt Robert Gorle, who was in charge of an 18-pounder. His role in the advance earned him a Victoria Cross, which was subsequently published in the *London Gazette* on 14 December 1918 as follows:

For most conspicuous bravery, initiative and devotion to duty during the attack on Ledegem on 1 Oct. 1918, when in command of an 18-pounder gun working in close conjunction with infantry. He brought his gun into action in the most exposed positions on four separate occasions, and disposed of enemy machine-guns by firing over open sights under direct machine-gun fire at 500 to 600 yards' range. Later, seeing that the infantry were being driven back by intense hostile fire he, without hesitation, galloped his gun in front of the leading infantry, and on two occasions knocked out enemy machine-guns which were causing the trouble. His disregard of personal safety and dash were a magnificent example to the wavering line, which rallied and retook the northern end of the village.

Gorle was decorated six months later by the King in the Quadrangle of Buckingham Palace on 14 June 1919.

Robert Vaughan Gorle was born in Southsea, Hampshire, on 6 May 1896. He was the son of Maj. Harry Vaughan Gorle DSO retired, late of the ASC, and of Ethel Catherine Gorle, who died in 1904. She was the eldest daughter of the Revd Canon Archdall, Rector of Glanmire, County Cork. Robert attended school at The Wells House in Malvern Wells before moving to Rugby. After leaving he emigrated to South Africa and took up farming in the Transvaal. On the outbreak of war, he decided to return to England and joined the Royal Field Artillery.

After leaving the Army in 1918, he returned to farming in Africa, but this time in north-eastern Rhodesia. Surprisingly, he decided to quit farming in order to become a librarian. His favourite pursuits were shooting and tennis.

In 1924 Robert married Ruth (née Thomas) and the couple were to have two children: a son, Timothy, and a daughter, Drucilla. In 1929 the Gorle family left Northern Rhodesia for Southern Rhodesia, where he was appointed sergeant-at-arms, as well as librarian, to the Legislative Assembly of Southern Rhodesia. Tragically, when only 40 years old, Gorle died of emphesema and pneumonia in Durban, Natal, South Africa, on 9 January 1937, after an eight-day illness. He was buried in Stella Wood Cemetery, Durban, Reference K, Grave 144.

After his early death one of his obituaries described him in the following way:

In the uniform of that office his splendid physique and fine bearing made him a figure of great dignity, but withal he was a man whose almost bashful modesty and natural charm endeared him to every member and official of the Southern Rhodesian

Parliament and public, he was also Librarian to the Legislative Assembly of Southern Rhodesia.

Two years after his death, a special memorial was placed over his grave, paid for by the Durban branch of the British Empire Service League. Gorle's widow was to outlive her husband by thirty-four years, dying of cancer in 1971. The couple's son, Timothy, became head of the Solusi College, near Bulawayo, and Drucilla worked as a doctor. Apart from the VC, Gorle had been awarded the 1914–15 Star, BWM and VM, and, at the present time, they are part of the Lord Ashcroft collection on display in the Imperial War Museum. At one time, Gorle's VC was owned by a collector, Kevin Patience, of Bahrain.

W. MERRIFIELD

Abancourt, France, 1 October

Sergeant William Merrifield was a member of the 4th Battalion (1st Central Ontario Regiment) CEF, and won his VC on 1 October 1918 during the fighting at Abancourt. The village was to the north of the German-held town of Cambrai. All four Canadian divisions were to take part in the advance towards the town on that day. The 2nd Division was to be prepared to move through the lines of the 3rd Division and then to cross the St Quentin Canal, exploiting the ground captured to the north-east of Cambrai. It was a very wet night, which made conditions treacherous, and the advance commenced with an artillery barrage which extended from Neuvilly-St-Rémy north-westwards to Epinoy.

The artillery played a significant role, firing more than 7,000 tons of ordnance, which contributed to the early success of the advance. However, later in the day, the 1st Canadian Division suffered a severe setback. The enemy resistance was mostly on the left, or northern, flank and was partly a result of the British 11th (Northern) Division's failure to make progress on the same day. The history of the CEF tells the story of what happened to two of the Canadian battalions:

> Attacking north of Bantigny Ravine, the 1st and 4th Battalions had been thwarted in attempts to free Abancourt by the heavy fire coming from in front of the British division. That formation, assigned the task of protecting the 1st Division's left, had been

halted by heavy uncut wire almost before it began to advance. The two Canadian battalions were pinned down all day at the line of the railway. The 1st Brigade's 388 casualties brought to more than a thousand the losses sustained by the 1st Division on 1 October.

It was during this fighting that Sgt William Merrifield won his VC, gazetted on 6 January 1919 as follows:

For most conspicuous bravery and devotion to duty during the attack near Abancourt on the 1st Oct. 1918. When his men were held up by an intense fire from two machine-gun emplacements, he attacked them both single-handed. Dashing from shell-hole to shell-hole he killed the occupants of the first post, and, although wounded, continued to attack the second post, and with a bomb killed the occupants. He refused to be evacuated, and led his platoon until again severely wounded. Sergt. Merrifield has served with exceptional distinction on many former occasions, and throughout the action of the 1st Oct. showed the highest qualities of valour and leadership.

He received his VC from the King at York Cottage, Sandringham, on 26 January 1919.

William Merrifield was born in Brentwood, Essex, on 9 October 1890. As a young man he emigrated to Canada and lived in Ottawa. At one point the family moved to Sudbury, where William became a fireman on the Canadian Pacific Railways for eighteen months. He joined the 97th Regiment (Algonquin Rifles), who were based in the same town, for a year.

After the war broke out he enlisted on 23 September 1914 from his home town at Sault Ste Marie, Ontario, with the 4th Battalion (1st Central Ontario Regiment) CEF. His service number was 8000. He had taken part in the Second Battle of Ypres in 1915 and was awarded the MM in early November 1917 at Passchendaele for 'serving with exceptional distinction'.

He left England and returned to Canada in April 1919 and was discharged from the CEF in the same month. He married Maude Bovington two years later. During a visit to the Dominion by the Prince of Wales in September 1919, the royal train was halted to allow Sgt Merrifield to climb on board. He had been demobilised by then, with the rank of lieutenant in the Canadian Militia.

Just over ten years later he met the Prince of Wales again, in November 1929, when he came to London as a member of the group of six Canadian Army VC winners who attended the House of Lords VC Dinner. His next meeting with royalty was in May 1939 during the King and Queen's visit to Canada, when he was a guest of honour at a celebration of their visit, in Toronto, held by the 4th Battalion, CEF.

In 1939 William Merrifield suffered a severe stroke, from which he never really recovered, and at the early age of 52 he died in Christie Street Military Hospital, Toronto, on 8 August 1943. He was buried in West Korah Cemetery, Sault Ste Marie, Ontario. His decorations were in family hands until they were donated to the Canadian War Museum in Ottawa in November 2005. Apart from the VC and MM, he was also awarded the 1914–15 Star, BWM, VM, and Coronation Medal for King George VI (1937).

Merrifield is also remembered with a statue in front of the courthouse of Sault Ste Marie, and the name of a public school in the city. There is also a small display at the Sgt William Merrifield VC Armoury in Bantford, Ontario.

F.C. RIGGS

Near Epinoy, France, 1 October

On 1 October 1918, during the battle of the Canal du Nord, the Canadian Corps, with the British 11th (Northern) Division under their command, was on the right wing of the First Army. Its orders were to secure the crossings over the Scheldt Canal, north of Cambrai, with the 11th Division guarding the left flank of the advance. The 6th (S) York and Lancaster Battalion (32nd Brigade, 11th Division) moved off at 5 a.m. from positions on the west side of the Douai–Cambrai road. They moved through several belts of wire which had been destroyed by artillery fire, but soon came up against a much tougher obstacle in the form of a great uncut belt of wire. The battalion was held up by intense shell and machine-gun fire, and suffered many casualties. D Company, on the left, was the only company able to get through the wire to reach an embankment. Lieuteannt Cook, in command of this company, led the attack at first, but when he was badly wounded, Sgt Frederick Riggs took over and led his men to the objective. Tragically, Riggs himself was killed in the action, and his posthumous VC was gazetted on 6 January 1919 as follows:

For most conspicuous bravery and self-sacrifice on the morning of 1 Oct. 1918, near Epinoy, when having led his platoon through strong uncut wire under severe fire, he continued straight on, and although losing heavily from flanking fire, succeeded in reaching his objective, where he rushed and captured a machine-gun. He later handled two captured guns with great effect and caused the surrender of 50 enemy. Subsequently, when the enemy again advanced in force, Sergt. Riggs cheerfully encouraged his men to resist, and while exhorting his men to resist to the last, this very gallant soldier was killed.

Further progress was made impossible by more uncut belts of barbed wire and the battalion dug in until they were relieved in the afternoon. Sergeant Riggs' body was never found and he is commemorated at the Vis-en-Artois Memorial to the Missing in France, 7 miles south-east of Arras, on Panel 9.

Frederick Charles Riggs was born in Bournemouth on 28 July 1888. At the age of 5 he was adopted by Mrs G. Burgum of 39 Capstone Road. He was educated at Malmesbury Park School, which was later demolished, and afterwards he worked for Messrs Pickford & Sons, the well-known carriers and furniture removers.

Riggs enlisted a month after the war broke out, on 4 September 1914, as a trooper in the 15th Hussars, and was later transferred to an infantry unit, the 6th Battalion, York and Lancaster Regiment, with the service number 20695. In 1915 he went with the battalion to France, then to Gallipoli, where he remained until January 1916 when the peninsula was evacuated. He then spent five months in Egypt, before once more returning to France. During the Battle of the Somme in 1916, he was severely wounded in the head and was sent home to convalesce. On recovering, he returned to France, but was killed when winning the VC. He had already won the MM. His family joked that his 'natural parting' was the result of a near miss by a German sniper.

Riggs' adoptive mother, Mrs Burgum, was invited to meet the King at an investiture at Buckingham Palace in March 1919, but she was unwell. Instead, the decoration was presented to her in her home by the Assistant Provost Marshal of Bournemouth, Maj. H.C. Wills, on 11 March.

On 12 March 1953, Riggs' decorations, which also included the 1914–15 Star, BWM and VM, were sold at Christies to Messrs Baldwin and Son for £180. The latter were acting on behalf of the York and Lancaster Regiment, who had set a top bidding price of £150. Baldwins gave the regiment first refusal at this sum and a short time later, at a special ceremony, the Regimental Museum took possession of the medals. Riggs' VC is now in the collection of the York and Lancaster Regiment, Clifton Museum, Rotherham, South Yorkshire.

There is also a plaque and portrait to his memory in the new Malmesbury Park School in Ascham Road, Bournemouth, which used to be in the original school building. At that time, every Armistice Day, the children would pay homage to the bronze plaque and portrait, displayed in the school hall. Riggs' former home at 39 Capstone Road was demolished in about 1974 to allow the construction of the Wessex Way and, later, instigated by Roger Coleman MBE, the local council decided to put up a plaque at No. 45, which is nearby. The plaque erected in 1995 gives brief details of Riggs' service life.

It is a remarkable coincidence that a second VC holder lived in the road at about the same time as Riggs. His name was Cecil Reginald Noble, and he was a corporal serving with the 2nd Battalion, Rifle Brigade, when he won his VC in 1915. He was born at No. 175. It is still standing and also boasts a plaque. Further local links with Riggs in Bournemouth include the naming of a road after him in Wallisdown, called Riggs Gardens.

W.H. JOHNSON

South of Ramicourt, France, 3 October

Sergeant William Johnson was a member of the 1/5th Territorial Force (TF) Battalion, Sherwood Foresters, 139th Brigade, 46th (North Midland) Division, who was awarded a VC on 3 October 1918. That day his battalion, together with their colleagues in the 1/6th TF and 1/8th TF Battalions, captured Ramicourt. The village was north of St Quentin and south-east of Gouy, and immediately to the east of the German-held Beaurevoir-Fonsomme Line. This was virtually the last section of the much-vaunted Hindenburg Line and consisted of strong barbed wire entanglements and a double line of shallow trenches, which were about 1ft deep. Every 50yd there were concrete machine-gun emplacements. The 137th Brigade was to their right and the 2nd Australian Division to their left, who were to attack at the same time as the 139th. The 1st Division, on the right of the 137th Brigade, were to capture Sequehart to the south.

The 139th Brigade were to take up positions during the night, roughly occupying a line on the west side of Joncourt and south-east of Ramicourt. In the small hours, Johnson's 1/5th Battalion was then to advance from these positions to attack Joncourt, together with Ramicourt to the north-east, and then, if successful, move on towards Montbrehain further to the north-east.

Three hours after beginning their journey, the companies were in position and, at 6.05 a.m., a six-minute barrage opened up, lifting as the companies moved off on a very misty morning. This mist led to the attackers being dependent on compass bearings. To the right the attack was not going well and, due to strong enemy resistance, several senior officers became casualties. According to the battalion history, the section of the Fonsomme Line to the south of Ramicourt was captured with the help of Sgt W.H. Johnson:

> Beyond the Fonsomme line the ground dipped gently to Ramicourt, about 2,000 yards away; then rose slightly for another 2,000 yards to Montbrehain, due east.
>
> The sunken roads to the south of Ramicourt were filled with the enemy, who were thus in a position to enfilade us.
>
> Heavy fighting continued round the sunken roads, but the resistance was finally overcome and many prisoners taken.

Ramicourt had yielded some 400 prisoners, but a much more unusual sight was the civilians who had dodged the enemy by sheltering in their cellars; most of them were subsequently evacuated. Montbrehain was reached two days later. However, before continuing their advance, an enemy-held machine-gun nest at Ramicourt Station was captured with the assistance of a tank.

William Johnson's VC was gazetted on 14 December as follows:

> For most conspicuous bravery at Ramicourt on the 3rd Oct. 1918. When his platoon was held up by a nest of machine-guns at very close range, Sergt. Johnson worked his way forward under a very heavy fire, and single-handed charged the post, bayoneting several gunners and capturing two machine-guns. During his attack he was severely wounded by a bomb, but continued to lead forward his men. Shortly afterwards the line was once more held up by machine-guns. Again he rushed forward and attacked the post single-handed. With wonderful courage he bombed the garrison, put the guns out of action, and captured the teams. He showed throughout the most exceptional gallantry and devotion to duty.

Johnson was presented with his VC by the King in the ballroom of Buckingham Palace on 29 March 1919.

William (Bill) Henry Johnson was a son of Frederick and Hanna Johnson and was born in Worksop, Nottinghamshire, on 15 October 1890, one of seven children. On leaving school he worked in the local Manton Colliery as a deputy, and his home during this time was at 1 Shelley Street, a respectable working class terrace. One of his main hobbies was bellringing, at which he became very proficient, being a member of Worksop Priory Church bellringing team.

On the outbreak of war in August 1914, and although he was a married man with three children, he decided to enlist and joined the Sherwood Foresters, with the service number 306122, serving mainly in France. After the award of his VC was made public in December 1918, his former colleagues at Worksop Priory Church rang a special peal of 1,260 changes, called '720 Kent Treble Bob', in his honour.

Johnson had been seriously wounded in 1918 and was in hospital at Trouville, where he underwent at least two operations, and later suffered from Spanish flu. After his demobilisation in 1919 he returned to Worksop, eventually becoming a checkweighman. During that year he was paraded through the town with the priory bells ringing. In March 1920 he was awarded the French *Medaille Militaire* and his mining colleagues clubbed together to present him with £100. Johnson eventually gave up colliery work in order to run a pub, the Mason's Arms, in Worksop. In addition, he was a scout master at his local church and later went on to lead a cadet force. He also took a keen interest in the local branch of the British Legion, eventually becoming its chairman. He attended occasional meetings of Victoria Cross holders, including the Garden Party at Buckingham Palace in June 1920 and the Prince of Wales' Dinner in the House of Lords in November 1929.

In 1925 he laid one of the foundation stones at Worksop Victoria Hospital Extension and he was present when Sir Horace Smith-Dorrien dedicated the town's war memorial.

Evidently he became restless running the pub, and decided to leave his hometown and move to Retford, and then to Arnold, about 25 miles from Worksop, where he was to spend the rest of his life.

On Armistice Day in 1931, Johnson attended the commemorations at Arnold parish church, which were followed by a march to the local war memorial at Arnold Hill Park to lay wreaths. Johnson was in charge of the ex-servicemen on parade and continued in this capacity each Armistice Day for several years. In 1934 Johnson was invited as a special guest to the reunion of the 8th Sherwood Foresters Battalion, which took place in Worksop.

When the Second World War broke out, Johnson became a member of the Home Guard, but was forced to resign owing to ill health. After he had moved to Arnold he took several jobs, at one time working for the Home Brewery Co., and he also became manager of the Arnold Ex-Servicemen's Club. In addition, he was a member of the National Defence Corps for many years. His last job was with one of the most famous of Nottinghamshire firms, that of Players' Tobacco, where he worked from 1941 until his death. He always kept up his bellringing, and, at one time, was a member of the St Paul's Church bellringing team in Daybrook. He frequently took part in special events, including those at St Peter's Church, Nottingham.

William Johnson died on 25 April 1945, at the early age of 54, after suffering a seizure while having breakfast at his home at 33 Nelson Road. An obituary in a local newspaper said that Johnson had been very concerned about the health of his son, Pte W.A. Johnson, who had been seriously injured in the war. W.A. Johnson had joined the Royal Artillery and, while serving in a searchlight unit, had suffered an injury to his leg which resulted in an amputation. A short time later his other foot also had to be amputated.

William Johnson's funeral took place with full military honours on 28 April at St Paul's, Daybrook, and he was buried at Redhill Cemetery, Nottingham, in grave number 4294, Section L, Grave 6. At the graveside the 'Last Post' was sounded and a special tribute was paid by Johnson's former bellringing colleagues, who rang a short course on handbells at the graveside. A fellow winner of the VC, Pte J. Caffery, followed Johnson's coffin, together with members of the family. The coffin was draped in the Union Jack and ex-servicemen of the Sherwood Foresters acted as pallbearers. It was an impressive gathering at the funeral, and included members of the Ex-Servicemen's Club, the Home Guard, and representatives from Players.

Johnson left a widow, Mrs Gertrude Johnson, and the son referred to above, as well as two daughters. Mrs Johnson lived on for a further sixteen years until 28 July 1961, and on her death she was buried next to her husband. Johnson's decorations also include the MM, BWM, VM and King George VI Coronation Medal (1937), and are in the possession of the Sherwood Foresters' Regimental Museum in Nottingham Castle.

In June 1991 the local council planted a Whitebeam tree in Johnson's memory in Worksop's Memorial Avenue Gardens, but a plaque at the tree's base was later stolen. A replacement plaque was rededicated on 8 August 2012. Other commemorations include a portrait, which hangs in a room in the town library, also in Memorial Avenue. With his local links, he is also one of the twenty names listed on the Nottingham and Nottinghamshire Victoria Cross Memorial in the grounds of Nottingham Castle, which was unveiled on 7 May 2010. Finally, in 2011, remedial work was carried out on his grave, which was paid for by his grandson Keith Johnson.

J. MAXWELL
Near Estrées, France, 3 October

The 5th Brigade of the 2nd Australian Division took part in its last engagement in the war when helping to breach the last section of the Hindenburg Line close to Beaurevoir and Montbrehain. The Australian Corps was to the left of the Brish 139th Brigade (see Vann and W.H. Johnson).

Lieutenant Joseph Maxwell was a member of the 18th Battalion AIF (5th Brigade, 2nd Division) and he won his VC near Estrées, 2 miles to the east of Bellicourt, during an attack on the Beaurevoir–Fonsomme Line on 3 October 1918. The action took place close to what is now the D932 Le Cateau road, in a position between the White Cottage, adjacent to the road, and the small village of Wiancourt.

At 9.40 a.m. the commander of the 5th Brigade, Brigadier General (Brig. Gen.) E.F. Martin, decided to call in his troops who were lying in front of the wire in a hazardous position. A barrage was then brought down on the vacated battlefield, which softened up enemy resistance, and, as a consequence, 200 Germans and eighteen machine guns were captured. However, it appears that Lt Maxwell, in charge of his company, had not been given any warning of the proposed bombardment. He had learnt from an English-speaking prisoner that a group of Germans in the adjacent post wished to surrender, but were afraid to give themselves up, although it is not clear whether this was a deliberate ploy.

Maxwell, together with two men, approached the post, where the small party was immediately surrounded and forced to give up their weapons. It seemed the war was over for this small Australian group, who were about to become prisoners of war. Then the five-minute barrage suddenly began and, taking advantage of the subsequent confusion, Maxwell drew out a pistol hidden in his respirator haversack and killed two of the enemy, before escaping with his men under heavy rifle fire. He then organised a group to capture the post.

For his gallantry, Lt Maxwell was recommended a VC, which was confirmed by the publication of a citation in the *London Gazette* on 6 January 1919 as follows:

> For most conspicuous bravery and leadership in attack on the Beaurevoir–Fonsomme line, near Estrées, north of St Quentin, on the 3rd Oct. 1918. His company commander was severely wounded early in the advance, and Lieut. Maxwell at once took charge. The enemy wire, when reached under intense fire, was found to be exceptionally strong and closely supported by machine-guns, whereupon Lieut. Maxwell pushed forward single-handed through the wire, and captured the most dangerous gun, killing three and capturing four enemy. He thus enabled his company to penetrate the wire and reach the objective. Later he again dashed forward and silenced, single-handed, a gun which was holding up a flank company. Subsequently, when with two men only he attempted to capture a strong party of the enemy, he handled a most involved situation very skillfully, and it was due to his resource that he and his comrades escaped. Throughout the day Lieut. Maxwell set a high example of personal bravery, coupled with excellent judgement and quick decision.

Maxwell received his VC from the King in the ballroom of Buckingham Palace on 8 March 1919.

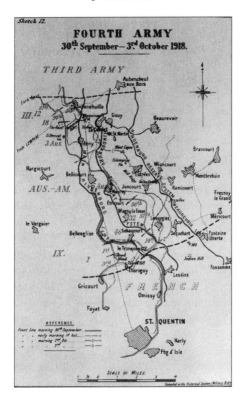

Joseph (Joe) Maxwell was born at Forest Lodge, a suburb of Sydney, in New South Wales, on 10 February 1896. He was the son of a labourer, Joseph Maxwell, and his wife, Elizabeth (née Stokes). On leaving school Joseph became an apprentice boiler-maker at an engineering works in Newcastle. On the outbreak of war he had a job with J & A Brown's Works in Hexham. Prior to enlisting in Sydney on 8 February 1915, he had served as a cadet for three years and spent two years as a member of the militia. He was sent to Liverpool Camp for training, before being posted to the 18th (New South Wales) Battalion, with which he served in Gallipoli in 1915, arriving there in August. After the evacuation of the peninsula and a spell in hospital with jaundice, he served in France and Belgium from March 1916 until 1918. In October 1916 he was promoted to sergeant. He returned to a training battalion in England and then briefly to France in May. He was sent back to an officer training school, but his career suffered a setback after he was involved in a brawl. He was sent back to his unit, but on 7 August 1917 he was promoted to warrant officer second class, then becoming a company sergeant major (CSM). It was as a CSM that he won his first gallantry medal, the DCM, on 2 September, near Westhoek, during the Third Battle of Ypres.

In this action he took over from the platoon commander, who had been killed, to lead an attack. About an hour later he noticed that the enemy was firing heavily on one of the captured positions. Maxwell dashed forward to this point and was able to lead several men to safety. On 29 September he was appointed a second lieutenant and made full lieutenant in the New Year. In early March 1918 he won his first MC while in charge of a scouting patrol to the east of Ploegsteert in Belgium. Having obtained the information he needed, he ordered his patrol to withdraw. However, spotting a small group of the enemy about 60yd away, he immediately recalled the patrol, then led a charge against the small group. The enemy sheltered in a trench, where they were attacked with rifles and bombs until they withdrew, leaving their casualties behind.

Five months later, on 8 August, close to Rainecourt on the first day of the Battle of Amiens, Maxwell earned a bar to his MC. Finding himself the only officer in his company who had not become a casualty, he took command and, preceded by a tank, led his men in an attack against their objectives. The tank was hit and, although his group were shaken by the explosion, Maxwell was able to rescue the crew of the vehicle before it burst into flames. He continued attacking until his company reached its objective. Maxwell also took part in the fighting for Mont St Quentin on 31 August/1 September. Amazingly, and in little more than a year, Maxwell had won the DCM, MC and bar, VC and French *Croix du Guerre*. He was only 22 when the war finished and his name was placed on the Retired List. Together with Lt Col. Harry Murray, Maxwell shares the unique honour of receiving four gallantry decorations

After returning to Australia in May 1919, Maxwell was discharged from Army service on 10 August. He tried his hand at several jobs, including gardening in Sydney, Canberra and in various New South Wales towns and cities. On 14 February 1921 he married Mabel Maxwell, a tailoress. The couple had one daughter, but the marriage lasted five years and was dissolved in 1926. Maxwell attended the New South Wales Dinner for the VCs in Sydney on 11 November 1929. In December 1930 he found himself in jail for not being able to pay his wife her divorce payments, but was set free when an army comrade paid the £30 fine. Two years later, in 1932, and with the assistance of Hugh Buggy, Maxwell wrote a book about the war titled *Hell's Bells and Mademoiselles*. At the time of publication he was working as a gardener in Canberra with the Department of the Interior. In 1933, during the trial of Alfred Jamieson for alleged housebreaking, Maxwell spoke eloquently in the man's defence as his former platoon commander. Jamieson had been of good character, but the war had affected him strongly so that he changed from being a good soldier to one who was often in trouble.

After the Second World War broke out in September 1939, Maxwell made several further attempts to enlist before achieving success in June 1940 in the state of Queensland, where he was not known. However, it was not long before his identity was discovered, at which time he was given a training position rather than being discharged. In 1946 he was in trouble again for being drunk and verbally abusive in public. In fact, throughout his life Maxwell had been in trouble with the authorities, including when he was in the army. He also contracted venereal disease.

In 1953 he was one of the Australian contingent invited to the Queen's Coronation and he was introduced to Queen Elizabeth and Prince Philip on 5 February 1954 at the Anzac Memorial in Hyde Park, Sydney. He was married a second time to a widow, Anne Burton, in the Registrar-General's Office on 6 March 1956 when he pretended that he was a journalist from Bondi. Three months later he attended the VC commemorations in London. In 1964, together with his wife, Maxwell attended the opening of the VC Corner in the Australian War Memorial, Canberra, but he was not happy with the prospect of his VC ending up in the collection, as he considered 'lumping' all the VCs together cheapened the award.

Maxwell was an unusual man, who appears to have been a tough bruiser and considerably destabilised by his war experiences. This resulted in what today might be called 'personality disorders'. He not only suffered from poor health but experienced difficulty in holding down a new job, and in his dealings with his wives and girlfriends he was less than honest, often passing himself off as someone else. Nevertheless, it should be remembered that he was a very heroic soldier, always ready to do a good turn for a former Army colleague.

Sadly, on 6 July 1967, Maxwell collapsed and died of a heart attack when walking in a street in Matraville, his home town. He had been an invalid pensioner for some time. His funeral service took place with full military honours at St Mathias Anglican Church, Paddington, Sydney, and his ashes were scattered in the Garden of Remembrance. Maxwell's decorations, which were a replacement set as he had managed to lose the originals, were presented by Anne Maxwell (who died in 1981) to the Victoria Barracks, Paddington. Subsequently the medal collection, together with a portrait and a brass copy of the VC citation, were unveiled by the Minister of Defence, Allan Fairhall, at the Maxwell Club for NCOs and other ranks. At the present time they are on permanent loan to the Australian War Memorial in Canberra and on display in the Hall of Valour. Apart from the VC, MC and bar, and DCM, they include the BWM, VM and Coronation Medals for 1937 and 1953.

During his lifetime Maxwell had become one of the most highly decorated Australian soldiers of the First World War. His name is commemorated in the Australian War Memorial in Canberra and with a wall plaque in the Eastern Suburbs Crematorium, Botany, Sydney. The Reference is 9209 and the plaque is on the Soldiers' Wall. He is also remembered with a plaque in the Soldiers' Club, Holsworthy Barracks, New South Wales. As with other holders of the VC, his name is listed on the Victoria Cross Memorial in the Queen Victoria Building, Sydney, and the Victoria Cross Park Memorial in Canberra.

W.H. COLTMAN

Mannequin Hill, North-East of
Sequehart, France, 3–4 October

Having already won two DCMs and two MMs, Lance Corporal (L. Cpl) William Coltman was already a highly decorated soldier before he added a VC on 3–4 October 1918 during the Battle of Beaurevoir. His battalion, the 1/6th North Staffordshires, 137th Brigade, 46th (North Midland) Division, was in action at Mannequin Hill, to the north-east of Sequehart. The hill is about halfway between the villages of Fontaine-Uterte and Montbrehain, near the north–south D283 road. The section of the Beaurevoir Line in this area ran north-easterly from in front of Sequhart and Estrees, and was virtually level with the road. The line was reached by the division at 10.30 a.m. on 3 October, but two and a half hours later the enemy began a strong counter-attack. Coltman was a stretcher-bearer and his citation, published in the *London Gazette* on 6 January 1919, takes up the story as follows:

For most conspicuous bravery, initiative and devotion to duty. During the operations at Mannequin Hill, north-east of Sequehart, on the 3rd and 4th Oct. 1918, L.-Corpl. Coltman, a stretcher-bearer, hearing that wounded had been left behind during a retirement, on his own initiative went forward alone in the face of fierce enfilade fire, found the wounded, dressed them, and on three successive occasions carried comrades on his back to safety, thus saving their lives. This very gallant N.C.O. tended the wounded unceasingly for 48 hours.

He was decorated by the King in the Quadrangle of Buckingham Palace on 22 May 1919, together with two other VC winners, George Kerr and Bellenden Hutcheson.

William Harold Coltman was born at Tatenhill Common, Rangemore, Burton-on-Trent, Staffordshire, on 17 November 1891. He was the eldest of five children and his father, Charles, died early in his life, leaving his wife, Annie, to bring up the children on her own. She did this partly by delivering milk by horse and trap, but later she married a man called Bannister, with whom she had further children.

William attended school in Rangemore, but left at the age of 13 in order to help in supporting his family. He took on employment as a gardener and worked for a short period at Duffield in Derbyshire. Later he returned to Staffordshire, where his home was at 60 Forest Road, Burton-on-Trent. He met a young lady, Eleanor May Dolman, while tending a garden at Repton, and the couple were later married at Burton Register Office on 8 January 1913. Both were active churchgoers. Soon after their marriage, Eleanor gave birth to a son, Charles, and later a daughter, Dorothy.

William Coltman, a diminutive 5ft 4in tall, was one of five brothers who served in the war. He enlisted in the 2/6th Battalion, North Staffordshire Regiment, in January 1915, before being transferred to the 1/6th in October. His service number was 241028. With his strong Christian beliefs, Coltman took the important decision at some point of telling his senior officer that to kill people would be against his religious beliefs, and he was allowed to transfer to the 'A' Company stretcher-bearer group. In January 1916 the division was sent to Egypt, but one month later it was back in France.

Coltman's division was involved in the disastrous diversionary attack at the village of Gommecourt on the Somme on 1 July 1916, in which his battalion lost thirteen officers and 292 other ranks. During this time, Coltman's 'devotion to duty' earned him the first of several Mentions in Despatches. Eight months later he was awarded the

MM for gallantry near Monchy, Arras, on 17 February 1917. The weather had been extremely misty when one of the battalion officers led a party out to repair wire in front of the trenches. However, when the mist suddenly cleared the enemy quickly opened fire on the group. The officer sent the party back, being himself the last to withdraw. On getting through the wire he was shot through the thigh and fell to the ground. Without hesitation, Pte Coltman went out and, with difficulty, managed to get the officer back through the wire. While doing so, he placed himself between the officer and the enemy, who were little more than 85yd away and were keeping the two men under rifle fire the whole time. The deed was written up in the *London Gazette* on 24 February 1917.

Coltman's second MM was gazetted on 23 June 1917. This time he had been in trenches close to the town of Lens, where he showed great gallantry and disregard for personal danger on three occasions. On 6 June a trench mortar bomb had exploded on the company ammunition dump, in which bombs and Very lights were stored. The subsequent explosions led to several casualties, and Coltman immediately began to remove the Very lights that were in the dump. On the following day the company headquarters was set on fire by a trench mortar bomb, causing several casualties. Again Coltman tended the wounded, among them a man who had both legs broken. A week later, on 14 June, after a tunnel through a railway embankment had been blown in, trapping twelve men, Coltman immediately organised a party to dig the men out and assisted the wounded along the trench. He was thus directly responsible for saving the lives of several men.

Coltman won his first DCM at the end of June and beginning of July 1917 when, at the height of the fighting, particularly during the attack on Liévin, Coltman continued with his heroic stretcher-bearer activities, even after the battalion had been relieved. He saved the lives of several men and, during the night, he scoured the battlefield for more casualties. Indifferent to danger, he was a splendid example to his colleagues. When he returned exhausted to his unit, he handed in more than thirty pay-books belonging to the battalion dead. He himself had been gassed and ended up in a field hospital.

On 28 September 1918 he won a bar to his DCM, just a few days before he won his VC. At Bellenglise, during the battle for the canals, he again cared for the wounded and carried several of them to safety despite heavy artillery fire. He continued this heroic work for two days, once again seemingly without any thought for his own survival.

After the war Coltman was always quick to point out that he did not win his gallantry medals by killing people, but rather by saving the lives of his comrades. As a stretcher-bearer he never used a rifle. He was discharged on 3 March 1919 and, fearing a fuss being made when he returned home to Burton-on-Trent, he decided to get off the train at Derby.

He had a secure job with the Corporation's Parks Department to which he gave loyal service for the rest of his working life. He also became a special constable with the Staffordshire Police Force. He was to attend almost all the VC winners meetings until his death, and these included the Garden Party at Buckingham Palace on 26 June 1920 and the Armistice Day ceremonies at the Cenotaph in November. In the 1920s, twin memorials were dedicated to the North Staffordshires and South Staffordshires at Whittington Barracks. They took the form of two obelisks, one surmounted by a Chinese dragon and the other by a sphinx.

In 1922, at Bellenglise, a memorial to the 46th (North Midland) Division was unveiled, with the deeds of the division inscribed on it, including the breaking of the Hindenburg Line, together with the capture of over 4,000 prisoners and seventy guns. In July 1929 Coltman talked with the Prince of Wales during the latter's visit to Burton-on-Trent, later meeting the prince at the dinner hosted by him on 9 November at the House of Lords. On the outbreak of the Second World War, Coltman stepped forward once again and took charge of the Burton cadets. He was commissioned in the Burton Army Cadet Force from 1939 to 1945 with the rank of captain. After the Second World War ended, Coltman attended the Victory Parade on 8 June 1946 and, ten years later, the VC Centenary Review in Hyde Park on 26 June 1956.

For many years Coltman gave dedicated service to the North Street Meeting House of the Brethren, where he also ran the Sunday School. In February 1963, at the age of 71, while still working as a corporation groundsman, he had to stop clearing the Wheatley recreation ground of snow in order to attend a special ceremony at the town hall. On his arrival, the mayor greeted him with a gift of a photograph commemorating his VC from 1918. The mayor was quoted in a newspaper as saying of the commemoration: 'I can't understand why it was not done before but I'm very happy that the town is doing something to put it right'. Coltman, gazing over the snowbound recreation ground, said: 'I bet the youngsters will be ready to give me a cheer when I get that lot cleared up for the last time'.

Coltman's home was at 6 Wheatley Lane, Winshill, Burton and, at the age of 82, he died at Outwoods Hospital, Burton, on 29 June 1974, and was buried with full military honours at St Mark's, Winshill. At the funeral, the Mercian Brigade Depot provided a band and firing party, while the Mercian Volunteers acted as pallbearers. The Victoria Cross Trust has since provided funding for the upkeep and maintenance of his grave.

In his will, Coltman left £7,884 net (£7,995 gross) and he left his decorations and medals to his son, Charles, on the understanding that they would be donated to the Staffordshire Regiment at Whittington Barracks Museum when he died. The decorations included the VC, DCM and bar, MM and bar, the French *Croix de Guerre*, 1914–15 Star, VM and MiD Oakleaf, Defence Medal (1939–45), Coronation Medals for 1937 and 1953, and Special Constabulary Long Service Medal.

At the Whittington Barracks, Coltman's name is commemorated in the Garrison Church on a memorial to all the Staffordshire Regiment VCs. The barracks also have a replica trench named after him. After he had been made a Freeman of the Borough, the Staffordshire Regiment commissioned Mr A.R. Todd to paint his portrait.

On 21 May 1977, a memorial plaque to Coltman was placed adjacent to the Burton-upon-Trent War Memorial, which was unveiled by Sir Arthur Bryan, the Lord Lieutenant of Staffordshire, in the presence of other dignitaries. After the dedication, a march past took place when the Lord Lieutenant took the salute at the entrance of the Memorial Gardens. The memorial was provided by donations from the Staffordshire Regiment, Staffordshire County Council and also individual subscribers.

Coltman's decorations made him the most highly decorated NCO of the First World War, but, more importantly, he was a man of great courage and was dedicated to the service of others.

In October 2003, a tree was named in his memory in the Staffordshire Regiment Grove in the National Memorial Arboretum. In November 2010 a new military medical HQ in Lichfield was named Coltman House, and was opened by Princess Alexandra. Also in recent years a road has been named after him in Tunstall, in the Potteries, about 1 mile from Burslem. At the time of writing, there is even talk of erecting a statue of him in his home town, though, being a self-effacing man, I am not sure that he would have approved of the idea.

G.M. INGRAM
Montbrehain, France, 5 October

On 4 October 1918, during the battle for the Beaurevoir Line, the 24th (Victoria) Battalion, 6th Australian Brigade, who had already been involved in the capture of the Beaurevoir sector the previous day and were therefore expecting a rest, were ordered to take part in another attack. Zero hour was to be 6.05 a.m. on 5 October. The battalion was to start from the village of Ramicourt, where Sgt William Johnson had just won a VC, and move north-eastwards in order to capture the village of Montbrehain, 600yd away across strongly defended enemy positions. The ground, a section of the Beaurevoir Line, was known to be rough and protected by a maze of wire and trenches. The battalion was to be accompanied by their colleagues, the 21st Battalion, as well as tanks to provide assistance. As the sun rose, the artillery barrage began and the Australians set off in its wake. Their advance was heavily counter-attacked by German artillery and machine-gun fire, but they still managed to continue, despite the late arrival of the promised tank support. The eleven tanks had been caught by heavy enemy shelling, which included the use of gas shells. However, when they did arrive they were able to clear the streets of Montbrehain. Heavy enfilade fire was coming from the direction of Doon and Mannequin Hills.

Lieutenant George Ingram was a member of B Company of the 24th Battalion, which was being sniped at and swept by machine guns. To the north-west of the village was a quarry which was defended by over 100 men and as many as forty machine guns, and the enemy could be seen lining its edge as a tank began to circle it. After his company commander was wounded, Ingram took over the attack, leading the charge on this fortress by jumping in among the enemy and shooting them. Sixty-three men subsequently surrendered.

While his men were mopping up the enemy positions, Ingram went on ahead, searching for machine-gun nests in the village. On locating a machine gun in a house, he managed to get into the house, and shot and killed the gunner who had been firing through a cellar ventilator at the rear. He then rushed through the rest of the building and found a group of about thirty Germans, whom he added to his tally of prisoners.

The fighting continued through the village and beyond, to the final positions on the north-east side. Despite the capture of so many prisoners, the rest of the Germans did not take things lying down and fought every inch of the way. As a result, the casualties of the 24th Battalion became so high that two companies from the 27th Battalion had to be brought up for close support. However, the line was finally taken at about 8 p.m., and was then linked up and consolidated. Even then the enemy continued to carry out raids against the Australians, but, although the Germans were desperate to hold on to Montbrehain, they finally had to admit defeat. The fight for the village had yielded 600 prisoners and the capture of 150 machine guns.

Lieutenant George Ingram's well-earned VC was gazetted on 6 January 1919 as follows:

For most conspicuous bravery and initiative during the attack on Montbrehain, east of Péronne, on 3 [should be 5] Oct. 1918. When early in the advance his platoon was held up by a strongpoint, Lieut. Ingram, without hesitation, dashed out and rushed the post, at the head of his men, capturing nine machine-guns, and killing 42 enemy, after stubborn resistance. Later, when the company had suffered severe casualties from enemy posts, and many leaders had fallen, he at once took control of the situation, rallied his men under intense fire and led them forward. He himself rushed the first post, shot six of the enemy and captured a machine-gun, thus overcoming serious resistance. On two subsequent occasions he again displayed great dash and resource in the capture of enemy posts, inflicting many casualties and taking 62 prisoners. Throughout the whole day he showed the most inspiring example of courage and leadership, and freely exposed himself, regardless of danger.

Ingram, the last Australian to win a VC in the First World War, was decorated by the King in the ballroom of Buckingham Palace on 15 February 1919.

George Morby Ingram came from Bendigo, South Yarra, Victoria, where he was born on 18 March 1889. His parents were George Ronald Ingram, a farmer, and his wife, Charlotte (née Hubbard). After leaving the state school at Lilydale, young George became an apprentice carpenter and joiner, and, on completing his apprenticeship, moved to Cauldfield, Melbourne, where he went into business as a building contractor. At the age of 14 he had joined the militia and was attached as a private to No. 7 Company of the Australian Garrison Artillery. On 19 January 1910, George married Jane Francis Nichols in a Congregational ceremony in East Prahran. The marriage was to last sixteen years before it was dissolved in 1926. There were no children.

Four months after the war began on 4 August 1914, George Ingram, by now a burly young man of nearly 14 stone, and 6ft tall, enlisted on 10 December from South Yarra with 3rd Battalion, Australian Naval and Military Expeditionary Force, serving initially in New Guinea. He was discharged as a corporal on 19 January 1916. Later the same day he enlisted in the AIF, being allotted to the 16th Reinforcements for the 24th Battalion (Victoria) AIF, which he joined in France in January 1917, with the rank of acting corporal. By 18 March he had been made temporary sergeant, and a few days later he was in action at Bapaume where he won the MM for 'great courage and initiative as a member of a bombing section, by excellent placing of his bombs'. He continued to serve in France, but was in hospital in England from April to June, and it was not until the end of June 1917 that he rejoined his unit. Three months later he was back in hospital again, and, on his return to the battalion on 10 October, he was made CSM.

Ingram was recommended for a commission in the 24th Battalion, which was confirmed on 20 June 1918. However, three days later, he was back in hospital with an illness, so it was not until 12 July that he was able to resume his duties as an officer. After the war he returned to Melbourne in 1919, where he was discharged on 2 June. He became a general foreman with E & A Frank Watts Pty Ltd. After his first marriage ended in 1926, he married a widow, Lilian Wakeling (née Hart), on 10 February 1927 at the Methodist parsonage, Malvern. He gave his occupation as 'farmer'. Two years later, on 11 November 1929, he attended the Melbourne VC Dinner.

In 1935 Melbourne's Shrine of Remembrance was completed and Ingram was chosen to be one of the earliest members of its 'permanent guard'. There had been 250 applications, from which just fourteen names had been chosen. Ingram also took part in the Second World War as a member of the Royal Australian Engineers, rising to the rank of captain. He was placed on the Retired List on 6 May 1944.

Ingram's second wife died in May 1951, but later that year, on Christmas Eve, he married another widow, Myrtle Lydia Thomas (née Cornell) and the couple were to have one son, Alex. Three years later, in 1954, Ingram attended the official unveiling of the shrine by the Queen and the Duke of Edinburgh in Melbourne on 28 February. At the ceremony the Queen unveiled an inscription and also set alight the flame to honour those who had died in the two world wars. The plaque read: 'To the glory and service of sacrifice, this perpetual flame was lit and this forecourt was dedicated by Her Majesty Queen Elizabeth the Second – 28th February 1954'. In 1956 Ingram was a member of the Australian VC contingent to be sent to London for the VC Centenary.

At the age of 72, Ingram died of coronary vascular disease at his home in Hastings, Victoria, on 30 June 1961, and was buried at Frankston Cemetery, Victoria, in the Methodist Section B/80. He is commemorated in a number of ways, including in the Australian War Memorial in Canberra, Victoria Cross Park Memorial and also with a street name in the same city. In Sydney he is remembered in the Victoria Cross Memorial in the Queen Victoria Building. In Melbourne in 1985, a special 50th anniversary commemoration at the Melbourne Shrine took place and, a year later, Ingram's widow took part in an Armistice ceremony, at which she wore her late husband's medals, which were then privately held. Ingram also has a commemoration on the foreshore in Hastings, close to the town's war memorial

On 27 May 2008 Ingram's decorations were sold at Sothebys, Melbourne, for $383,760 (£187,000). They were purchased by an anonymous buyer, who later presented them to the Australian War Memorial in Canberra. Apart from the VC and MM, they included the BWM, VM, War Medal (1939–45), Australia Service Medal (1939–45) and Coronation Medals for 1937 and 1953.

J. TOWERS
Méricourt, France, 6 October

On 6 October 1918 the 2nd Cameronian (Scottish Rifles) (59th Brigade, 20th Division) were occupying the ruined village of Méricourt, to the east of the Beaurevoir Line. The village was halfway between Fontaine-Uterte and Fresnoy-le-Grand and, when orders were issued for the village to be evacuated, the order failed to reach a small party of thirty men from the battalion's B Company, who were then almost surrounded by German machine-gunners. Realising that the group was going to be completely cut off, a volunteer was requested to go out and lead the group back to the company lines. Five men were killed in the attempt before Pte James Towers, a company runner, decided to volunteer for the task.

Setting out under heavy cross-fire, and moving deftly from shell-hole to shell-hole, he managed to crawl through the wire entanglements; in doing so, he came across the body of Frank Dunlop, one of his best friends, who had been a previous volunteer. Keeping close to the ground, he had to be extremely careful, knowing that the enemy was watching the top of the embankment where he lay. He was well aware that five men had died before him and concluded that it would be best to 'surprise' the vigilant foe, so he leapt over the embankment and found himself almost on top of a machine-gun nest of Germans. However, Towers was so agile and speedy that he had vanished almost before the enemy knew of his presence. Eventually he reached the trapped men, staying with them overnight, before leading them back to safety in the half-light of dawn, all the while dodging the danger spots on the way. The small party recovered the bodies of their comrades who had been killed. Private James Towers was awarded a VC for this deed, which was published in the *London Gazette* on 6 January 1919 as follows:

> For most conspicuous bravery and devotion to duty at Méricourt on 6 Oct. 1918, when, under heavy fire, five runners having failed to deliver an important message, Private Towers, well aware of the fate of the runners who had already attempted the task, volunteered for the duty. In spite of heavy fire opened on him as soon as he moved, he went straight through from cover to cover and eventually delivered the message. His valour, determination and utter disregard of danger were an inspiring example to all.

Towers was presented with his VC in the Quadrangle of Buckingham Palace on 8 May 1919. When asked about his VC in his later years, Towers replied:

> I joined up as a youngster for a bit of fun, but it didn't turn out like that. We were young men, old before our time. I felt then, that I had to go to the help of these lads, after all they were my pals. I had been in worse situations than that before, and no medals were awarded, but that's how it was.

James Towers was born on 8 September 1897 in Church House Farm, Broughton, Preston, and attended Emmanuel Boys' School. Later he worked on his father's dairy farm in Broughton and, still under-age, he enlisted in the West Lancashire Artillery in July 1915. When his age was discovered Towers was discharged. Later he tried again, enlisting in the 5th Dragoon Guards in August 1916, and then transferred to the infantry, joining the 2nd Battalion, The Cameronian (Scottish) Rifles. His service number was 30245 and he left for France in December 1916.

After winning the VC in October 1918, he was welcomed home by the inhabitants of Broughton and soon after, in January 1919, he was discharged from the Army. Towers returned to his father's farm at

Broughton and, after his father retired, James set up in business himself. In 1920 Towers attended the Garden Party for holders of the VC at Buckingham Palace, and later in the year was present for the burial service of the Unknown Warrior in Westminster Abbey. In November 1929 he was a guest at the House of Lords Dinner for VCs.

After the Second World War he took part in the 1946 Victory Parade in London, and ten years later he attended the VC Centenary at Hyde Park. In fact, he managed to attend most of the other VC commemorations as well, often accompanied by his wife, Ethel.

From about 1971 his health began to fail, and he particularly suffered from arthritis. Six years later he died in Preston Royal Infirmary on 24 January 1977 at the age of 80. At his funeral, which was followed by cremation in Preston Crematorium, those in attendance included men from the Scottish Rifles, officials from the VC/GC Association and members of the Preston Council of Ex-Servicemen. His ashes were dispersed on the crematorium lawns.

At the time of Towers' death, his home was at Mericourt, Lightfoot Green, Bartle, Preston. He left a widow and a married daughter, Mrs Marion Castle. In his will he left £14,264 net (£14,464 gross). On 30 June 1983 his decorations, which included the VC, BWM and VM, were sold at Sothebys for £7,500, and again on 7 April 2005 in Sydney by Noble Numismatics. This time they fetched £90,000 ($222,000).

Towers also has a road named after him in his hometown of Preston: James Towers VC Close, on the Lonsdale estate.

J.H. WILLIAMS
Villers-Outreaux, France, 7/8 October

By early October 1918 the Third Army had already captured most of the German Hindenburg defences, but the 38th (Welsh) Division had not been used in this action. However, it still had a role to play, as orders for it to advance were received on 3 October. It was to capture the village of Villers-Outreaux, to the east of the Beaurevoir Line and north-east of the village of that name. The 115th Brigade of the 38th (Welsh) Division left the village of Sorel-le-Grand on the morning of 4 October, and the 10th South Wales Borderers, who were part of the same brigade, reached Bony by noon. Later in the day, the 10th South Wales Borderers were to take over from the 2nd Royal Munster Fusiliers, in order to be ready to advance on the morning of 5 October. They were then to move in a northerly direction, before later moving to the right and swinging eastwards. The brigade duly moved northwards, but, on reaching Aubencheul-aux-Bois on 6 October, they found that the enemy had already left. Two platoons from the 10th South Wales Borderers were sent out eastwards towards Villers-Outreaux: one managed to seize a quarry, while the other took up positions in a sunken road to the south-west of Villers-Outreaux. During the night, patrols found that the enemy defences were strongly held, with machine-gun positions protected by a thick belt of uncut wire. It was now abundantly clear that the enemy would not give up its hold on Villers-Outreaux without a strong fight and, through 7 October, the Borderers were under heavy fire and pinned down on the exposed ground. The enemy held Mortho Wood, together with a building called Pierre Mill, which caused particular problems for the attackers.

Despite this hold-up, the division was to continue its advance against Villers-Outreaux with an attack at 1 a.m. on 8 October. The role of the Borderers would involve a move in a north-easterly direction, to the east of Villers-Outreaux, the idea being to cut the village off. To the left the 17th Royal Welch Fusiliers were also to move past the village, so that once it had been isolated the 2nd Royal Welch Fusiliers, with the assistance of two tanks, could take control of it. The final objective was Walincourt, along the Premont–Esnes road.

Though the plan looked sensible on paper, the reality turned out to be something quite different, as almost at once the Borderers got caught up in the uncut wire and at the same time machine-gun fire opened up on the trapped men. The darkness simply added to the confusion. However, one section of the battalion, under Maj. Monteith, was able to reach its objective. That it succeeded was due mainly to the extreme gallantry of CSM John Henry Williams. For a time the rest of the 115th Brigade was held up, although eventually the 2nd Royal Welch Fusiliers, duly assisted by three tanks, managed to enter the village by 11 a.m., which by then had fallen. At the end of the day the Borderers, who by then had been reorganised, dug in for the night to the south-east of Walincourt. Their losses had been very high, but they had accomplished their task. The gallant CSM John Henry Williams' VC was gazetted on 14 December as follows:

> For most conspicuous bravery, initiative, and devotion to duty on the night of 7–8 Oct. 1918, during the attack on Villers-Outreaux, when, observing that his company was suffering heavy casualties from an enemy machine-gun, he ordered a Lewis-gun to engage it, and went forward under heavy fire to the flank of the enemy post, which he rushed single-handed, capturing 15 of the enemy. These prisoners, realising that Company Sergt.-Major Williams was alone, turned on him and one of them gripped his rifle. He succeeded in breaking away and bayoneting five enemy, whereupon the remainder again surrendered. By his gallant action and total disregard of personal danger he was the means of enabling not only his own company, but also those on the flanks to advance.

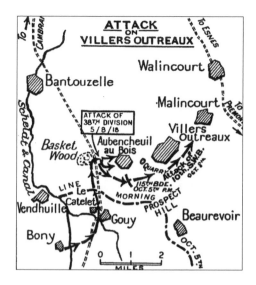

Williams, who had been severely wounded by shrapnel in his right arm and leg, was discharged on medical grounds nine days later on 17 October. On 22 February 1919 he was awarded four medals by the king – a record for one investiture. They were the VC, DCM, MM, and a bar to the MM. Williams had still not recovered from his severe wounds at the time of the presentation, as the wound in his arm had opened up and required treatment. Photographs taken at the time show him with his arm in a sling.

John (Jack) Henry Williams was born on 29 September 1886 at Nantyglo, Monmouthshire, a son of Henry and Elizabeth Williams. His father worked in the boiler-shop at Ebbw Vale, and his mother was a schoolteacher. John attended the Briery School in Ebbw Vale until he was 12 and then began work at the Ebbw Vale Iron & Coal Co. Ltd in the smith's shop at Marine Colliery. In 1906 he was working at the Cwm Colliery as a blacksmith, and in the same year enlisted in the South Wales Borderers with the service number 20408, but soon bought his discharge. At the beginning of the war in 1914, Williams was one of the first men to enlist with a battalion formed solely from

Ebbw Vale. It was to be a unit formed as part of Lloyd George's Welsh Army Corps. However, it was not until 12 November 1914 that the swearing-in took place and, after initial training, the 631 men who formed the battalion left Ebbw Vale as part of the 10th South Wales Borderers, bound for Colwyn Bay on 29 December. On 1 January 1915 Williams was promoted to sergeant. In 1916, between 10 and 12 July, he won the DCM for his bravery in the fight for possession of Mametz Wood on the Somme: 'He handled his men in the attack with great courage and skill. He has performed constant good work throughout.' Williams won a MM for bravery at Pilkem Ridge on 31 July 1917 on the opening day of the Third Battle of Ypres. Two months later he was promoted to company sergeant major on 2 October. On the 30 October he won a bar to his MM for bravery during a raid in the Armentières sector, in which he also brought back a wounded comrade.

When Williams won his VC in October 1918, he received a letter of congratulation from the lieutenant colonel in command of the 10th South Wales Borderers, in which he wrote the following:

> I am writing to wish you my most heartiest congratulations on your being awarded the V.C. All ranks of the battalion are delighted and send their heartiest congratulations. I thank you also for bringing to the battalion and the regiment such glorious honour. Those of us who know you know full well how much you deserved winning the Victoria Cross. I hope you are recovering from your wound, and will have a long and happy life to enjoy your well-deserved honour … Again wishing you all the best and many congratulations …

Other officers of the regiment also sent letters of congratulation.

After being discharged as medically unfit, he was appointed Commissionaire at the General Offices of the Ebbw Vale Company, and was given free house-coal and lighting. The town also presented him with a gold watch. In 1920 he attended the VC Garden Party at Buckingham Palace on 26 June. In 1921, at Cardiff Arms Park, which had been turned into a giant parade ground, Williams was introduced to the Prince of Wales during his visit to South Wales. The prince took a special interest in Williams, as he had been the only man to receive four gallantry medals from the King at the same time. A contemporary press photograph shows the two men in Army uniform talking together. In 1924 Williams took part in a wreath-laying ceremony at the newly erected Cenotaph in Newport, at which the Duke of York was present. In March 1927 his wife Gertrude died. The couple had had eleven children, five boys and six girls. In June of the following year, Williams was present at the unveiling of the National War Memorial in Cardiff, where he met the Prince of Wales a second time. In 1929 he represented the 10th South Wales Borderers at the unveiling of a memorial to the 24th Battalion at Gheluvelt, near Ypres. Also in 1929 he attended the House of Lords Dinner, presided over by the Prince of Wales. In that same year, however, the Ebbw Vale Company went into bankruptcy, which resulted in Williams being transferred to the housing department as a rent collector. He moved from Garden City, where his wife had died, to a house in Willowtown. In 1936 Williams met the Prince of Wales for a fourth time when the prince visited South Wales to see the poor conditions and high unemployment there. This was the visit when the prince spoke out about what he saw of unemployment and poverty, saying: 'Something must be done.' The comments bordered on the political and were widely reported in the press.

In 1937 Williams was reinstated as Commissionaire at the General Offices when the new works started up. Meanwhile, he married again, this time to Morfydd Rees of Aberbeeg, a telephonist at the General Offices. The couple moved to a company house at 4 The Dingle. In the Second World War, Williams served as a captain in the Home Guard in Ebbw Vale. When peace returned he attended the Victory Parade on 8 June 1946, and also attended a VC Dinner at the Dorchester Hotel.

At the age of 66 John Williams died on 7 March 1953 in St Woolos Hospital, Newport, Monmouthshire, and was buried in Ebbw Vale Cemetery alongside his first wife and one of his daughters. Thousands of local people lined the route of his funeral cortège. He was survived by his second wife, Morfydd, along with five sons and five daughters.

At some point the headstone for Williams's grave was removed during cemetery clearance work and not replaced. When it was later discovered that his grave was unmarked, a fund was set up to provide a suitable replacement headstone for the local hero's grave.

A service of rededication took place on 21 October 1990 after a commemorative parade had passed through Ebbw Vale. Tragically, one of Williams' sons, Harry Williams, died on the way to the ceremonies, but a granddaughter and grandson were present, with the former wearing her grandfather's medals for the occasion. Apart from his VC, DCM, and MM and bar, Williams was also awarded the 1914–15 Star, BWM, VM, Coronation Medal (1937) and the French *Medaille Militaire*. His portrait used to hang in the Ex-Servicemen's Club in Ebbw Vale, and a plaque commemorating him is on the first floor of Ebbw Vale Town Civic Centre. Other commemorations include a hall being named after him at The Centre, Abertillery, Gwent, and a memorial in Havard Chapel, Brecon Cathedral, Powys. There also used to be a commemoration in the offices of Richard Baldwin & Thomas in Ebbw Vale. Williams' medals and a portrait are in the collection of the South Wales Borderers Museum in Brecon.

C.N. MITCHELL

*Canal de l'Escaut, North-East of
Cambrai, France, 8/9 October*

By the beginning of the second week of
October 1918, the British First Army,
which included the Canadian Corps, had
reached a line about 1 mile to the west of
Cambrai. The line ran in a north-westerly
to south-easterly direction. As the Allies
wished to limit the damage done to the city
of Cambrai, their plan was to encircle it.
The divisions to the right and in the centre
had no specific obstacles to overcome, but
to the left the Canadian Corps had the task
of crossing the wide Canal de l'Escaut.
Most of the bridges had already been
destroyed and those which survived would have been prepared by the
enemy for demolition at a moment's notice.

The plan for the Canadian Corps on the night of 8–9 October
was for the 2nd Division to make the initial canal crossing, followed
by the 3rd Division which would cross on its own front, in order
to establish bridgeheads in Cambrai. The position selected for the
Canadian attack was the bridge named Pont d'Aire (close to the D61
road), across the Canal de l'Escaut. This would allow the Canadians
to reach the village of Escaudoeuvres to the east. The situation was
complicated by the fact that, in addition to the main bridge, there
were also two further obstacles in the form of millstreams about 20ft
wide to the west of the canal.

Most of the following details are based on accounts written
by Capt. Coulson Mitchell, which differ at certain points from

accounts of the action in the *Official Histories*. Mitchell was a member of the 4th Battalion, Canadian Engineers, 2nd Canadian Division, who through his extreme gallantry won his VC at the Pont d'Aire in preparation for the Canadians to cross the canal. The 4th Battalion, Canadian Engineers, led by Capt. Mitchell, were instructed to prevent the enemy blowing up the main bridge before the Allies reached it.

Mitchell's small group left the jumping-off trench in Tilloy Wood, to the north of Cambrai, at midnight, accompanied by A Company from the 26th Battalion. The engineers moved quickly for about 1½ miles before reaching a road where they parted company with the infantry, who were to remain there for a couple of hours. The road led to the first millstream, which they reached at about 2.00 a.m., only to find the crossing destroyed, leaving a 20ft gap. Mitchell sent a couple of runners back with this information. The sappers located a footbridge across a stream about 100ft to their left, but this ended at a door in a brick wall which opened into a warehouse. The group then sought out the second millstream, where they discovered a stone arch that appeared to be unmined. Two more runners were sent back with this information, and also to act as guides to lead the infantry to the second bridge. Assistance then came from the artillery, who provided a box barrage around the bridges to protect them from the enemy.

Depleted by the number of runners who had to be used for communication, Mitchell's party was down to four. Years later, Mitchell said the men became quite excited when they ran across the 500ft area towards the main canal bridge. The bridge was found to be a double-span steel girder, with a concrete base which rested on two abutments, together with a pier and canal locks in the middle of the stream. The bridge was about 15ft above the water and there was a towpath on each side of the canal. The sappers felt their way very gingerly across the bridge, after a while locating the various wires that were connected to the German explosives, and finally reached the far side of the bridge, which was about 200ft long. Mitchell sent one man back as look-out to guard the western end of the bridge and left another sentry at the German end. After the fuses had been cut, there was a shout from one of the sentries who had shot two of the enemy when they had suddenly appeared from the back of a building to the left of the bridge. It was now about 4 a.m. and dawn light was beginning to show. The three remaining men were wondering what was going to happen next when a third German appeared on the scene, but Mitchell disposed of him. Mitchell and his colleague, Sgt Jackson, then quietly slipped into the cold water of the river to search for the explosives. Finding a large box of explosives close to one of the 75ft steel girders, they cut the electric circuit and began a search for similar charges.

Suddenly the Germans realised what was happening and began to tackle the small group. Down to just three men, they were 'yelling like madmen' in an effort to convey to the enemy that they were up against a whole battalion. Surprisingly, the group of Germans scuttled off, which allowed Mitchell's men to finish the job of cutting any remaining fuses; as it became lighter, they dismantled the four main charges, which they threw down on the towpath. They then came across a small party of twelve Germans who were only too anxious to give themselves up, together with a group of eight more. The small group had managed to save the bridge, which allowed the advance of the Canadian infantry to continue, followed by the field artillery. For their role in capturing this bridge intact, Sgt Jackson and the sapper who had held the German end of the bridge were both awarded the DCM. Captain Mitchell won a VC, which was gazetted on 31 January 1919 as follows:

For most conspicuous bravery and devotion to duty on the night of 8–9 October 1918, at the Canal de l'Escaut, northeast of Cambrai. He led a small party ahead of the first wave of infantry in order to examine the various bridges on the line of approach and, if possible, to prevent their demolition. On reaching the canal he found the bridge already blown up. Under a heavy barrage he crossed to the next bridge, where he cut a number of 'lead' wires. Then, in total darkness, and unaware of the position or strength of the enemy at the bridgehead, he dashed across the main bridge over the canal. The bridge was found to be heavily charged for demolition, and while Capt. Mitchell, assisted by his N.C.O., was cutting the wires, the enemy attempted to rush the bridge, in order to blow the charges, whereupon he at once dashed to the assistance of his sentry, who had been wounded, killed three of the enemy, captured 12, and maintained the bridgehead until reinforced. Then, under heavy fire, he continued his task of cutting wires and removing charges, which he well knew might at any moment have been fired by the enemy. It was entirely due to his valour and decisive action that this important bridge across the canal was saved from destruction.

Mitchell remained with the 4th Battalion in its advance towards Mons and, at the time of the Armistice, was in the area of Elouges. A week later the unit marched towards the Rhine, which it crossed at Bonn on 13 December. He remained with the Army of Occupation and returned to England on 1 April 1919. Two days later he was decorated by the King in the ballroom of Buckingham Palace and returned home to Winnipeg later in the month.

Coulson Norman Mitchell, later known as 'Mike', was born at Ross Street, Winnipeg, on 11 December 1889. He was the third son of Mr Coulson Nicholas Mitchell and his wife, Mary Jane. Mitchell's father also came from a military background, which included serving in the 90th Winnipeg Rifles. After Coulson's birth the family moved to a terraced house in Edmonton Street. Coulson was educated at Mulvey Public School and Winnipeg Collegiate Institute, and while at school he became a keen sportsman. In 1912 he graduated in engineering at the University of Manitoba. Before the war Mitchell worked as an electrical engineer with the Foundation Company of Canada on projects both in Manitoba and British Columbia. When the war broke out he was working on the construction of the Transcona elevator and was keen to see the job completed before enlisting.

On 10 November 1914 Mitchell joined the Canadian Engineers as a sapper, being posted to 4 Field Company in Ottawa. In December a signal company was set up and Mitchell, together with other university graduates, joined the 2nd Divisional Signal Company. Mitchell remained with this unit until May 1915, having a pretty easy time in the hilly country around Ottawa with 'flag and heliograph'. Later, he was transferred to the Canadian Railway Construction Corps and, leaving New Brunswick on 14 June 1915, sailed for England.

He arrived in Plymouth on 26 June, and then moved to Longmoor Camp, Hampshire. He remained in England for two months before he and his unit moved to France on 26 August. From Calais they proceeded to Alveringen in Belgium, where the unit was attached to the Belgian Army and their role was to build a narrow gauge track as far as the support line. When this job was completed, the unit returned to Longmoor Camp on 5 October.

In November 1915 Mitchell was promoted to sergeant and recommended for a commission in the Canadian Engineers; he was made a lieutenant on 28 April 1916. In the following month he was transferred to the 1st Canadian Tunnelling Company, which he joined in Belgium in July; he was posted to the left half-company operating between Verbrandenmolen and the Ypres–Comines Canal, and was sent up to the Bluff. Mitchell's work was 90ft below ground level, and he was later involved in the capture or destruction of German tunnels at the Bluff. He was in that area until the end of the year, and it was during this period that he won the MC on 11 December, gazetted on 13 February 1917. The citation states that 'he was cut off from our lines for twelve hours'. On 24 May he was promoted to captain.

At the beginning of January 1918 the 1st Canadian Tunnelling Company was moved to Vimy Ridge in readiness for the much-heralded German Spring Offensive, which began at the end of March. The 1st and 2nd Tunnelling Companies were broken up in the summer and the personnel distributed among the newly formed engineer battalions. Mitchell was posted to D Company of the 4th Battalion, Canadian Engineers, taking part in the Battle of Amiens in August. During the period from 2 September to the Armistice he was in the areas of Drocourt–Quéant, the Canal du Nord, Cambrai and Valenciennes. In 1919, after being demobilised as captain, Mitchell returned to Winnipeg to rejoin the Foundation Company of Canada as manager of a high-power electrical station in British Columbia. Later, in 1926, he joined the Power Corporation and became the general superintendent of construction and development of steam and hydro-electric power plants for their subsidiaries and other companies.

Mitchell attended the House of Lords VC Dinner in November 1929, returning home on the *Duchess of Atholl* on 22 November 1929. In 1930 he joined 16 Field Company, 4th Reserve Engineers (M), as a captain, remaining with them for three years. In 1936 Mitchell attended the unveiling of the Vimy Ridge Canadian Memorial and took his 82-year-old father with him. While in France, Mitchell revisited the Pont d'Aire bridges where he had won his VC. In 1940 Mitchell was asked to raise a company of pioneers and, with the rank of major, take it overseas. The unit sailed for England in August and he remained with it for eleven months, before being appointed OC 11 Field Company, Royal Canadian Engineers. In February 1942, as a lieutenant colonel, he was transferred to the 1st Royal Canadian Engineer Reinforcement Unit and remained in that position as OC of the Training Wing. In September 1943 he returned to Canada, working at National Defence HQ on special duties. In April 1944 he was appointed to command the Royal Canadian Engineer Training Centre at Petawawa. There he was responsible for the training of officers and other ranks in units serving overseas. The training programme was 'hard and intensive'.

In 1944 Mitchell was involved in the building of a Legion Hall at Chilliwack, British Columbia, which was opened in May that year. Also in 1944 he was active in raising money for the erection of a memorial at Vedder Crossing to the memory of members of the Canadian Corps who had been killed in battle. At the end of the war, Mitchell was a key figure in a campaign to build the first permanent married quarters. In September 1946, after very distinguished war service, Mitchell left the Army and returned to his home in the town of Mount Royal, Quebec. He continued working as an executive with the Power Corporation until he finally retired in 1957.

Mitchell had always taken a keen interest in the Canadian Legion and, in 1942, the 'Norman Mitchell VC Branch' was named in his honour. He was also instrumental in suggesting a housing project, which was built on a street named after him. In 1956 he attended the VC Centenary commemorations in London. In 1973 the married quarters he had campaigned for were renamed 'Mitchell Gardens', and a memorial cairn to his own achievements was unveiled by him on 12 October. Mitchell had never let his association with the Royal Canadian Engineers lapse and he later became a member of the VC/GC Association, attending several of their meetings over the years.

At the age of 88, Coulson Mitchell died on 17 November 1978 at his home at Mount Royal, while watching television. Even among the hallowed ranks of winners of the Victoria Cross, Mitchell stands out as a very courageous and public-spirited man. His funeral took place at the Mount Royal United Church on 21 November and he was buried at Pointe-Claire Field of Honour Cemetery, Quebec, Section M, Grave 3051. He left behind a widow, Gertrude Hazel Bishop, who died in her mid 90s in 1985; she was buried next to her husband. There were two daughters from the marriage.

Mitchell was commemorated in several ways. A mountain in Jasper National Park, Alaska, was named after him to mark his work in bridge-building on the Alaska Highway, and a street in Mount Royal was named after him. He is also commemorated with the Royal Canadian Legion Post in Montreal. In 1980 the Royal Canadian Engineers Museum at Chilliwack, British Columbia, was able to acquire not only Mitchell's decorations, but also a large collection of documents, maps and photographs. The medals, in addition to the VC and MC, included the 1914–15 Star, BWM, DM, Canadian Volunteer Service Medal and clasp (1939–45), Coronation Medals of 1937 and 1953, the Canadian Centennial Medal and the Jubilee Medal of 1977. The museum already owned Mitchell's uniform and the weapon that he was using at the time of winning his VC, and provides a permanent exhibit to honour the only Canadian military engineer to have won a VC. If readers wish to visit the site of Mitchell's VC action, which hasn't changed a great deal since 1918, then they would be advised to go around Cambrai in a north-easterly direction and take the D61 road to Morenchies.

W.E. HOLMES
Cattenières, France, 9 October

On 9 October 1918 in the area of VI Corps, to the south-east of Cambrai, the 2nd Battalion, Grenadier Guards (1st Guards Brigade, Guards Division) passed through the lines of the 2nd and 3rd Divisions. Their objective was the railway line to the east of the village of Wambaix, and then to occupy this line as far as the VI Corps boundary. Their task was duly achieved on 9 October, as they found the enemy had disappeared. The Guards then moved north-eastwards towards the Cambrai–Le Cateau road in order to capture the villages of Cattenières and Estourmel, and later the small hamlet of Igniel-le-Petit. However, further progress was opposed and attempts to outflank the German machine-gun posts were unsuccessful. Nevertheless, at 1 a.m. on 10 October, the 2nd Grenadier Guards, moving from Cattenières towards the main road (now the N43), captured the village of Boistrancourt, which lay on a north–south ridge commanding the Cambrai–Le Cateau road.

It was during the fighting for Cattenières that Pte William Holmes of the 2nd Grenadier Guards won a posthumous VC, which was gazetted on Boxing Day 1918 as follows:

For most conspicuous bravery and devotion to duty at Cattenières on 9 Oct. 1918. He carried in two men under the most intense fire, and while he was attending to a third case he was severely wounded. In spite of this he continued to carry wounded, and was shortly afterwards again wounded with fatal results. By his self-sacrifice he was the means of saving the lives of several of his comrades.

Holmes' body was taken to the village of Carnières to the north-east, which was captured a day after he was killed. A week later the Guards Division created the Extension to the Communal Cemetery, to the north-east of the village, and buried Holmes there in Plot I, Row B, Grave 3. The cemetery is about 5 miles to the east of Cambrai, on the west side of the D97 road to Avesnes-les-Aubert. There used to be a German cemetery close by, which was later removed. Holmes' company commander wrote of his deeds as follows:

It really was a most extremely gallant act to go on carrying when he was already wounded; unfortunately he only got another twenty yards. I cannot say how sorry I am, not only for his own sake, but also because the company loses such a gallant man, who always, both in and out of the line, showed such a good example.

Second Lieutenant B.R. Osborne, in a letter to Pte Holmes' mother, stated that: 'Private Holmes was acting as a stretcher-bearer in his platoon, and was hit in the throat while trying to get a wounded man back to the aid post ... May I add that he was one of the best men in my platoon, always cheerful, and loved by everybody.'
Two of Pte Holmes' friends in the platoon also wrote to his parents:

In your loss it will be a great comfort to you to know that Edgar died the bravest of deaths whilst trying to save a wounded comrade. His loss to us will be very great, as we have been close comrades for the last four years. He was always the life and soul of our platoon. We cannot really express the depths of our sympathy for you in your great bereavement, but we hope you will be able to seek consolation in the fact that he died a hero's death.

Holmes' posthumous VC was presented by the King to his parents in the ballroom of Buckingham Palace on 29 March 1919.

William Edgar Holmes was born at Wood Stanway, Gloucestershire, on 26 June 1895, the second son of Edward Holmes, a timber feller on the Stanway Estate, and of Ellen Elizabeth Holmes, daughter of Mr and Mrs Stanley. William went to school at Church Stanway and later worked as a groom on the estate. Holmes joined the Gloucestershire Regiment in July 1913 and transferred to the 2nd Battalion Grenadier Guards on 21 October 1913. His service number was 16796. It is known that, in the following year, he took part in the Retreat from Mons and the First Battle of Ypres.

During this first winter of the war, Holmes suffered from severe frostbite and was invalided home before two of his toes were amputated in hospital. He returned to France in 1915 and continued to serve in France and Flanders, and was twice wounded before winning his VC in October 1918.

After the war, Holmes was commemorated in the Roll of Honour in St George's Church, Didbrook, Gloucestershire. There is also a wooden bench to Holmes' memory in the churchyard. In 1959 his father, Edward, appeared as a contestant on a BBC radio programme called *Have a Go*, which was conducted by Wilfred Pickles. During the programme Holmes described how his son won his Victoria Cross more than forty years earlier.

Holmes' decorations were purchased by his regiment in 1985 and, apart from the VC, included the 1914 Star with clasp ('5th Aug–22 Nov 1914'), BWM and VM, and are held by the Grenadier Guards Division in Wellington Barracks, London. The date for the Mons Star clasp is 8 November.

In 2000 a small exhibition relating to Holmes' career was put on display at the Almonry Heritage Centre in Evesham, Worcestershire.

W.L. ALGIE
North-East of Cambrai, France, 11 October

On 11 October, 5 miles to the north-east of Cambrai, the 4th and 6th Canadian Brigades of the Canadian Corps of the First Army attacked at 9 a.m., and the enemy replied strongly with artillery and machine-gun fire. In particular, the 6th Brigade met heavy resistance from their objective, the village of Iwuy. The Germans defended Iwuy by piling up stacks of lumber and this, together with masses of wire, allowed them to maintain a steady fire against the Canadian attackers. In addition, the enemy could be seen bringing up more guns in small handcarts, to enfilade the Canadian positions.

Lieutenant Wallace Lloyd Algie won his VC during the fighting as a member of the 20th Battalion, Central Ontario Regiment, 4th Brigade, 2nd Canadian Division. Assessing the situation, Algie called for volunteers in order to thwart the enemy intentions. His thinking was that, if his group moved to the left, beyond the battalion boundary, then they could perhaps clear out the east end of the village. Taking a leading role he rushed forward, used his revolver to shoot the crew of a machine gun and, after turning it on the enemy, his group was able to cross a railway embankment. He then rushed a second machine gun and killed its crew; in the process he cut off the escape of an officer and ten enemy troops, forcing them to surrender. With the use of the captured machine guns he then cleared the east end of the village of the enemy:

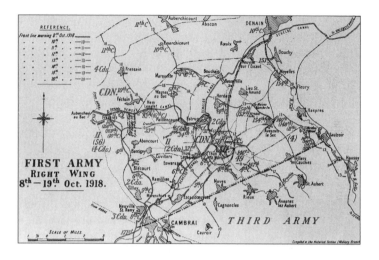

Having placed his men in a good position and showed them how to use the German machine-guns, he went back for reinforcements, but was killed in bringing them forward. The posts he had established were able to hold their positions until the situation was relieved by the troops on the left occupying the village.

By early afternoon Algie's group, together with troops of the 28th and 31st Canadian Battalions, were able to completely clear the village. After the capture of Iwuy, the town of Le Cateau fell the next day and the Allies reached the Solesmes–Le Cateau road to the east of Cambrai. Algie's VC was gazetted on 31 January 1919 as follows:

> For most conspicuous bravery and self-sacrifice on the 11th Oct. 1918, north-east of Cambrai, when with attacking troops which came under heavy enfilade machine-gun fire from a neighbouring village. Rushing forward with nine volunteers, he shot the crew of an enemy machine-gun, and, turning it on the enemy, enabled his party to reach the village. He then rushed another machine-gun, killed the crew, captured an officer and ten enemy, and thereby cleared the end of the village. Lieut. Algie, having established his party, went back for reinforcements, but was killed when leading them forward across the railway.

His valour and personal initiative in the face of intense fire saved many lives and enabled the position to be held.

Algie was buried at Niagara Cemetery, Iwuy, Row C, Grave 7, which is 5 miles north-east of Cambrai, and his posthumous VC was presented to his father by the Lieutenant Governor of Toronto on 28 March 1919.

Wallace Lloyd Algie was born in Alton, Ontario, on 10 June 1891. The family home was 1155 King Street and his parents were Rachel and James Algie, who had practised medicine for twenty-five years in Peel County. In about 1908 the family moved to Toronto and settled at 75 Dewson Street. Wallace was educated at Alton Public School and, after he left, took up banking, working in various branches in Toronto and Vancouver. He graduated from the Royal Military Academy of Canada and served with The Queen's Own Rifles of Canada as a lieutenant, and also for four months with the 40th Regiment.

One of Wallace's brothers had already enlisted and Wallace joined up in Toronto in April 1916. After basic training, Wallace was drafted from the Reserve of Officers to the 95th Battalion, and by October he was serving with the 20th Battalion, arriving in France in 1917.

On 23 March 1995 Wallace's VC, in its original Hancocks' fitted case of issue, was sold at Glendinings to Lord Ashcroft for £17,800. At the present time it is in his collection at the Imperial War Museum. Algie's other decorations would have been the BWM and VM, which presumably are in private hands.

F. LESTER
Neuvilly, France, 12 October

On 11 October, during the early stages of the move towards Le Cateau and the River Selle, the 10th Lancashire Fusiliers (52nd Brigade, 17th (Northern) Division) were to the south-west of the village of Inchy, close to the Cambrai–Le Cateau road. While there the battalion received orders to attack the village of Neuvilly on the River Selle, about 4,000yd north-north-west of Le Cateau. The brigade plan was for the 12th Manchesters from the north and the 9th Duke of Wellington's Regiment to the south to cross the Selle bridges at 5 a.m. The two battalions were then to make good the railway line under the protection of a creeping barrage. Subsequently, they would occupy high ground to the north-east.

B Company of the 10th Lancashire Fusiliers were to support the Manchesters and A Company were to support the Duke of Wellington's. Their objective was to mop up any remaining Germans in Neuvilly, then occupy a position behind the Manchesters to the north.

Shortly after midnight, the battalion moved up to its assembly positions to the west of the River Selle, reaching their positions by 4 a.m. On the left of the attack, the Manchesters managed to cross the river to consolidate their positions and then began to clear the village from the north-west to the south-east. There was no hold-up to their advance. However, on their right things were not going quite so smoothly, as The Duke of Wellington's were unable to reach the top of the ridge, despite having crossed the river to reach the railway.

They met with stiff resistance when attempting to clear the eastern side of the village and also met opposition from houses and a factory to the south-east of the cemetery.

It was during the capture of the village itself that Pte Frank Lester of the 10th Lancashire Fusiliers Lester won his VC when he was a member of a party of seven men led by an officer. During the clearing of the village, he entered a house by the back door and shot two of the enemy as they tried to get out through the front door. Lester's VC citation, gazetted on 14 December 1918, takes up the story:

> For most conspicuous bravery and self-sacrifice during the clearing of the village of Neuvilly on 12 Oct. 1918, when with a party of about seven men under an officer, he was the first to enter a house from the back door, and shot two Germans as they attempted to get out by the front door. A minute later a fall of masonry blocked the door by which the party had entered. The only exit into the street was under fire at point-blank range. The street was also swept by the fire of machine-guns at close range. Observing that an enemy sniper was causing heavy casualties to a party in a house across the street Private Lester exclaimed, 'I'll settle him,' and, dashing out into the street, shot the sniper at close quarters, falling mortally wounded at the same instant. This gallant man well knew it was certain death to go into the street, and the party opposite was faced with the alternative of crossing the fire-swept street or staying where it was and being shot one by one. To save their lives he sacrificed his own.

Neuvilly had been partially captured, but it was not until five days later that it was completely in British hands. Lester's heroic action was witnessed by his officer, who later wrote to his parents and also brought Lester's gallantry to the notice of Lt Col R.E. Cotton DSO, OC of the 10th Lancashire Fusiliers. In a letter to Frank Lester's father, Cotton wrote:

> Your son's superb action is one of the bravest acts I can recall in this terrible war. He has added one more VC to the record of the regiment, which has more VCs to its credit than any regiment in the British Army.

I have seen the spot where the gallant deed was done in the village of Neuvilly, north of Le Cateau. It was a day of gallant deeds, and two Military Crosses, one Distinguished Conduct Medal, and three Military Medals were gained that day by the battalion.

The colonel also included an annotated map, on which he had marked the spot of Lester's death.

Lester is buried in Row B, Grave 15, in the Neuvilly Communal Cemetery Extension, which lies to the north of the village on the north-east side of the road to the town of Solesmes. Lester's posthumous VC was presented to his mother in the ballroom of Buckingham Palace on 22 February 1919.

Frank Lester was born at West View, Huyton, Liverpool, on 18 February 1896, the second son of a market gardener, John Lester, and his wife, Ellen. When he was still very young the family moved to Hoylake on the north coast of the Wirral, where Frank attended Hoylake National School in Trinity Street, leaving in 1910. Afterwards he took up the joinery trade, but gave this up two years later when his family moved the short distance to Irby, where he helped his father in the market garden business. The Lester family were apparently very musical and both Lester's parents were very accomplished, being members of the Hoylake Temperance Choir and also the Congregational Choir. Later, Frank Lester became the organist of a small methodist 'tin chapel' at Irby, Wirral. He had also become a member of the Boys' Brigade.

On 30 March 1916, when he had just turned 20, Lester enlisted in the Army and was given the service number 51674 when he joined the 10th Battalion, South Lancashires. He was 6ft tall and had a strong physique. He was soon made a sergeant-instructor in training camps and served at Press Heath, Shropshire, and Kinmel Park, North Wales. It appears that Army discipline came easy to him after his service with the Boys' Brigade.

In June 1917 Lester transferred to the Lancashire Fusiliers, but had to relinquish his rank and revert to private when posted to the 10th Battalion in France in December 1917. A few months later, on

21 March 1918, the first day of the German Spring Offensive, Lester was one of the few survivors from a large group who had been overwhelmed by the German advance. During this time he was slightly wounded and spent some time in hospital in Rouen. Lester regained his stripes and returned to England shortly afterwards, being stationed at Cromer in north Norfolk. He returned to France in September 1918.

After his death when winning a VC, Frank Lester was 'claimed' by several churches and is consequently commemorated at several places. His elder brother, Edwin, is often remembered on the same memorial: he served as a sergeant in the 4th Cheshires and died in Palestine on 9 July 1917; he was buried in Tel-El-Fara Cemetery, but later his remains were disinterred and reburied in Israel.

Frank's life is commemorated with a display at the Wirral Museum at Birkenhead Town Hall, Merseyside. His name was one of seven local holders of the VC unveiled by the Mayor of Wirral and Ian Fraser VC in Birkenhead Town Hall on 29 March 1984. However, this board has been updated and the replacement was unveiled on 22 February 2012 by a local historian, Mr Denis Rose, and Melba Fraser, widow of Ian Fraser VC, and is to be found in Wallasey Town Hall. The twelve men's names listed on the second memorial board include all Wirral VC recipients, as well as those from the Ellesmere Port and Neston districts. The same twelve names are listed on a VC plaque at the Birkenhead Cenotaph. It is hoped that in 2014 a VC/GC Association display will be set up in the ground floor main stairwell in Birkenhead Town Hall.

A plaque to Lester's memory was set up in the library in Thurstaston Road, Irby; it is on the left as one enters the building. It was restored in 2012 as it had been damaged by sunlight. His name is also listed on the Hoylake and West Kirby War Memorial, Grange Hill, West Kirby, Merseyside. Two miles from Birkenhead, Frank is remembered at the Holy Cross War Memorial in Woodchurch. A plaque to his name was erected in the Methodist Chapel, Irby, where he had played the organ before the war. The then 'tin chapel' was replaced in 1936 by a more permanent building. In Hoylake itself, a marble plaque was erected in the now defunct United Reformed Church and he is also remembered with an oak plaque at Hoylake Evangelical Church. His name is listed on the family grave at Holy Trinity churchyard, Trinity Road, Hoylake, where his rank is given as corporal.

Frank's name is also listed on the war memorial at St Barthomew's, Thurstaston Church, both inside the building and outside. The parish was once part of Cheshire, but later became Merseyside. Finally, the names of the two brothers are listed in a Book of Remembrance in Chester Cathedral.

Frank's father, who had been predeceased by all his four children, died in 1941. Frank's VC was purchased by Lord Ashcroft at a sale by Morton & Eden on 18 April 2002 at a hammer price of £78,000 and is on display at the Imperial War Museum, together with the BWM and VM, and his original grave cross.

H.B. WOOD

St Python, France, 13 October

After the crossing of the Canal du Nord, the 2nd Battalion, Scots Guards (3rd Guards Brigade, Guards Division), were next involved in crossing the River Selle. This river ran through the German-held town of Le Cateau in a north-westerly to south-easterly direction. Early on 12 October, soldiers from the enemy trenches opposite the 24th Division, on the Guards' left, were seen retiring towards the village of Haussy, a few miles to the north-west of Le Cateau. At first the Guards decided to stand fast, as it became clear that the enemy had an organised defence on their front. At around midnight, patrols of the 2nd Scots Guards moved towards the northern part of St Python, took a few prisoners, then reached the left bank of the Selle. The enemy resisted strongly and it became clear they were not going to surrender St Python without a strong fight.

The slopes of the right bank of the Selle were held by well-hidden machine-gun positions, and trench mortars from the St Python–Solesmes road bombarded the local Haussy–St Python railway. By 6.30 a.m. on 13 October, the Scots Guards had three platoons in positions to the north of St Python, and two more to the south and west. Other parts of the battalion were in positions in line with the railway. The main road bridge in the village had been destroyed, together with all other river crossings. The river was not particularly wide, but it was in flood and was quite wide enough to present a formidable obstacle.

The day was spent mainly clearing the enemy out of the part of St Python west of the Selle, and trying to get across the swollen river. Not only were the Germans well dug in, but local civilians who had not yet left the village were now adding to the confusion, getting mixed up with the enemy attacking force. Slowly, the northern part of the village was cleared, but the southern part provided stiff opposition. To the south-west, bitter hand-to-hand fighting took place and it was at this time that Cpl Harry Wood won his VC.

Wood led his platoon opposite the church where the main road bridge had been destroyed. Their task was to clear the western side of the village, then to secure a crossing of the river. The ruined bridge had to be taken first, but it was covered by enemy snipers who were well entrenched. The platoon was under very heavy machine-gun fire when Wood decided to take a direct hand in events. At great personal risk, he crawled along the top of the bridge, managing to shoot three of the German machine-gunners and putting a fourth out of action. Still exposed to enemy fire, he rushed back to his platoon and gathered up a Lewis gun, then went back over the bridge to fire on the remaining machine guns and their crews, managing to put them out of action as well. He gained a VC for this action, which was gazetted on 14 December 1918 as follows:

For most conspicuous bravery and devotion to duty during operations at the village of St Python, France, on 13 Oct. 1918. The advance was desperately opposed by machine-guns, and the streets were raked by fire. His platoon sergeant was killed, and command of the leading platoon fell to him. The task of the company was to clear the western side of the village and secure the crossing of the River Selle. Command of the ruined bridge had to be gained, though the space in front of it was commanded by snipers. Corpl. Wood boldly carried a large brick out into the open space, lay down behind it, and fired continually at these snipers, ordering his men to work across while he covered them by his fire. This he continued to do under heavy and well-aimed fire until the whole of his party had reached the objective point. He showed complete disregard for his personal safety, and his leadership throughout the day was of the highest order. Later, he drove off repeated enemy counter-attacks against his position. His gallant conduct and initiative shown contributed largely to the success of the day's operations.

Later in the day, the Royal Engineers brought forward bridges, ready to throw across the river during the night. That evening, Wood's battalion was relieved and went into billets at St Hilaire. Wood received his VC from the King in the ballroom of Buckingham Palace on 22 February 1919.

Harry Blanshard Wood was born on 21 June 1881 at Newton-on-Derwent, east of York. His birth was registered in Pocklington, a nearby village. As with so many of the details of his life, there is inconsistency about whether he was born in 1881 or 1882. Whichever year he was born, he was the son of John, who was an agricultural labourer, and Maria Wood (née Dey), and he attended school at Strensall, near York. Later, the family moved into the city of York itself and made their home at 13 Grange Street. After leaving school, Wood worked at York station as a cleaner before enlisting with the Scots Guards on 4 February 1903; he was physically well suited for a Guards Regiment as he was 5ft 10in tall. His enlistment papers show that he had blue eyes, brown hair and a fresh complexion. By 1908 he had moved up the promotion ladder to lance sergeant, but this was as far as he was to go because he was later charged with drunkenness and reduced to the ranks.

In February 1911, after nearly eight years with the Colours, Wood was transferred to the Army Reserve as a private; he was recalled on 5 August 1914. He served with the 2nd Battalion, Scots Guards, from October 1914, his service number being 4796. Early in the war, Wood trained as a sniper, and one of the first stories about him tells of one occasion when he was on outpost duty. He lost contact with his comrades, but came across a Belgian soldier in the same plight in No-Man's-Land. For several days, so the story goes, the two men were in great danger of capture and lived off root crops and apples until they established contact with some Belgian cottagers. The Belgians looked after the two men, providing them with civilian clothes and forged passports, which allowed them to cross over the border into Holland.

Wood returned to England and then re-embarked for France a few months later.

In the autumn of 1915, Wood took part in the Battle of Loos, the first battle in which the newly formed Guards Division was involved. A few months later, in February 1916, Wood's thirteen years' service (his service was extended by one year) was completed, and he returned to civilian life. However, the Army had other ideas for his future and, in January 1917, after a break from military duties of only eleven months, he was recalled to the Colours. When living at home at 15 Worcester Street, Gloucester, with his mother, he had missed the Battle of the Somme. When recalled, Wood was given a new service number, 16444, and drafted into the 3rd Scots Guards. He appears to have moved from Gloucester to Bristol at about this time. For unknown reasons, Wood was not involved on the Western Front for some time as he remained in the United Kingdom until February 1918. He was by then a lance corporal.

Wood returned to France a few days after the German Spring Offensive was launched in March 1918, then at the end of the month he returned to the 2nd Scots Guards, being promoted later in the year. It was when serving with this battalion in September that he won the MM for an ingenious piece of work. Having lost his bearings in No-Man's-Land, he arrived at the enemy trenches. At the same time, he unfortunately made a noise which attracted a group of Germans, who quickly surrounded him. Reacting quickly, he shot two of them and wounded another. The Germans were slow to respond, and Wood took the wounded man hostage, before getting clean away. Later, Wood's captured German was discovered to have important papers on him. In November, when Wood was discharged from the Scots Guards, he was awarded a small disablement pension, initially of 6s a year.

Returning briefly to York on 17 February 1919, five days before he was presented with his VC by the King, Wood was met by a civic party at the railway station and driven in a procession of motor cars to the Mansion House. A couple of days later, Wood was the guest of honour at a West Yorkshire Regimental dinner, where he was presented with a wristwatch. Soon he was given a job in Bristol as a commissionaire with the Anglo-American Oil Company, and shortly afterwards his employers awarded him £100 and his workmates pre-sented him with a gold watch. He lived first at 34 Sydenham Road, Knowle, and then 14 Windsor Terrace, Totterdown. There had been a plan for Wood to set himself up in business somewhere in the south of England, but it came to naught. After being in the public eye for several months, Wood was arrested in London in September for being drunk and disorderly, and was subsequently bound over. During this period it seems that Wood's nerves were very badly affected by his experiences in the war, which may have contributed to his early death. In February 1920, Wood met the King when he was running a stall at the annual Ideal Homes Exhibition, and in June of the same year he attended the Garden Party for VC winners at Buckingham Palace. In November he attended the ceremonies at the Cenotaph and the burial of the Unknown Warrior in Westminster Abbey, being one of fifty holders of the VC who provided the guard of honour.

In early July 1924, while on holiday in Teignmouth with his new wife, the couple were walking along a street when a car suddenly mounted the pavement. Seeing that her husband's life was in extreme danger, Mrs Wood pushed him out of the way, only to be pinned against a wall herself. Although she suffered only a few cuts and abrasions, her husband, possibly because of his nervous state, was so shocked that he became immediately unconscious and fell into a coma from which he never recovered. Wood was taken back to Bristol Mental Hospital where he died after six weeks on 15 August 1924. Wood's funeral service took place six days later in Bristol Cathedral, where he had lain in state. His coffin was drawn on a gun-carriage with an escort from the Scots Guards. The cortège was led to the Arnos Vale Cemetery by the band, pipes and drums of his former regiment, and he was buried in Grave 1737 of the Soldiers Corner.

Wood died intestate and information about his widow is scanty, but it appears that she remarried. After Wood's death his VC became part of a collection owned by Lady Desborough, and, on her death, it was auctioned at Christies on 11 December 1953. The VC, together with four other medals, was keenly sought by Wood's relatives, who dipped into their savings but could only muster a bid of £120. York Corporation promised a further £40 and Mr William Lee, an antiques dealer from Stonegate, York, was planning to find the balance himself in order to present the medal to Wood's family. Representatives of the Scots Guards Association, who were also keen to purchase the medal, dropped out of the bidding when the price rose to £200. The bidding went up to £240, and the decoration was duly purchased by William Lee, who then presented it to Wood's sister, Mrs Agnes Hughes of Kilburn Road, York. It was displayed on her parlour sideboard, alongside a picture of her brother. The plan was for the family to hold the decoration for a year, and that on 31 December 1954 it should be passed to the military section of the Castle Museum at York. Apart from the VC and MM, Wood's other medals were a 1914 Star with clasp, BWM and VM.

Wood's grave in Bristol became neglected, but it was later replaced by a local branch of the Scots Guards Association. A new stone, which lists his date of birth as being 1882, replaced the original with the birth date of 1881 on 27 October 2001. A plaque commemorating his life was also erected at his former school at Strensall, York, and his name is listed on the war memorial at Bristol Cathedral.

Although he died in peacetime in 1924, there are active plans for adding his name to the those servicemen listed on the War Memorial in Wilberfoss, just over 1 mile to the north of Newton-on-Derwent. Pocklington, which is 5 miles to the east of Newton-on-Derwent also has Wood's name on the local war memorial.

The recorded facts about Wood's life are often conflicting, and at this distance in time it is not always possible to obtain the full story with the greatest of accuracy. However, despite his drunkenness and the continuous problems of keeping a job, Wood did win the nation's highest military honour after all.

Canal du Nord (Peter Batchelor)

Sanders Keep Military
Cemetery (Peter Batchelor)

Lt Col Viscount Gort

Bourlon Wood (Peter Batchelor)

The canal at Marcoing (Peter Batchelor)

Marcoing (Peter Batchelor)

Scole Council School

Felixstowe War Memorial (*East Anglian Daily Times*)

Tyne Cot Memorial, Belgium (Donald C. Jennings)

Lt Col B.W. Vann (Vann family)

Sgt James Crichton

Crevecoeur (Peter Batchelor)

Vis-en-Artois Cemetery, France (Peter Batchelor)

Lt Joseph Maxwell

Lt Joseph Maxwell's portrait, with a brass copy of the VC citation, Victoria Barracks, Sydney, Australia

The funeral of L. Cpl H.B. Wood

Solesmes, France (Peter Batchelor)

VC group photograph, 8 May 1919. Left to right: Pte James Towers, CSM Thomas Caldwell, Lt Col Harry Greenwood, CSM Martin Doyle, Sgt John Daykins

The site of the Moulin J. Jacques (Peter Batchelor)

37721 A/CSM JAMES CLARKE . VC
BORN 06·04·1894 . DIED 16·06·1947
AGE 53

Rochdale Cemetery, Lancashire (Donald C. Jennings)

Sambre–Oise Canal, France (Peter Batchelor)

Pont-sur-Sambre, France (Peter Batchelor)

Norfolk Military Cemetery, near Albert, France (Peter Batchelor)

J. JOHNSON
South-West of Wez-Macquart,
France, 14 October

Second Lieutenant James Johnson of the 2nd Battalion, Northumberland Fusiliers, was attached to the 36th Battalion (178th Brigade, 59th Division) to the south-west of Wez-Macquart, south-east of Armentières, when he gained a VC on 14 October.

At 4 a.m., 13 and 14 Platoons of the 36th Battalion, under the command of 2/Lt Johnson and Lt Woodward respectively, were involved in attacking a German-held ridge. The attack was not given artillery support. Corporal Edward Foulkes, a subsequent witness to Johnson's VC actions, had previously been observing the enemy's movements on the ridge over a period of several days. However, when the attack was being prepared, Foulkes found that he had been left behind. On catching up with Lt Johnson, he was told that he was a 'bloody fool', but that since he had bothered to come on the raid he might as well make himself useful: 'As the men on our left were held up by heavy fire, he [Johnson] told me to rally them, silence the machine-guns doing the damage, and take the enemy trench'. Foulkes duly captured the trench and later witnessed one of the deeds for which Johnson was awarded the VC. Foulkes' account of the event is as follows:

As our people escaped from their ditch, the enemy came down their trench and some came across the open firing from the hip, but Mr Johnson stood his ground, emptied his revolver into the enemy and took his wounded servant in his arms. As he was doing this I picked up a rifle and a bandolier of ammunition. I used as cover the dead West Riding lad on his stretcher and kept the enemy from Mr Johnson until he came up to me.

Then I guided him to the log bridge. A stream of bullets whined by us as we had crossed. The lad in the officer's arms moaned and we saw that he had been killed. We were about 20 yards from the safety of our trench but Mr Johnson talked tenderly and said, 'He was a good lad and he's having a decent burial.' We reached the cover of our trench in which was a platoon of the Royal Scots Fusiliers who had relieved us. The survivors of the West Riding officers, Lieutenant Smith, embraced me when he saw me and said, 'I thought you were dead ... '.

On Christmas Eve 1918, Foulkes was sent for by Maj. Gen. Sir Neville Smythe VC, GOC 59th Division. According to Foulkes, he gave him an Army Council telegram and said:

'You are the proper one to take this to Mr Johnson.' When I gave it to the officer, he read it, waltzed me round his billet and then threw every piece of his shaving kit through the window. A runner came with a note which read, 'Brigadier Stansfield desired Lieut Johnson VC, to dinner this evening.' My officer gave the runner a 10 franc note and said, 'Tell the sender you can't find me. The corporal's name should be placed with mine. I'm taking him to be photographed.'

Johnson's VC was gazetted on 26 December 1918 as follows:

For most conspicuous bravery and devotion to duty south-west of Wez Macquart on the morning of 14 Oct. 1918, during operations by strong patrols. He repelled frequent counter-attacks, and for six hours under heavy fire he held back the enemy. When at length he was ordered to retire he was the last to leave the advanced position, carrying a wounded man. Three times subsequently this officer returned and brought in badly wounded men under intense enemy machine-gun fire. His valour, cheerfulness and utter disregard of danger inspired all.

James Johnson was presented with his VC in the Quadrangle of Buckingham Palace on 14 June 1919, at the same ceremony in which R.V. Gorle and D.G. Johnson received their VCs. Johnson was also presented with various gifts by the staff of the Newcastle Infirmary, where he used to work before the war.

James Johnson was born in Widdrington, Northumberland, on 31 December 1889. When war broke out he was working as a clerk in the Newcastle Infirmary, and enlisted on 13 October 1914, joining the Northumberland Fusiliers. Three and a half years later he was commissioned in the 2nd Battalion on 29 May 1918.

He was demobilised at the end of 1918, and in 1920 attended the VC Garden Party at Buckingham Palace, then the House of Lords Dinner in November 1929. He lived in Jesmond, Newcastle, and was a businessman with connections with Bedlington, Morpeth, Northumberland. He was also a member of the Auxiliary Division of the Royal Irish Constabulary. Towards the end of his life, he moved from north-east England and held a job in the Plymouth City Treasurer's Office, starting work there in July 1941. His job dealt with the rating assessments of buildings. Johnson, who lived at 2 Salisbury Road, Plymouth, died in the City Hospital on 23 March 1943 at the early age of 53. He was unmarried. His funeral took place at Searles Chapel of Repose on 27 March, followed by cremation at Efford Cemetery, Reference 2857. Only one member of his family attended his funeral, but Plymouth City Council was represented, and members of the Old Contemptibles Association, the British Legion, and his former regiment were present. His sister, Chris, sent a wreath in the design of a Victoria Cross. His ashes were scattered in the Garden of Remembrance.

Although Johnson seems to have been a solitary man, he did have two close friends in Plymouth, a Mr and Mrs Ramsey of 1 Evelyn Street, St Budeaux, who probably organised the funeral. In his will, Johnson left his VC to his regiment and it is now in the collection of the Royal Northumberland Fusiliers, Alnwick Castle. His other medals included the 1914–15 Star, BWM, VM and King George VI Coronation Medal.

Edward Foulkes won the DCM and MM during the First World War and later became a Methodist minister. He was awarded the MBE for his work. He and Canon Lummis, the expert on the lives of holders of the Victoria Cross, corresponded until both were well into their 80s.

J. MCPHIE

*Near Aubencheul-au-Bac,
France, 14 October*

Corporal James McPhie was a member of 416 Field Company, Royal Engineers (TF), 56th (London) Division. The division was under the command of the Canadian Corps in the area of the Canal de la Sensée, north-west of Cambrai and close to the village of Aubencheul-au-Bac. 416 (Edinburgh) Field Company was one of three Royal Engineers field companies which were part of the 56th Division, and it was under the command of a Canadian, Maj. C.R. Dain. A few days before McPhie gained his posthumous VC, his company was detailed for special training in the use of cork-float bridges, a new way of crossing stretches of water at great speed.

On the night of 12–13 October a sapper officer, Lt Arnold, together with several sappers, proceeded to a pre-selected spot to gather a number of cork-floats in order to make a cork bridge. The cork-floats were packed very closely together, then placed in a wire mesh to hold them firmly. The resulting structures were about 5ft high and 3ft square. On the top was placed a metal construction, designed to hold lightweight duckboards. These, together with the floats, produced a sort of light footbridge. This bridge was then to be built out until the other side of the canal was reached. Once across, a board was to be dropped into position to bridge the gap to the bank. The principle was probably sound, but in reality it did not quite work. The construction became quite lively under the weight of the men using it. As its buoyancy was very poor, the troops were ordered not to crowd, but to leave at least a 6ft gap between each man. Despite this, the men using it had to be very agile in order to avoid a dunking in the canal.

The crossing point selected was in the grounds of a badly damaged château, the cellars of which were used as an infantry headquarters. Further along on the enemy side of the canal, and only about 8yd from the bridge, was a large building which appeared to be a sort of storehouse. It was obvious that the Germans would use this building to obtain a perfect view of any bridging attempts.

The attack on 13 October was made at first light, when a large body of troops from the 1/2nd London (56th Division) managed to make the crossing to the far bank of the canal, albeit under heavy shell-fire. They were acting as a patrol, but found they were unable to remain there and were ordered to retire. This journey was far more difficult as, not surprisingly, there was continuous sniper fire coming from the storehouse. Unfortunately, there was too much crowding by the troops trying to get back and the bridge broke, leaving a number of men trapped on the enemy side of the canal.

During the enemy bombardment, Lt Arnold had been wounded and died when sheltering in the château. His death was immediately reported to Maj. Dain, who decided that a further attempt should be made to rescue the sappers then trapped on the far side of the canal.

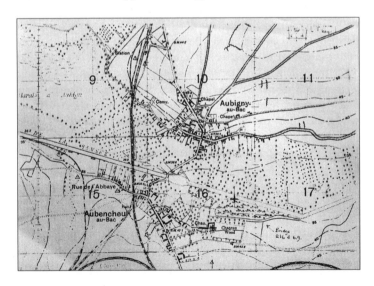

Another officer, Lt Norburn, together with a small party, was ordered to return to the bridge and try to repair it. However, it was impossible to save the isolated men as the sniper fire from the storehouse pinned down anyone in the vicinity. It was then decided to wait until the next day. The night turned out to be very clear, with the moon rising early, which helped the engineers continue with their preparations. Fresh floats and boards were collected from close to the château, where they had been kept. During the day, Cpl James McPhie arrived with a party of five sappers in order to take over the maintenance of the bridge, which they succeeded in repairing. A pre-arranged artillery barrage began at dawn in order to cover the return of the isolated party, most of whom managed to cross safely, although the bridge was smashed again. The bridge over the canal, or 'McPhie's Crossing' as it became known, was about 600yd to the east of the village itself.

McPhie and another sapper ran out onto the bridge to repair it once more. When they saw this was not possible, they jumped into the canal, which was only about half full, and for a short while they held the broken sections of the bridge together, enabling more men to use it. However, tragedy then struck when the two men were hit by sniper fire. McPhie was fatally wounded when shot in the face and his colleague, Sapper Cox, was hit in the arm and leg, but managed to drag McPhie onto the bridge and hold him up. The enemy saw what was going on and opened up with machine-gun fire, and this time McPhie was hit in the back. Cox was hit by the same gun in the thigh, yet he still managed to hold on to the mortally wounded McPhie until he saw that the latter was dead. Another sapper, Hawkins, then threw a line to Cox and, at great risk to himself, managed to pull him to shore. He was taken to the dressing station, but lived only two days and was buried at Boisleux, south of Arras. McPhie was buried 4 miles from Cambrai at Naves Communal Cemetery Extension, Plot II, Row E, Grave 4. His VC was gazetted on 31 January 1919 as follows:

For most conspicuous bravery on 14 Oct. 1918, when with a party of sappers maintaining a cork-float bridge across the Canal de la Sensée, near Aubencheul-au-Bac. The further end of the bridge was under close machine-gun fire and within reach of hand grenades. When infantry, just before dawn, were crossing it, closing up resulted and the bridge began to sink and break.

Accompanied by a sapper, [McPhie] jumped into the water and endeavoured to hold the cork and timbers together, but this they failed to do.

Corpl. McPhie then swam back, and, having reported the broken bridge immediately started to collect material for repair. It was now daylight. Fully aware that the bridge was under close fire and that the far bank was entirely in the hands of the enemy, with the inspiring words, 'It is death or glory work, which must be done for the sake of our patrol on the other side,' he led the way, axe in hand, on to the bridge, and was at once severely wounded, falling partly into the water, and died after receiving several further wounds. It was due to the magnificent example set by Corpl. McPhie that touch was maintained with the patrol on the enemy bank at a most critical period.

McPhie's VC was presented to his mother, Elizabeth McPhie, in the ballroom of Buckingham Palace on 3 April 1919.

James McPhie was the son of Allan and Elizabeth McPhie, and was born at 21 Salisbury Place, South Bridge Street, Edinburgh, on 18 December 1894. The family home was 112 Rose Street. He was educated at South Bridge School and, at the age of 17, joined the Territorial Army early in 1912, where his service number was 422047.

After his death, a subscription fund was raised on behalf of his widowed mother, which came to £744. The fund was used to provide Mrs McPhie with an annuity of 22s 3d per week and this, together with the balance of £14, was presented to her by the Lord Provost of Edinburgh. After the war, Mrs McPhie unveiled a plaque in St Giles Cathedral, Edinburgh, to the memory of the Royal Engineers who had died in the First World War.

In 1961 surviving members of McPhie's company clubbed together to pay for a seat in memory of James McPhie and of other comrades who fell in action. It was placed in Princes Street Gardens, below the Scots Greys Memorial. After Mrs McPhie died, her son's VC was passed to her other son, John, who had served in the same unit as a lance corporal; he had not taken part in the operation, but helped to bury his brother the next day. John then presented the decoration on loan to the Imperial War Museum at a ceremony that took place on 27 September 1963. Three years later, in 1966, it was gifted to the museum by James McPhie's sister, Elizabeth Missingchuk of Edmonton, Alberta, at a ceremony at the Imperial War Museum, when she unveiled a case containing her brother's VC. A number of veterans from the action were traced, and they attended the ceremony, wearing their medals. John, eighteen months younger than his brother and now a retired insurance official, also attended. James's was probably one of the first Great War VCs acquired by the museum, which also holds his service medals, including the BWM, VM and Territorial Force Medal (1914–1918). Apart from his decorations, the museum also holds his Next of Kin Memorial plaque, his RE Service badge and his Imperial Service Badge. A scroll from the Edinburgh Union of Upholsterers, of which McPhie had been a member, is in the archives of the Royal Engineers Museum in Gillingham, and his framed photograph used to be displayed in what later became a Territorial Army Hall at Longstone in Edinburgh. A special McPhie exhibit is also on display at the Royal Engineers Museum.

Those readers attempting to retrace James McPhie's VC action will unfortunately have difficulties, as this part of the canal has been made considerably wider than it would have been in 1918.

M. MOFFATT
Near Ledegem, Belgium, 14 October

By October 1918 the static warfare on the Western Front was changing into a war of movement, and, with the aid of tanks, the Allied infantry were making real progress. However, the Germans were still determined to fight for every yard of ground.

In Belgium on 13 October 1918, the 2nd Battalion The Prince of Wales's Leinster Regiment (88th Brigade, 29th Division) moved up to assembly positions in readiness for an assault on Ledegem the following day. The area was 9 miles to the east of Ypres.

The Battle of Courtrai began in the early morning along the whole of the Flanders front, from Dixmude to the Lys. The Leinsters were to lead the attack on what were known to be very strong enemy positions, but the Germans were aware of the impending attack and were planning to respond with artillery and trench mortar fire, together with poison gas. The advance of the Leinsters in the mist was at first successful, with the 88th Brigade crossing the Menin–Roulers road, and reaching Ledegem at about 9 a.m. During the advance, Pte Martin Moffatt's section of the Leinsters was held up by severe fire from a fortified farmhouse, at which point he decided to take matters into his own hands and gained a VC for his bravery. Moffatt's VC action was witnessed by the battalion chaplain, Capt. John Moran MC of South Wales, who recommended him for the VC.

The citation was gazetted on 26 December 1918 as follows:

For most conspicuous bravery and devotion to duty on 14 Oct. 1918, near Ledegem, when, advancing with five comrades across the open, the party suddenly came under heavy rifle fire at close range from a strongly held house. Rushing towards the house through a hail of bullets, Private Moffatt threw bombs, and then working to the back of the house, rushed the door single-handed, killing two and capturing 30 of the enemy. He displayed the greatest valour and initiative throughout.

The day had been very successful for the Leinsters, who captured a total of eleven field guns, sixty machine guns and 240 prisoners.

Moffatt remained in the frontline for the next four weeks, until the Armistice, and was decorated with the VC in the Quadrangle of Buckingham Palace on 12 June 1919. On the same occasion, Admiral of the Fleet Sir David Beatty and Field Marshal Sir Douglas Haig were both presented with the insignia of the Order of Merit. Private Moffatt followed these two war leaders and 'was all of a fluster'.

Martin Moffatt was the son of Mr and Mrs Martin Moffatt, and was born in Knappagh Road, Sligo, Ireland, on 15 April 1882, being one of eleven children. He attended St Vincent's National School, but left at the age of 14. He then became a seaman, working out of Sligo Harbour. Later, in 1913, he was involved in a strike over the non-payment of wages to seamen looking after cattle on board ship.

When the war began he joined the 6th (Service) Battalion of the Connaught Rangers, beginning his training at Kilworth Camp in September before moving on to Fermoy. Moffatt's service number was 18321. His training took about a year and his division, the 16th (Irish) Division, left Ireland for England in order to complete it. They left for France on 10 December 1915. The division then served a period of trench familiarisation for some three months in the Hulluch–Loos area, becoming responsible for its own sector in March as part of I Corps, still in the same area. Towards the end of April 1916, the division was subjected to severe German gas attacks and suffered 1,260 gas casualties, of whom 338 died.

At the end of August 1916 the Connaughts were on the Somme at Guillemont, where they were involved in heavy fighting, along with the 7th Leinsters, losing their commanding officer, Lt Col J.S.M. Lenox-Conyngham. A few days later they were in action at Ginchy and Moffatt took part in both of these battles. In June 1917 the 16th Division, together with the 36th (Ulster) Division, took part in fighting at Messines and at Wytschaete, and in the spring of 1918 it suffered such heavy casualties that it was taken out of the line and reconstructed, although not with Irish regiments. Those men who survived were transferred to other Irish battalions and men from the 6th Connaughts were amalgamated with the 2nd Leinsters.

Moffatt was demobilised in 1919 and, after receiving his VC from the King on 12 June, he returned to a public reception at his home in Sligo. In view of the political situation in 1919, it was surprising that Moffat was given a huge welcome with half of the town coming to a standstill. Even the train bringing him home had difficulty in getting into the station, so great was the crowd which had turned out to greet him. When news of his VC reached his hometown, a testimonial fund was set up for him and it raised £134. He was presented with a £100 war bond, £30 in cash, an inscribed gold watch from the 2nd Leinsters, a silver cigarette case bearing the regimental crest and, finally, a gold-centred silver medal given by Mr and Mrs McHugh of George's Street, Sligo. Moffatt was the last Irishman to win the VC in the Great War and, in 1920, he attended the Garden Party for VC holders at Buckingham Palace. Moffatt's deeds even inspired an anonymous ballad-style poem, which refers to his birth in a cottage in Knappagh, only half a mile from Sligo.

In October 1921 Moffatt married Annie McNiff and they had five children: four girls and a boy, Joseph, who sadly died at the age of 3 in 1933. In November 1929 he attended the House of Lords VC Dinner. In 1934 he met up again with Capt. John Moran MC, who by now had become Father Moran, when the two men were on an ex-servicemen's pilgrimage to Lourdes; the last time they had met was in Belgium, when Father Moran was witness to Moffatt's VC action. John O'Neill was also on the pilgrimage and, presumably, the three men had a lot to talk about! Subsequently, the men exchanged Christmas cards. While in Lourdes an Irishman from Sligo, Mr Carroll, who had been a pilgrim to the shrine, died suddenly and no fewer than seven holders of the VC acted as his pallbearers, including Moffatt. Moffatt used to attend the Armistice Day Parade every year at the Sligo War Memorial.

Moffat was employed for many years as a harbour constable, but a few days after he was relieved of these duties he was found drowned, close to Rosses Point, on 7 January 1946. He had been missing for two days and *The Times* reported the incident:

> Moffatt, who lived at Emmelt Place, Sligo, had been missing since January 5, until a few days later his body was recovered from the sea at Rosses Point, some miles from Sligo. The actual place where his body was found was on the seashore near Garda Barracks at Rosses Point. The news of the find was conveyed to the Sligo Guards by Sgt. A. Kelly. At the inquest held on Wednesday it was stated that he had suffered from a weak heart, and had been drawing a 100 per cent war disability pension. A verdict was returned of 'Death from drowning', there being no evidence to show how he entered the water.

Moffatt's funeral took place in the local cathedral and the burial was in Sligo's town cemetery. His widow and his four daughters attended the funeral, and ex-servicemen accompanied the cortège to the cemetery. Two files of ex-servicemen under the charge of John Fallon of the British Legion formed up at the graveside. His wife, Annie, outlived her husband by seventeen years, dying in 1963. A decade later, Moffatt's VC exploits were written up in the children's comic, *Victor*.

On 21 October 1991 his decorations, which also included the Belgian *Croix de Guerre* and *Décoration Militaire*, the 1914–15 Star, the BWM, VM and King George VI Coronation Medal, together with a parchment showing a Mentioned in Despatches, were sold at Christies to Lord Ashcroft for £17,400 and are on display in the Imperial War Museum. The Sligo County Museum also has a Moffatt display.

J. O'NEILL

Near Moorsele, Belgium, 14 October

On 14 October 1918 three men gained the VC during the Battle of Courtrai in Belgium: two at Ledegem, Thomas Ricketts and Martin Moffatt, and a third, John O'Neill, near Moorsele, north of Menin.

Like Pte Moffatt, Sgt John O'Neill was a member of the 2nd Battalion The Prince of Wales's Leinster Regiment (88th Brigade, 29th Division), which moved out of Ypres towards the heavily contested ground around the strongly held town of Courtrai. They advanced slowly to a point between the villages of Ledegem and Moorsele, some 6 miles from Courtrai, where the attack ground to a halt when checked by two machine guns and an artillery battery firing over open sights.

Sergeant O'Neill, leading a small group of only eleven men, decided to charge the German battery. The small party successfully overcame the enemy positions and some of the captured guns were turned against the German lines. Elevating them as high as possible, they loosed them off in the vague direction of the enemy. Later that day the HQ of the Leinsters was set up in the former German battery command post.

Six days later, O'Neill was once again involved in an action which was part of his VC citation, when he charged a machine-gun position single-handed, with only one man to cover him. Both of O'Neill's actions were witnessed by Capt. John Moran MC, an officer in the 2nd Leinsters, who had also witnessed Moffatt's VC action. O'Neill's citation appeared in the *London Gazette* on 26 December 1918 as follows:

For most conspicuous bravery and devotion to duty near Moorsele on 14 Oct. 1918, when the advance of his company was checked by two machine-guns and an enemy field battery firing over open sights. At the head of eleven men only he charged the battery, capturing four field-guns, two machine-guns and sixteen prisoners. Again, on the morning of the 20th Oct. 1918, Sergt. O'Neill, with one man, rushed an enemy machine-gun position, routing about 100 enemy and causing many casualties. Throughout the operations he displayed the most remarkable courage and powers of leadership.

Sergeant John O'Neill was presented with his VC by the King at Buckingham Palace on 4 August 1919. The Prince of Wales, as colonel-in-chief of the Leinster Regiment, was also present at the investiture, as was Field Marshal the Duke of Connaught.

John O'Neill, the son of Samuel O'Neill and his wife, Agnes (née Devan), was born at 13 Forsythe Street, Airdrie, Lanarkshire, on 27 January 1897, and was baptised on 11 February 1897. His father worked in a nearby colliery and, after John left school, he followed his father into the coalmining industry. The war broke out when O'Neill was 17 and he eventually joined the 2nd Leinsters, his service number being 4119.

By all accounts he seemed a pretty fearless soldier who relished leading from the front. In addition to his VC, he won the MM as a result of his actions in an attack on Hill 63, and was also awarded the French *Medaille Militaire*. On 5 August, the day after being presented with his VC, he was awarded the Freedom of the Burgh of Hamilton. He was also presented with a monetary gift of more than £400. On 6 February 1920 the Prince of Wales drove to Colchester, where he presented honours and medals to about 100 officers and men of the Leinster Regiment. The prince was met by O'Neill on the outskirts of the city and was driven to the barrack square. Four months later, O'Neill was also present at the VC Garden Party on 26 June 1920 at Buckingham Palace.

On 18 February 1922 he married Kathleen O'Neill Flanagan, a dressmaker from Hamilton, and the couple set up home at 19 Moore Street, Hamilton. They were to have two daughters. In the same year, after the disbandment of the Leinsters, O'Neill returned briefly to the coal mines. However, less than a year later, on 25 April 1923, he enlisted as an aircraftsman in the RAF, working up to the rank of sergeant with a specialism as an armourer. For a time he served on the aircraft carrier HMS *Glorious*.

On 9 November 1929 he attended the House of Lords VC Dinner. In 1934 an ex-servicemen's pilgrimage to Lourdes attracted much press attention, and one of the photographs published at the time showed Father John Moran and Martin Moffatt shaking hands, with O'Neill looking on. At this time O'Neill was still in the RAF and was serving in Scotland. Moran and O'Neill had not met since the war and O'Neill had no idea that the former captain was now a priest.

On 27 July 1939, after sixteen years of service, much of which was with the Marine Branch of the RAF, O'Neill was discharged. With war once more imminent, it was not long before O'Neill was back in uniform, this time as a commissioned officer in the Pioneer Corps in 295 Company, part of 17 Group Army Pioneer Corps, based in Huyton. One of his duties was to act as part of a military escort to 2,250 deportees bound for Australia on the ship *Dunera*. This voyage, which has been well documented, proved to be the darkest period of his life because, for reasons that are not readily apparent, O'Neill behaved almost like a German concentration camp guard. According to a transcript of an interview with Walter Fliess, an internee on board the *Dunera*, O'Neill bullied his charges in a brutal and sadistic manner.

For three years from the summer of 1941, the pioneers carried out work defending Liverpool Docks and also often took part in fire-watching duties during air raids on the city. In recognition of this service, the members of the Liverpool United Warehouse Keepers Conference presented the pioneers with the Alexander Cup at a ceremony on 19 September 1944, this being the first piece of silverware acquired by the fledgling corps which had been founded in October 1939. O'Neill, with other members of 295 Company, was billeted in Hoylake and West Kirby.

John O'Neill died suddenly in Hoylake of heart trouble on 16 October 1942, and he was given a full military funeral at Hoylake Holy Trinity Church, before being buried in the Trinity Road church-yard, Grave 8. On 29 March 1984 his was one of seven gilded names listed on the Roll of Honour that was unveiled by the Mayor of Wirral and Ian Fraser VC in the newly decorated parlour of Birkenhead Town Hall. The roll helped to mark the special connection between the City of Liverpool and the Royal Pioneer Corps. Also in the 1980s, a CWGC VC headstone was set up at O'Neill's grave as he had died while on active service.

On 19 April 2002 a memorial arch to the fourteen men from Lanarkshire who had won the VC, including O'Neill, was unveiled by Dr John Reid, the then Secretary of State for Northern Ireland. On 31 October 2004 his headstone was refurbished and an additional memorial plaque added to its base, which linked his First World War service with the Leinster Regiment. A revised replacement VC board, this time listing the names of twelve men linked with the Wirrall and including the Ellesmere Port and Neston districts, was unveiled in Wallasey Town Hall on 22 February 2012 by its instigator, Mr Denis Rose, and Melba Fraser, widow of Ian Fraser VC. The same twelve names are listed on a VC plaque at the Birkenhead Cenotaph. In 2014 it is hoped to have a VC display set up in the ground-floor main stair-well in Birkenhead Town Hall.

O'Neill's decorations were due to be sold in 1962, but were stolen from Messrs B.A. Seaby, a numismatics firm, on 13 February. They have never been found. Apart from the VC, MM and the French *Medaille Militaire*, they would have included the 1914–15 Star, BWM, VM, King George VI Coronation Medal and Belgian Knight of the Order of Leopold II.

T. RICKETTS

Near Ledegem, Belgium, 14 October

In October 1918, during the advance to victory, the 1st Battalion Royal Newfoundland Regiment (28th Brigade, 9th (Scottish) Division), was involved in an attack from Ledegem, 9 miles to the east of Ypres, on

the morning of 14 October 1918. It was very misty and, at 5.35 a.m., the Royal Newfoundlanders moved over a ridge, through some barbed wire entanglements, to descend the other side of the ridge, before crossing a beet field to reach a shallow ditch 300yd beyond. By then the mist had begun to lift and one of the companies was held up by a German field battery, which was firing at point-blank range from the shelter of two farmhouses. The shallow ditch gave very little protection and the company began to take heavy casualties. The men

were trapped, and it was at this point that Pte Thomas Ricketts seized a Lewis gun and worked forward, together with L. Cpl Matthew Brazil MM of B Company, his section commander, to try to outflank the enemy battery and prevent any more casualties. Moving from the far right of the ditch, the two men advanced in short rushes over the open ground, but when 300yd from the farmhouses they ran out of ammunition. Immediately, Ricketts returned for more ammunition and, picking up two carriers, returned to his colleague. However, L. Cpl Brazil was nowhere to be seen. By now the enemy gunners were taking shelter in the partially destroyed farm buildings, so, grabbing his chance, Ricketts rushed forward. Firing from the hip, he planted the gun in the doorway of one of the buildings and the whole crew quickly surrendered. By his presence of mind in anticipating the enemy's intentions and his utter disregard of personal safety, Pte Ricketts secured the further supply of ammunition which directly resulted in these important captures and undoubtedly saved many lives. It's possible that Ricketts had been spurred on by the news that his elder brother George had recently been killed in the Battle of Cambrai.

Brazil was awarded the DCM and, two months later, on 14 December, the announcement of Ricketts' VC was made at a parade by Maj. Bernard, who read out the official citation and then congratulated the private. Nearly a month later, on 13 January, Ricketts left the regiment, returning to England for his investiture. His VC was gazetted on 6 January 1919 as follows:

> Near Ledegem on 14 Oct. he volunteered to go with his section commander and a Lewis-gun to attempt to outflank a battery causing casualties at point-blank range. Their ammunition was exhausted when still 300 yards from the battery. The enemy began to bring up their gun teams, Private Ricketts doubled back 100 yards under the heaviest machine-gun fire, procured ammunition, dashed back again to a Lewis-gun, and by very accurate fire drove the enemy and the gun teams into a farm. His platoon then advanced and captured the four field-guns, four machine-guns and eight prisoners. A fifth field-gun was subsequently intercepted by fire and captured.

Thomas Ricketts was anxious to return home to Newfoundland in order to resume his studies, and on 18 January he received a message informing him the King had agreed to invest him with his VC at York Cottage, Sandringham, the following day, which was a Sunday.

The young Canadian travelled by train to Wolferton, the nearest station to the royal residence. Here he was met by an equerry with a car, who explained the formal procedure before he met the King. Once at York Cottage, Ricketts was given a splendid lunch, which he ate in a room by himself. In the afternoon he was taken to meet the King, who was not in uniform but in civilian clothes, and who, as well as presenting him with the VC, talked to him for at least ten minutes. While at Sandringham, Ricketts was also introduced to other members of the royal family. At that point he was the youngest holder of the VC in the Army. On 29 January Ricketts was promoted to sergeant and he left Liverpool for home the following day.

Thomas Ricketts was the son of John Ricketts, a fisherman, and Amelia, and was born at a small fishing settlement in White Bay called Middle Arm, on the Baie Verte Peninsula, Newfoundland, on 15 April 1901. His mother died when he was still very young and he was probably brought up by an aunt. Overstating his age, which was 15, Ricketts joined the Newfoundland Regiment in St John's on 2 September 1916, with the service number 3102, and went overseas four months later when he carried out training at Ayr, Scotland. He left for France on 10 June 1917 and first saw action at Steenbeek at the Battle of Langemark in August. His regiment was part of 28th Infantry Brigade of the 9th Division. Three months later, during the Battle of Cambrai, he was wounded in the right leg at Marcoing on 20 November. After a five-month break, during which time he spent eighteen days in hospital in Wandsworth, he returned to the Western Front on 4 April 1918. By now his regiment had been honoured with the 'Royal' as a prefix.

In addition to becoming one of the youngest men to win the VC in the First World War, Ricketts was also awarded the French *Croix de Guerre*. It was presented at Holickshen on 27 September by the commander of II Corps, Lt. Gen. Sir Claud Jacob.

He left the Army after he returned to Canada in early 1919, but his demobilisation wasn't formally completed until 1 July. Returning to St John's on 10 February, he was given a huge welcome and acclaimed by the whole town. He was drawn in a sleigh by young men through the streets of the capital. A fund was set up for his college education, which reached more than $10,000 (£5,000). At one point he was considering a career in medicine, but decided on pharmacy instead. He attended a course at Bishop Field College and, in 1925, entered an apprenticeship. In 1937 he opened his own drug store in Water Street, St John's.

In November 1929 he attended the House of Lords Dinner. On 17 July 1962 he attended a Garden Party at Buckingham Palace given by the Queen for members of the VC/GC Association, and on the same day he also attended a banquet given by the Lord Mayor of London for the Association at the Mansion House. On the next evening he attended a dinner for the Association, which took place at the Café Royal in Regent Street, London. It appears that Thomas Ricketts was a very shy and modest man, and disliked having his photograph taken.

Sadly, Ricketts suffered from poor health for many years and, at the early age of 65, he died of a heart attack on 10 February 1967 while working in his drug store. Three days later he was given a full military funeral and his remains lay in state for three hours before the funeral at St Thomas' Anglican Church. Large crowds turned out on an extremely cold day to line the route of the procession. His decorations were placed on the flag-draped coffin. The cortège included a guard of honour drawn from the Royal Newfoundland Regiment and the Royal Canadian Legion. Also represented were men from the Royal Canadian Mounted Police, Newfoundland Constabulary. Local dignitaries, including Prime Minister J.R. Smallwood, walked behind the coffin.

Ricketts was buried in the Anglican Cemetery, St John's, and many of the nearby graves belong to former members of the Royal Newfoundland Regiment. A three-volley salute was fired by the Royal Newfoundland Regiment and veterans dropped poppies into the open grave. The 'Last Post' and 'Reveille' were then sounded.

Ricketts left a widow, Edna (née Edwards), a daughter and a son. A painting of him is displayed at the Royal Canadian Legion in Corner Brook, Newfoundland. For many years his VC was on display at the Confederation Building, but in the early 1980s it was returned to his family. On 10 June 1972 a monument to the memory of Thomas Ricketts was unveiled in St John's, near the site of his pharmacy store, which described him as a 'Soldier-Pharmacist-Citizen'. A play based on his life 'The Known Soldier' was first performed in Newfoundland in 1982. In October 2002, a display about his service life was opened in the Royal Newfoundland Regiment Room in the Canadian Forces Station. On 22 October 2003 his widow donated his decorations to the Canadian War Museum, Ottawa. Apart from the VC and French *Croix de Guerre*, his medals included the BWM, VM, and Coronation Medals for King George VI (1937) and Queen Elizabeth II (1953).

R.E. ELCOCK

South-East of Capelle Ste Catherine, Belgium, 15 October

On 14 October 1918, beyond Ledegem and to the north of Menin, the 9th (Scottish) Division attacked towards the Courtrai–Roulers railway. Once this line was taken, the advance could continue towards the River Lys by capturing the river crossings. By noon they had reached a small ridge called Steenen Stampkot, but here the enemy resistance became more determined. The infantry did manage to reach a wood called Laagacapelle, but they were pinned down by German artillery firing from Hill 40, some 500yd to the east.

On the following day, the 27th Brigade, with the 11th (S) Royal Scots leading, managed to move quickly forward under a smokescreen towards the enemy gun positions on Hill 40. At the same time they managed to clear Laagacapelle Wood, but on leaving its eastern side they were immediately pinned down by two machine guns. It was at this point that L. Cpl (A/Cpl) Roland Elcock, in charge of a Lewis gun team, achieved the seemingly impossible. He dashed forward amid a hail of bullets and killed the two men who were firing one of the guns. He then promptly turned this gun on to the other machine-gun team, accounting for both men. The advance was then able to resume and the battalion moved rapidly down the slope. The 12th (S) Battalion, which had followed the 11th into the wood, then swung southwards to drive the enemy from Steenbeek and also from the southern part of Hill 40. Three days later, at Harlbeke, to the north-east of Courtrai,

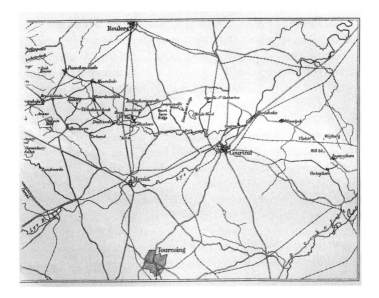

Elcock again captured an enemy machine-gun position when the advance had reached the River Lys. He was awarded the VC for these two actions, which was gazetted on 26 December 1918 as follows:

> For most conspicuous bravery and initiative south-east of Capelle Ste Catherine on the 15th Oct. 1918, when in charge of a Lewis-gun team. Entirely on his own initiative, Corpl. Elcock rushed his gun up to within ten yards of enemy guns, which were causing heavy casualties and holding up the advance. He put both guns out of action, captured five prisoners, and undoubtedly saved the whole attack from being held up. Later, near the River Lys, this non-commissioned officer again attacked an enemy machine-gun and captured the crew. His behaviour throughout the day was absolutely fearless.

Elcock was presented with his VC by the King in the ballroom of Buckingham Palace on 13 February 1919.

Roland Edward Elcock was born at 52 Alma Street, Wolverhampton, Staffordshire, on 5 June 1899, the son of Mr and Mrs George Henry Elcock (formerly of Kingswinford). He attended the Causeway Lake School, then, at the age of 14, obtained work as a clerk at the Labour Assembly Room in Alderman J. Whitaker's office in Queen Square.

In October 1914, when still only 15, he enlisted in the Army, joining the 1/6th (TF) Battalion, South Staffordshire Regiment, and was sent overseas to Egypt. The battalion had only been established for two months. When it was discovered that Elcock was underage, he was discharged and sent back home. He then worked for a time at the Wolverhampton Corporation Electricity Works in Commercial Road, but re-enlisted in June 1917 when he was 18, and this time he became a member of the 11th (S) Royal Scots, serving with them in France and Belgium, with the service number 27148. During the war he also won the MM. In 1919 he was demobilised and was once more employed in his old job with the Wolverhampton Corporation Electricity Department. In 1920 he attended the VC Garden Party at Buckingham Palace.

In 1921 Elcock and his brother, together with their mother, had to leave their home in Wolverhampton as the land was required for cultivation. Two years later, Elcock decided to go abroad and he obtained a position in the Indian Government's Posts and Telegraph Service as an engineer. Initially based in Lahore, he worked on telegraphs and telephones. At one time, when he was Assistant Divisional Superintendent of Telegraphs, Calcutta, he had an accident with a rifle when it jammed and a cartridge exploded in his face. Prompt action, followed by an operation, saved his sight and prevented any lasting damage. He was unable to attend the House of Lords VC Dinner in 1929, but did have some home leave. At the beginning of 1930 he returned to India, this time obtaining a post with the Indian Telegraph Department in Upper Burma. In July 1933 he married Amelia Burnside (née Rowe), a lady from Jersey. In 1936 he was on the north-West Frontier of India and, by then, had become Director-General of Posts and Telegraphs at a time when there were disturbances in the Khyber Pass area.

On the outbreak of the Second World War, Elcock joined the Indian Army with the rank of major, but when he was about to leave for active service with his regiment he was struck down by a mysterious liver illness from which he never fully recovered. He returned to his civilian job and died at Dehra Dun, United Provinces, India, on 6 October 1944, at the age of 45. He was buried the following day in St Thomas' Churchyard.

Elcock left his decorations to his brother, George, and, in addition to the VC and MM, they included the 1914–15 Star, BWM, VM, King George VI Silver Jubilee Medal (1935) and King George VI Coronation Medal (1937). They were sold by Roland's daughter at Christies on 18 February 1958 to the Royal Scots Museum, Glencorse Barracks, Midlothian, for £650. The money received in the sale contributed financial assistance for Mrs Elcock. At the present time, the Regimental Museum houses them in Edinburgh Castle.

H.A. CURTIS

East of Le Cateau, France, 18 October

In the small hours of 18 October 1918, the 50th (Northumbrian) Division moved forward to the east of Le Cateau. Their objective was a ridge 2,000yd to the east of the Le Cateau–Arbre Guernon road, which ran in a south-easterly direction from Le Cateau. The second objective was the village of Bazuel, to the south-east of Le Cateau, and the division was then to capture a line from Bazuel to the Baillon Farm road. The first objective was quickly taken, but when members of the 2nd Royal Dublin Fusiliers (149th Infantry Brigade) entered Bazuel, they came up against six enemy machine guns. It was during the subsequent action that Sgt Horace Curtis won his VC, which was gazetted on 6 January 1919 as follows:

For most conspicuous bravery and devotion to duty east of Le Cateau on the morning of the 18th October 1918, when in attack his platoon came unexpectedly under intense machine-gun fire. Realising that the attack would fail unless the enemy guns were silenced, Sergt. Curtis, without hesitation, rushed forward through our own barrage and the enemy fire, and killed and wounded the teams of two of the guns, whereupon the remaining four guns surrendered. Then, turning his attention to a trainload of reinforcements, he succeeded in capturing over 100 enemy before his comrades joined him. His valour and disregard of danger inspired all.

Horace Curtis was presented with his VC by the King in the ballroom of Buckingham Palace on 8 March 1919.

Horace Augustus Curtis was the fourth of five children of a gamekeeper and was born in St Anthony-in-Roseland, near Portscatho, Cornwall, on 7 March 1891. His home was at Glenburn, St Newlyn East, where he was later commemorated. After leaving school he was employed as a china clay worker until September 1914, when he enlisted in the army soon after war had been declared. On 12 September he attested into The Duke of Cornwall's Light Infantry (DCLI) at Bodmin and was allocated the service number 15833. However, as recruiting in Ireland was not as successful as in England, Curtis became one of the many English recruits to be transferred to an Irish regiment. Hence, four days later, he moved to the 7th (S) Battalion of the Royal Dublin Fusiliers and was given the new service number 14107. He then left for Ireland for basic training at the Curragh in County Kildare. His brigade, the 30th, moved to Dublin in February 1915 and left for England three months later, to continue their training in Basingstoke. His division, the 10th (Irish), left Devonport for Egypt on 11 July and landed at Suvla Bay, on the Gallipoli Peninsular, on 7 August. After suffering very high casualties during the fighting against Turkish forces, the division left for Salonika and then Egypt in October.

On 7 February 1916 Curtis was promoted to lance corporal, and was then promoted to sergeant on 17 November; he was also Mentioned in Dispatches on 21 July 1917. Two months later, the 10th Division left for Alexandria and took part in fighting in Palestine. The 7th Royal Dublin Fusiliers was one of several battalions transferred from the 10th Division and arrived in France in June 1918. On the 6th Curtis was one of the men from the battalion to be absorbed into the 2nd Battalion and, a fortnight later, and due to him suffering from malaria, he left for England and became a patient in Bermondsey Military Hospital. He also had some much overdue leave in Cornwall between 24 July and 3 August. He returned to France on the 19 August and was back on frontline duty on 21 September.

After winning the VC in October 1918, Curtis returned to England on 31 January 1919 when he was awarded twenty-eight days' demobilisation leave. On 23 March he was transferred to Class 'Z' Army Reserve.

On 30 October the Lord Lieutenant of Cornwall presented him with £150, which had been paid for by subscriptions from his colleagues in the local china clay industry. He was finally discharged on 31 March 1920. A few weeks later, on 5 May, he became a member of the 5th (TF) Battalion DCLI on a three-year engagement, and in June he attended the Buckingham Palace Garden Party for VC holders. During this period he was promoted to sergeant and, on 27 August 1920, to WO2 (CSM). He was transferred on 20 December 1921 to the 4/5th DCLI and left the Army on 19 May 1923. He then returned to his former job, but never had any wish to draw attention to his war record, being both shy and modest.

In the same year he married Rose Phillips at St Colomb, Cornwall, and the couple had one daughter, Kathleen Hilary. In 1929 he attended the House of Lords VC Dinner. In the Second World War he became a member of the local Home Guard and, in June 1946, he attended the Victory Parade in London.

During the mid 1960s Curtis became very ill and was virtually paralysed. He finally died in hospital at Redruth on 1 July 1968, and three days later his funeral took place at Newlyn East Methodist Church. His coffin was covered with a Union Jack and the large congregation included former members of the Home Guard, as well as the British Legion. He was cremated at Penmount Crematorium, Truro, and his ashes scattered in the Garden of Remembrance.

Apart from his VC, which is on display as part of the Lord Ashcroft collection in the Imperial War Museum, his other decorations are in private hands. They consist of the 1914–15 Star, BWM, VM and Coronation Medals for King George VI (1937) and Queen Elizabeth II (1953).

J.B. DAYKINS
Solesmes, France, 20 October

On 19–20 October 1918 the 2/4th (Hallamshire) Battalion (TF), The York and Lancaster Regiment (187th Brigade, 62nd (2nd West Riding) Division), was detailed to carry out a special mission as part of the divisonal advance towards the village of Solesmes, on the River Selle, about 5 miles north-west of Le Cateau. The regimental history described the plan as follows:

At Zero minus thirty, [the battalion] was to cross by the bridges over the river in the southern divisional area and form up on the eastern banks of the river. At Zero it was to go forward, one company attacking the factory immediately south of the railway triangle, a second company the northern area of the railway triangle and the southern portion of Solesmes, the remaining two companies to advance along the railway as far as the crossings south-east of Solesmes and then turn inwards and attack the town from that direction.

The night of the 19th/20th October was very wet and the battalion moved off from its billets at Quiévy at 10.30 p.m. and marched to the River Selle in pouring rain. They reached the western bank of the river two hours later and found the river much swollen. It was then decided to move the troops across to the opposite bank earlier than Zero minus thirty minutes. The crossings were successful and this was mainly because of the bridges that the Sappers had constructed earlier in the night, although some men had to wade through water up to their waists.

The factory in the village was duly captured, together with a few prisoners and two machine guns. The battalion then moved on to the railway, mopping up as they went, while the enemy was resisting the advance from a château. More prisoners and guns were then taken.

The second phase of the operation then began, which was to capture the high ground overlooking Romeries, and it was during this fighting that Cpl (A/Sgt) John Daykins won his VC when he led his No. 7 Platoon up the main street of Solesmes as far the church, meeting with heavy opposition along the way. Halfway along the street he shot a machine-gunner who was just about to open fire on his platoon, and the gun position was rushed. Then, 50yd from the church, heavy fire was opened from a second machine gun and the enemy also threw bombs at the party. When more of the enemy began to emerge from cellars, the Yorkshire platoon became surrounded and the men became completely isolated for thirty minutes. Daykins' VC was gazetted on 6 January 1919 and tells the story as follows:

For most conspicuous bravery and initiative at Solesmes on 20 Oct. 1918, when, with twelve remaining men of his platoon, he worked his way most skillfully, in face of heavy opposition, towards the church. By prompt action he enabled his party to rush a machine-gun, and during subsequent severe hand-to-hand fighting he himself disposed of many of the enemy and secured his objective, his party, in addition to heavy casualties inflicted, taking 30 prisoners. He then located another machine-gun which was holding up a portion of his company. Under heavy fire he worked his way alone to the post, and shortly afterwards returned with 25 prisoners and an enemy machine-gun, which he mounted at his post. His magnificent fighting spirit and example inspired his men, saved many casualties, and contributed very largely to the success of the attack.

On 4 November, a week before the Armistice, Daykins was once more in the thick of the fighting and this time gained a MM for bravery in the field (*London Gazette*, 20 August 1919).

At the end of the war, Daykins remained in the Army and served with the 62nd Division, which was the only Territorial division to be part of the Army of Occupation in Cologne. It was during this period that the award of his VC was announced. Six months after the war ended, he was presented with his VC by the King in the Quadrangle of Buckingham Palace on 15 May 1919.

John Brunton Daykins was born at Ormiston Farm, Hawick, near Roxburgh, Scotland, on 26 March 1883, the eldest son of John and Bessie Daykins (née Brunton). A short time after his birth, the family moved first to Sunnyside and then to Kaimend Farm. During this time, two more sons were born and, later, a daughter. When John junior was 2 years old, his father, together with his uncle, Samuel Brunton, took over the tenancy of Howden Farm on the Marquess of Lothian's estate at the end of 1885, and the family moved to Jedburgh.

John went to school in the town from May 1889 until 1896, before completing his education in Kelso. In his youth, John was very practical with his hands and was a keen member of Jedburgh Rifle Club, which was to prove useful to him in the Army. Soon after war broke out, John Daykins enlisted on 13 September in the Lothians and Border Horse Yeomanry, and was posted to A Squadron. For the next eight months the squadron was involved in training at Haddington, before moving to Salisbury Plain in May 1915.

On 21 September the squadron moved to Southampton and left for France with the 26th Division cavalry. The squadron arrived at the front in time to be involved in the final stages of the disastrous Battle of Loos in 1915, but soon afterwards it was posted to Salonika, where Daykins remained until February 1916. As losses mounted on the Western Front, he returned to France with reinforcements for B Squadron. They took part in holding Vimy Ridge in the spring of 1916 and moved to the Ypres Salient in May, where they were involved in heavy fighting in the area of Mount Kemmel. In September 1916, by now a sergeant, he went down with trench fever and was taken back to recuperate in an Amiens hospital.

After the Somme battle was over in November, more officers were needed and it was decided that Daykins should return to England to be commissioned. However, when medically examined at Salisbury Plain, he was found totally unfit to serve and so was discharged from the Army.

On returning to his home, he 'champed at the bit' and twice tried to re-enlist. He was successful on his third attempt, becoming a trooper in the Westminster Dragoons at the beginning of 1917. He joined the regiment at Aldershot, but was immediately posted to the 2/4th Battalion, the York and Lancaster Regiment, with the service number 205353. He returned to Flanders in the spring of 1917, serving with the battalion later in the year in the Passchendaele campaign. In the following March, Daykins was with the 62nd Division when the German Spring Offensive began, and he continued to be involved in the fighting for most of that year.

When he returned home in May 1919, after the investiture in London, he received a great welcome. He arrived at the ceremony in a horse and carriage specially provided for him, with a second carriage made available for his family. At one point the horses pulling Daykins' carriage were replaced by soldiers, and on reaching the town hall he was carried shoulder-high. He signed the Burgess Roll and received his 'Burgess Ticket' in a silver-mounted cask, which was made of wood from the ancient Capon Tree. The 'Burgess Ticket' was a sort of licence or certificate which gave the bearer permission to trade in the town, but in Daykins' case it was the equivalent of being given the 'Freedom of the City'. He was also presented with other gifts from people in the town. In a speech of reply, Daykins thanked everybody, saying that he felt proud to have brought some little distinction to the town. Daykins returned to work at Howden Farm and, on his father's death in June 1924, took over the tenancy.

He attended the Garden Party for VC holders at Buckingham Palace on 26 June 1920, and the Unknown Warrior Service at the Cenotaph and Westminster Abbey in November of the same year. In November 1929 he attended the House of Lords VC Dinner.

Daykins died on 24 January 1933, as a result of a freak accident. He was at home in the evening when he heard a disturbance outside in the garden; taking up his gun he went out to find out what was going on. When he failed to return his sister left to look for him and found him dying of gunshot wounds. An ambulance was called, but he died on his way to the Edinburgh Royal Infirmary. He was only 49 years old, unmarried and lived with his mother and sister. He was buried in the family plot in Castlewood Cemetery, Jedburgh, Grave 1431.

Daykins left his VC to his sister, Mrs Elizabeth Swanston, and in 1957 she presented his medals to the York and Lancaster Regiment, and they were put on display at the regimental museum in Rotherham. At the time of writing the museum is in the throes of being relocated. Apart from his VC and MM, the decorations include the BWM and VM. The guns that Daykins captured at Solesmes were mounted in his hometown, but in 1940 they were removed for scrap and melted down for the war effort. In 1981 Daykins' name was commemorated in Hawick with the naming of a street: Daykins Drive. In September 2000 Daykins was one of three VC holders who had plaques to their memory unveiled outside the Royal British Legion branch in Jedburgh.

A.R. WILKINSON

Marou, France, 20 October

After the Hindenburg Line had been breached, the German Army was determined to make a stand on the River Selle, but on 20 October 1918 they had to give up the village of Solesmes to the north of Le Cateau and on the Selle, although they did put up strong resistance in the small hamlet of Marou, slightly to the east of the town. It was during this fighting that Pte Alfred Wilkinson of the 1/5th Manchester Regiment (127th Brigade, 42nd (East Lancashire) Division), won his VC, which was later gazetted on 6 January 1919 as follows:

> For most conspicuous bravery and devotion to duty on 20 Oct. 1918, during the attack on Marou, when four runners in succession having been killed in an endeavour to deliver a message to the supporting company, Private Wilkinson volunteered for the duty. He succeeded in delivering the message, though the journey involved exposure to extremely heavy machine-gun and shell fire for 600 yards. He showed magnificent courage and complete indifference to danger, thinking only of the needs of his company, and entirely disregarding any consideration for personal safety. Throughout the remainder of the day Private Wilkinson continued to do splendid work.

Wilkinson was presented with his VC by the King in the ballroom of Buckingham Palace on 22 February 1919. Six other men were awarded the VC at the investiture.

Alfred Robert Wilkinson was the second son of Alfred and Sarah
Wilkinson (née Swift) and was born in Leigh, Lancashire, on
5 December 1896, and baptised eight days later. The family of four
boys and three girls had their home at 1 Brideoake Street and later
moved to 59 Bradshawgate. Alfred was educated at St Joseph's
Roman Catholic Day School and then at a junior school in Leigh from
1903 until 1909. As a young man he became a member of the Young
Men's Society at his local church. After leaving school he became a
piecer at the Mather Lane Spinning Company in Leigh, where his
father had previously worked as a spinner. It was a hazardous job.

He enlisted in the Army in Atherton, near Wigan, on 14 December
1914, becoming a member of the 2/5th Manchester Battalion (TF)
with the service number 3120. His battalion was part of 199th
Infantry Brigade, 66th (2nd East Lancashire) Division. Having joined
them in Southport, Wilkinson went with them to the Crowborough
area in Sussex in May 1915. He continued training with the 2/5th,
before moving to Colchester in Essex the following March. On
30 July, with the new service number 43839, he was sent as one of the
reinforcements to the 18th (S) Battalion in France. Wilkinson probably joined this battalion in Busnes in early August. The battalion was
part of the 30th Division and was engaged in the Battle of the Somme
until November.

In early November Wilkinson sprained his ankle and was admitted
to 43rd Casualty Clearing Station (CCS). All was not well as, eight
days later, he was transferred to 16th General Hospital at Étaples and
didn't return to his battalion until 23 December.

For much of 1917 the battalion had a relatively 'quiet' time,
although it ended the year on the Passchendaele front. The battalion, which was the junior member of the 90th Infantry Brigade, was
disbanded on 19 February 1918. At this point Wilkinson became
a member of the 1/5th Manchesters (TF), just prior to the German
Spring Offensive.

Four months after he won the VC in October 1918, Wilkinson
was granted a fortnight's leave and promoted to lance corporal.
When on leave he returned home to Leigh, where he was presented
with a gold watch by fellow members of the St Joseph's Boys' and

Young Men's Society. In addition, the directors of the Mather Lane Spinning Company presented him with an illuminated address, together with £50. He was also given 500 war certificates, together with the sum of £442 10s 6d, which had been raised by public subscription.

After his VC investiture, Wilkinson returned to Belgium to rejoin his battalion. He was back in England in April and played an active role in the Victory Parade on 19 July. Two of his three brothers had died in the war.

On 26 June 1920 Wilkinson attended the Garden Party in the grounds of Buckingham Palace, and the House of Lords VC Dinner in November 1929. He took time off work in order to attend the dinner and his pay was docked by his employers, the Leigh Operating Spinner's Association; however, when the press discovered this, there was such an outcry that he was quickly reimbursed. On 22 October 1932 he married a fellow Catholic, Grace Davies, of Hazel Grove, West Leigh, at the Church of the Twelve Apostles, and they were to have one daughter. The couple also ran a sweet shop at 34 Leigh Road.

Together with five other Catholic VC holders, Wilkinson went on a pilgrimage to Lourdes in September 1934. Four years later, he was presented to the King and Queen when they visited Leigh in May. In the late 1930s he and his wife gave up the sweet shop business. Wilkinson then worked for the Bickershaw Colliery as a tester in the surveyor's laboratory. On the outbreak of the Second World War, he joined the Leigh Special Constabulary, and also assisted in Home Guard duties. The family home at this time was 113 Etherstone Street, Leigh.

Sadly, at the early age of 43, Alfred Wilkinson died as the result of a tragic accident on 18 October 1940, the same day on which he had been offered a commission in the Pioneer Corps. An inquest into the cause of his death revealed that he had died from gas poisoning while on duty at the Bickershaw Colliery, Planks Lane, Leigh. He was found by Harold Webb, a brickworks clerk at the colliery, who saw the slumped figure through an office window. Webb summoned assistance and Wilkinson was taken to the local infirmary, but he was declared dead on arrival. The coroner's official verdict was one of 'death by misadventure'. It was revealed at the inquest that a dead sparrow had become wedged in a ventilation pipe, which may have contributed to Wilkinson's death from carbon monoxide poisoning.

Alfred Wilkinson was buried with full military honours in Leigh Borough Cemetery five days later, after a funeral service at St Joseph's Church, which was attended by many local dignitaries. A large congregation attended the requiem mass at the church and the procession route to the cemetery was lined with spectators. Three separate organisations shared the task of carrying the remains of their comrade: the Knights of St Columba, the Special Constabulary and the British Legion. At the head of the procession was a group of men from the Leigh Home Guard, led by Sgt Maj. Gill, who had been Wilkinson's company sergeant major when he won his VC in 1918. The soldiers from the Home Guard were followed by the Bickershaw Colliery Band. At the end of the service a rifle volley was fired over the grave by the Home Guard and a member of the British Legion sounded the 'Last Post' and 'Reveille'. Flags in the town were also flown at half-mast.

Over the years the Wilkinson family grave in Leigh, Plot IU 99, became neglected, but is now in a good state of repair. Its headstone takes the form of a cross of black marble. This was paid for jointly by the Manchester Regiment and Wigan Borough Council. On 20 April 1995 a Circular War Memorial Plaque dedicated to Tameside VC winners was unveiled, although no names are listed. Wilkinson's name is remembered in the VC Book of Honour in the Regimental Chapel in Manchester Cathedral. He also has a commemorative plaque in Wigan Town Hall and one in Leigh Town Hall, which was installed on 27 January 2005.

Alfred Wilkinson left a widow and daughter. His widow later remarried. His decorations were privately held until 9 June 2006 when they were purchased by Lord Ashcroft at a sale by Dix Noonan Webb of London, and they are now on display in the Imperial War Museum. As well as the VC they include a BWM, VM and King George VI Coronation Medal (1937).

D.S. McGREGOR
Near Hoogmolen, Belgium, 22 October

Lieutenant David McGregor was a member of the 6th Battalion, the Royal Scots (Lothian Regiment), and the 29th Battalion Machine Gun Corps (29th Division), and he won a posthumous VC close to Hill 66 at Hoogmolen, near Courtrai to the north-east of Menin, on 22 October 1918. It was gazetted on 14 December 1918 as follows:

For most conspicuous gallantry and devotion to duty near Hoogmolen on 22 Oct. 1918, when in command of a section of machine-guns attached to the right platoon of the assaulting battalion. In the assembly position he concealed his guns on a limber under the bank of a sunken road. Immediately the troops advanced at zero they were subjected to intense enfilade machine-gun fire from Hill 66 on the right flank. Lieut. McGregor fearlessly went forward into the open to locate the enemy guns, and having done so, realised that it was impossible to get his guns carried forward either by pack or by hand without great delay, as the ground was absolutely bare and swept by a hail of bullets. Ordering the teams to follow by a more covered route, he went to the limber, got on to it, and lying flat, told the driver to leave cover and gallop forward. This the driver did, galloping down about six hundred yards of absolutely open road under the heaviest machine-gun fire into cover beyond. The driver, horses and limber were all hit, but Lieut. McGregor succeeded in getting the guns into action, effectively engaging the enemy, subduing their fire and enabling the advance to be resumed. With the utmost gallantry he continued to expose himself in order to direct the fire of his guns, until, about an hour later, this very gallant officer was killed whilst observing fire effect for the trench mortar battery. His great gallantry and supreme devotion to duty were the admiration of all ranks, and especially the officers and men of the 1st Border Regt., who witnessed this extraordinary action.

McGregor was buried by 29th Divisional burial officers a mile to the east of Courtrai at Staceghem Communal Cemetery, Row A, Grave 1, and his VC was presented to his parents in the ballroom of Buckingham Palace on 15 February 1919.

David Stuart McGregor was born in Craig's Road, Corstophine, West Edinburgh, on 16 October 1895, the son of a clothier, David McGregor, and his wife, Annie. He went to school at George Watson's College and, later, to George Heriot School, which is close to Edinburgh Castle and which has always enjoyed a close association with the Royal Scots, in particular its Territorial battalions, before the war began.

McGregor's first job when he left school in 1911 was as an apprentice at the Commercial Bank of Scotland, becoming an associate of the Scottish Bankers' Institute. Two years later he joined the Midlothian Royal Field Artillery (TF). When war broke out, he volunteered for service abroad and was commissioned with the 1/6th Royal Scots (TF) in 1915, and in May the following year he was sent to Egypt. He was then transferred to France, where he took part in much of the fighting throughout 1916. He was trained for machine-gun work and posted to the 29th Machine Gun Corps, with whom he was serving at the time of his death. He was a keen sportsman, being a particularly fine swimmer, and he was also a keen rugby player and golfer.

In 1921 the Roll of Honour for the George Heriot School was published: out of the 2,657 boys connected with the school who took part in the war, no fewer than 461 had been killed. Nearly a hundred had not reached the age of 20 when they died.

On 21 June 1976 a small ceremony took place at Edinburgh Castle when the colonel of the Royal Scots accepted the donation of McGregor's VC from a relative, Mr James McGregor. This gift completed their museum's collection of all seven VCs won by the regiment. His other decorations were the BWM and VM. McGregor was also one of seven members of the Machine Gun Corps to win a VC in the Great War.

F.G. MILES

Bois l'Evêque, France, 23 October

During the Battle of the River Selle, to the east of Le Cateau, on 23 October 1918, the 25th Division attacked on a 2,000yd front, with the aim of capturing Pommereuil and clearing the Bois l'Evêque in an advance of some 8,000yd. The 1/5th Gloucesters (75th Brigade) were given the task of mopping up the north-eastern part of the wood. After advancing some 300yd the battalion met with stiff resistance, from machine-gun nests which had not yet been dealt with, in a sunken road close to a mill. These machine guns protected the west side of the Bois l'Evêque. For five hours there was heavy fighting, during which Pte Francis Miles won his VC, which was gazetted on 6 January 1919 as follows:

For most conspicuous bravery and initiative in attack on 23 Oct. 1918, during the advance against the Bois l'Evêque, when his company was held up by a line of enemy machine-guns in the sunken road near the Moulin J. Jacques. Private Miles alone, and on his own initiative, went forward under exceptionally heavy fire, located a machine-gun, shot the gunner, and put the gun out of action. Observing another gun near by, he again advanced alone, shot the gunner, rushed the gun and captured the team of eight. Finally, he stood up and beckoned to his company, who acting on his signals, were enabled to work round the rear of the line and to capture 16 machine-guns, one officer and 50 other ranks. It was due to the courage, initiative and entire disregard of personal safety shown by this very gallant soldier that the company was enabled to advance at a time when any delay would have jeopardised seriously the whole operation.

Miles was presented with his VC in the Quadrangle of Buckingham Palace on 30 May 1919.

Francis George Miles was born in Clearwell, near Coleford in the Forest of Dean, Gloucestershire, on 9 July 1896, the son of Christopher George Miles and Mrs Frederick Clack. He attended the Clearwell Church of England School and left this at the age of 13, afterwards working for a mining firm, the Princess Royal Colliery Company.

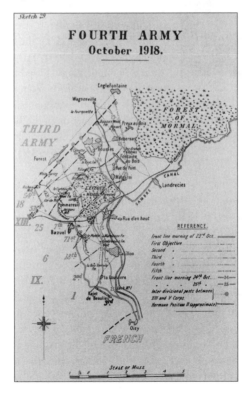

Miles grew into a short, thick-set young man. He enlisted on 28 December 1914, with his stepfather, in the 9th Gloucesters, who were training in Cheltenham. The following April, Miles left for further training at Fovant, near Salisbury. On 21 September he embarked for France, but at some point his foot became infected and, subsequently, he spent some time in hospital. During this period his battalion left for Salonika without him, so when he left hospital he was attached to the 8th Battalion, and later to the Royal Engineers as a tunneller, where his mining experience came in useful. In July 1917 Miles was injured in a mine explosion which killed most of his colleagues. He then returned to England, where he spent some time in hospital at Halifax. On recovering, he returned to the Gloucesters and joined the 1/5th Battalion, with the service number 17324. In November he was sent with this battalion to Italy, where he remained until September 1918, when his regiment was sent to France to join the 75th Brigade, 25th Division.

In January 1919, when news of his VC was first made known, Miles was at home and the announcement was made at Clearwell Castle by Maj. Vereker.

On 31 May, a day after he was invested with his VC, Miles returned to Gloucestershire for two official welcomes. First he was warmly welcomed in Clearwell village by the Mayor and Mayoress of Gloucester, together with the City's High Sheriff, and this was followed by a second welcome at Coleford. The 'capital' of the Forest of Dean, Coleford was also the birthplace of another holder of the VC, Capt. Angus Buchanan, who gained his decoration in Mesopotamia. Francis Miles was welcomed home enthusiastically and carried the 2½ miles back to Clearwell. He was demobilised later in the year and returned to Bream Colliery, but his health was poor. As a mark of respect his wage packets were always marked F.G. Miles VC.

In June 1920 he attended the Garden Party at Buckingham Palace, but was unable to attend the House of Lords VC Dinner in November 1929. In 1934 he attended a function in Colston Hall, Coleford, in his honour. On the outbreak of the Second World War he joined the Pioneer Corps. In 1946 he took part in the Victory Parade on 8 June and also in the Hyde Park Centenary VC Review in 1956.

For much of his later life, Miles continued to suffer from very poor health as a result of shell-shock and deafness, and he died in

Clearwell on 8 November 1961, aged 65. He was buried at St Peter's Church, Clearwell. In 1973 a plaque to his memory was unveiled in the church, and in November 1985 a new regimental headstone was dedicated at his grave. The ceremony was arranged by the Gloucestershire Regimental Comrades. A local newspaper reported that the whole of the village had turned out to pay homage to the former miner who had won the nation's highest honour. Five regimental associations took part in the service and the quarter-mile march from the church to the cemetery was led by the Coleford Band. By 2003 the grave had fallen into a poor state and the headstone was replaced on 22 May 2004.

Until 2005 Miles' decorations were in private hands, before they were sold at Morton & Eden on 25 May for a hammer price of £72,000. They were purchased for the Ashcroft Trust and are on display in the Imperial War Museum. Apart from the VC they include the 1914–15 Star, BWM, VM, WM (1939–1945) and Coronation Medals for King George VI (1937) and Queen Elizabeth II (1953). The display also features his identity tags and a pair of German binoculars presented to him. In the early 1980s the District Council of the Forest of Dean commissioned a painting of Miles's VC deed by the military artist David Rowlands.

H. GREENWOOD

Ovillers, France, 23–24 October

During the Battle of the River Selle (17–25 October), A/Lt Col Harry Greenwood, commander of the 9th King's Own Yorkshire Light Infantry (KOYLI) (64th Brigade, 21st Division), won his VC at Ovillers, a village 3 miles north of Le Cateau, during the advance to the Selle. As the advance continued, it was held up from time to time in order to deal with enemy machine-gun nests.

The 9th KOYLI was checked in its advance by fire from an enemy machine-gun post to the west of Ovillers, which caused a great many casualties. Greenwood, always a man to lead from the front, managed to outflank the post and subsequently rushed it single-handed to kill or capture its occupants.

Just outside Ovillers he came across another machine-gun post and dealt with it in a similar fashion. Later, when the front of the battalion was facing a position to the west of Duke's Wood, in front of Vendegies, the attackers found themselves almost surrounded by the enemy. However, Greenwood, together with his colleagues, managed to repulse the enemy and pursue them as they fled. Greenwood was awarded the VC, which was gazetted on 26 December 1918 as follows:

> For most conspicuous bravery, devotion to duty and fine leadership on the 23rd–24th Oct. 1918. When the advance of his battalion on the twenty-third was checked, and many casualties caused by an enemy machine-gun post, Lieut.-Colonel Greenwood single-handed rushed the post and killed the crew.

At the entrance to the village of Ovillers, accompanied by two battalion runners, he again rushed a machine-gun post and killed the occupants. On reaching the objective west of Duke's Wood his command was almost surrounded by hostile machine-gun posts, and the enemy at once attacked his isolated force. The attack was repulsed, and, led by Lieut.-Colonel Greenwood, his troops swept forward and captured the last objective, with 150 prisoners, eight machine-guns and one field-gun. During the attack on the Green Line, south of Poix du Nord, on 24 Oct., he again displayed the greatest gallantry in rushing a machine-gun post, and he showed conspicuously good leadership in the handling of his command in the face of heavy fire. He inspired his men in the highest degree, with the result that the objective was captured, and in spite of heavy casualties, the line was held. During the further advance on Grand Gay Farm Road, on the afternoon of 24 Oct., the skillful and bold handling of his battalion was productive of most important results, not only in securing the flank of his brigade, but also in safeguarding the flank of the division. His valour and leading during two days of fighting were beyond all praise.

Greenwood's VC, together with a bar to his DSO, was presented to him in the Quadrangle of Buckingham Palace on 8 May 1919. Others who received their VCs on the same day included CSM Martin Doyle, Sgt Thomas Caldwell, Sgt John Daykins and Pte James Towers.

Henry (Harry) Greenwood was born in Victoria Barracks, Sheet Street, Windsor, on 25 November 1881, the son of Charles Greenwood, a sergeant in the 2nd Grenadier Guards, and Margaret Greenwood (née Abernethy), who came from County Tipperary, Ireland. The family lived in the married quarters at the time of Greenwood's birth.

In 1899 Greenwood enlisted in the City of London Imperial Volunteers (CIV) and served in the South African War from January 1900. The Volunteers served alongside the Regular troops, but in October were ordered home by Lord Roberts. In the same month Greenwood took part in a parade to St Paul's Cathedral from

Paddington station, followed by a reception at the Guildhall given by the Lord Mayor. After the war, Greenwood returned to South Africa when he joined the South African Constabulary. He also became associated with a businessman who had mining interests, Sir Robert Williams, for whom he worked as his private secretary. In 1909 he married Helena Anderson from Newcastle-on-Tyne and the couple went on to have three children, all girls.

Greenwood returned to England, where he became a member of the Territorial Force from its inception in 1908. When the First World War broke out he left the employment of Sir Robert to re-enlist from the Reserve of Officers, and was posted to the KOYLI, travelling to France with them in September 1915. He quickly got caught up in the thick of the fighting and, as a captain, he won the MC, gazetted for action on 26 September, near Hill 70 at Loos 14 January (1916 *London Gazette*). Later, with the rank of temporary major, he won his first DSO, which was gazetted on 26 July 1918. The DSO was awarded for his work on 23 March 1918 during the German Spring Offensive. Together with Pte H. Wright and a lance corporal from the 1st East Yorks, he moved to a place where the wire joined the Péronne–Longavesnes road, taking advantage of the mist after a German attack had been broken up. Here they found two machine guns lying on the road, which they turned on the enemy, causing heavy casualties and securing many prisoners. The citation was as follows:

> For conspicuous gallantry and devotion to duty during two heavy attacks, made under cover of mist, which were repulsed, but a hostile machine-gun detachment which succeeded in getting within 50 yards of the line suffered the troops severely and an officer and two men ran back to cover. The battalion being very short of machine gunners owing to casualties, Greenwood, with an NCO rushed out with greatest daring, found an officer and men hiding in a hollow with a heavy-machine gun, and made them carry it back, being all the time under intense fire. The gun was used later on the enemy with great effect.

Greenwood was appointed OC of the 9th KOYLI, with the rank of acting lieutenant colonel. On 23 August the battalion moved up during the Battle of Amiens in order to support an attack which was due to commence at midnight. At dusk the battalion moved round the village of Beaucourt, to the south side of the River Ancre, which had been turned into a formidable obstacle with the use of dams and other artificial constructions. On this day, 24 August, Greenwood won a bar to his DSO while leading an attack on a German position; he then helped to repel two German counter-attacks, holding his ground until he was relieved. It was during this action that he was wounded by 'friendly fire' when several shells from heavy batteries fell among men of the 9th KOYLI as they approached the Grandcourt–Thiepval road after clearing some dug-outs in Battery Valley. Greenwood himself was blown off his feet and thrown against a post, which resulted in internal injuries. He carried on for five more days before going to a dressing station and handing over command of the battalion to Maj. Walsh. He returned to his battalion on 15 October 1918. The citation for the bar to his DSO was published in the *London Gazette* on 2 December 1918 as follows:

For conspicuous gallantry during an attack. Although ill, Greenwood refused to leave his battalion and led the first line to the attack, and after being injured by the bursting of a shell captured the first objective. On reaching the second objective he organised his battalion and another, and took up a defensive position from which he beat off two enemy counter-attacks and held his ground until relieved. Next day when the advance was held up by very heavy machine-gun fire, he made daring reconnaissance, with the result that he succeeded in getting round the enemy's flank. Throughout he set a splendid example of pluck and devotion to duty to all ranks.

By the end of the war Greenwood had been awarded the French *Croix de Guerre* and was also Mentioned in Despatches several times. His other decorations from the conflict included the 1914–15 Star, BWM and VM. He had also been wounded three times during his war service. He left the Army in 1919 and rejoined Sir Robert Williams & Co.

In June 1920 he attended the VC Garden Party at Buckingham Palace and, later in the year, was a member of the VC Honour Guard for the interment of the Unknown Warrior on 11 November.

Later, Greenwood travelled extensively on business in Africa. During the 1930s his family moved to 77 Home Park Road,

Wimbledon, a house which overlooked the golf course. The house still stands, but has been divided up into flats.

After the Second World War began in 1939, Greenwood volunteered for the Army in the following year, although he was already 58. He was too old for service overseas, but he did serve as a colonel in the Pioneer Corps for the rest of hostilities, becoming commander of No. 12 Pioneer Depot in the West Midlands. For his work in merging various depots under a single command he was awarded the OBE in 1944. In January 1942 Greenwood was closely involved with a programme of raising funds for warships during Aldridge Warship Week. After the war ended in 1945, Greenwood took part in the Victory Parade in London in June 1946 and, in addition, attended various regimental reunions. He also attended a special dinner for holders of the VC at the Dorchester Hotel in London.

Harry Greenwood, always a vibrant personality, died at home at the age of 66 from stomach cancer on 5 May 1948. He had suffered from this illness for a long time. He was buried at Putney Vale Cemetery, Block N, Grave 71, Headstone C, and later one of the main paths in the cemetery was named after him. Other paths are also named after holders of the VC who are buried in the cemetery. Nearly 50 years later, a commemorative plaque to him was unveiled at Victoria Barracks in Windsor on 8 April 1997, in the presence of Col Pat Porteous VC, who won his decoration at Dieppe in the Second World War.

In 1998 an exhibition was arranged in Windsor by Derek Hunt to commemorate winners of the VC who had a link with the area, and these men included Harry Greenwood and Oliver Brooks VC. Mr Hunt has done much research work on the life of Harry Greenwood, including writing a book which he self-published in 2003. In the book, entitled *Valour Beyond All Praise: Harry Greenwood VC*, he revealed that Greenwood had also fathered a son and not just three girls. Greenwood's decorations were in private hands until 17 July 2002, when they were donated by his family to the KOYLI in Doncaster. They are considerable and, apart from those mentioned, include the MC, Queen's South Africa Medal (1899–1902), King's South African Medal (1902), 1914–15 Star, BWM, VM, Defence Medal (1939–45), War Medal(1939–45) and King George VI Coronation Medal (1937).

F.W. HEDGES
North-East of Bousies,
France, 24 October

To the north-east of Le Cateau, on 24 October 1918, Capt F.W. Hedges of the Bedfordshire Regiment, attached to the 6th Battalion, Northamptonshire Regiment (54th Brigade, 18th Division), gained a VC when his battalion was attacking north-east of Bousies. They were ordered to advance as far as the hamlet of Hecq, on the south-western edge of the Mormal Forest. The advance began at 4 a.m. with A and B Companies advancing 500yd over wooded country, which was very difficult terrain. C and D Companies then passed through their lines and C Company, led by Capt. Hedges, reached Hecq at about 6 a.m. Here they discovered that it was very strongly held by the enemy, who immediately launched a counter-attack. The Lewis guns dealt with this attack, but when C Company emerged from the edge of the wood they found their way still barred by two German machine guns.

At about 2 p.m., on hearing that the line on his left was intending to make a determined advance, Hedges also decided to make a move. With the help of Sgt Gibson, he managed to capture the machine guns, together with some enemy prisoners. His VC was gazetted on 31 January 1919 as follows:

> For most conspicuous bravery and initiative during the operations north-east of Bousies on the 24th Oct. 1918. He led his company with great skill towards the final objective, maintaining direction under the most difficult conditions. When the

advance was held up by machine-gun posts, accompanied by one sergeant and followed at some considerable distance by a Lewis-gun section, he again advanced and displayed the greatest determination, capturing six machine-guns and 14 prisoners. His gallantry and initiative enabled the whole line to advance, and tended largely to the success of subsequent operations.

A few days later, on 4 November, in the Mormal Forest, Hedges received a severe head wound which required treatment for several months. He had also been injured by gunshot wounds in his right shoulder and was back in England on 8 November. However, he was fit enough to receive his VC from the King in the Quadrangle of Buckingham Palace at an investiture on 15 May 1919.

❖❖❖

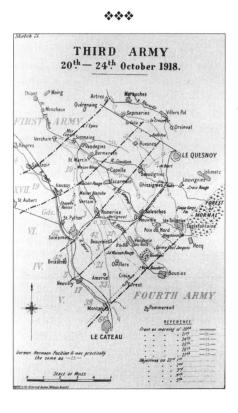

Frederick William Hedges was born in Umballa, India, on 6 June 1896, the third of four soldier sons and the seventh of nine children of Mr and Mrs H.D. Hedges of 23 Lansdowne Road, Hounslow. Mr Hedges had served for many years in the Army as a bandmaster. Some records indicate that Frederick was born in 1886, while others record 1896. He was educated at Grove Road Boys' School and at Isleworth County School.

He enlisted on 6 August 1914 after the outbreak of war and his height is recorded as 5ft 8½in. He was given a medical two days later and posted as rifleman 2182 with the 1/9th County of London Battalion (Queen Victoria's Rifles), with whom he served for several months. The riflemen arrived in France on 5 November 1914, as part of the 13th Infantry Brigade of the 5th Division, and at the end of the month they served in the trenches in front of Messines in the First Battle of Ypres. During this period, Hedges was invalided home from France with frostbite and sent to No. 3 Northern General Hospital in Sheffield on 29 January. On recovering in mid-March, he was transferred to the 3/9th Battalion of the London Regiment and became a member of B Company in April 1915. He was commissioned into the 9th (S) Battalion, Bedford Regiment on 5 July 1915 and served as a musketry officer. On 12 July he was transferred for training at the Felixstowe School of Instruction.

For some time Hedges carried out his musketry officer's duties at a home station, but finally returned to France in early September 1916 and transferred to the 6th Battalion. He was in time to serve in the final stages of the Battle of the Ancre on the Somme between 13 and 15 November. In the following year he took part in the Battle of Arras at Easter, when he was severely wounded in the right hand. He was sent to hospital in Rouen and was then transferred to England where he underwent seven-and-a-half months of treatment, firstly at No. 5 Southern General Hospital in Portsmouth and, later, at Queen Victoria's residence, Osborne House on the Isle of Wight. On recovery in July 1917 he became a machine-gun instructor, and on 12 October he was sent to the 3rd Reserve Battalion until he was declared fit again for foreign service on 25 September 1918. He was then posted to the 6th (S) Northampton Battalion as his previous battalion had been disbanded. By now he had been promoted to full lieutenant.

Hedges was passed fit for light duties on 2 May 1919 and, in the same year, he was presented with a public testimonial and the local schools in Isleworth were granted a day off. A procession was organised in his honour, which began at his home in Lansdowne Road, with a band of the ASC leading it. The band was followed by the County School Cadet Corps, with sixty boys from Grove Road School acting as escort. Hedges was in a car and accompanied by his parents and his fiancée, Miss Mollie Kenworthy. The route was lined by schoolchildren as far as the Hounslow Council Chamber. After inspecting the guard of honour, Hedges was invited into the Council House, where a band played 'See the Conquering Hero Comes'. He was then presented with a gold watch and chain, along with a war bond for £100. Part of this welcome was captured on film by *Pathé News*. On 26 July Frederick married Mollie at Holy Trinity Church, Hounslow.

After the war Hedges relinquished his commission on 14 April, but still retained his rank of lieutenant. From 19 June 1919 he was in charge of No. 8 Group, Prisoner-of-War (POW) Camp, Fulwell, Guildford, and on 27 September, while on duty, he was involved in an accident when travelling on a motorbike, which left him with a compound fracture of the right leg. Later in the year he was discharged. His service file notes that he attended several medical boards and, at some point, was advised to apply for a 'wound gratuity'.

Hedges was fortunate to secure a job with the Cornhill Insurance Company, where he was to stay for the rest of his working life.

In June 1920 he attended the Garden Party for VC holders at Buckingham Palace and his address in the 1920s was The Avenue, Sunbury-on-Thames, Teddington. In 1922 he attended the unveiling of a memorial to the eighty-one members of Isleworth County School who had died in the war. This took the form of a handsome oak screen, and was erected in the assembly hall. Hedges had been a leading light behind the setting up of the memorial and was himself secretary of the memorial committee. Sadly, after the war the Roll of Honour at Isleworth County School was lost, possibly when the school became a large comprehensive.

In February 1924 Hedges' wife, Mollie, gave birth to a son in Hounslow and the couple named him John Grosvenor. In November 1929 Hedges attended the House of Lords VC Dinner.

In the 1930s both Hedges and his wife were extremely active in British Legion affairs, and Hedges often assisted ex-soldiers with their claims for disability allowances. He also very often attended old comrades' reunions of the Bedfordshire Regiment. In November 1939 he was elected chairman of the Teddington Legion Branch, having previously served as vice-chairman, and in 1941 he commanded the Teddington British Legion Service. Throughout the Second World War Hedges served in the Civil Defence Service. His son, John, also became a member of the Home Guard and his duties involved guarding the Thames crossings at risk of invasion. Tragically, John died as a result of a drowning accident on the Thames in Sudbury in 1941 when he was only 17 years old. It would appear that his parents never got over their loss as he had been the centre of their lives.

Probably in the late 1940s, the Cornhill Insurance Company decided to send Hedges to run their office in Leeds and the couple moved northwards to live in Harrogate. Sadly they were never at home in Yorkshire, although Mollie was able to visit her mother more easily, until 1950 when she died. At some point Hedges took to drinking and this, together with his being retired early in 1954 and the anniversary of his son's death, brought him to a very depressed state.

On 29 May 1954 Hedges took his own life by hanging himself from the banisters of his home at 60 Duchy Road, Harrogate. At the subsequent inquest two days later, he was described as having suffered from neurosis and depression for several years, having recently retired early from his job as Cornhill manager in Leeds. One feels that this verdict only told part of the story.

Hedges was cremated at Stonefall Crematorium, Wetherby Road, Harrogate (Ref 3934), four days after his death. His VC and four other decorations were first sent on loan to the Leeds City Museum, but are now in the care of the Bedfordshire and Hertfordshire Regiment in Wardown Road, Luton. His medals also included the 1914 Star with clasp ('5 Aug–22 Nov'), BWM, VM and Coronation Medals for King George VI (1937) and Queen Elizabeth II (1953).

W.D. BISSETT

East of Maing, France, 25 October

A few days after the River Selle had been successfully crossed, the objectives of the 51st (Highland) Division of the First Army to the south of a line from Denain to Valenciennes were as follows: they were to reach a line through the village of Gaumont Farm (halfway between Quérénaing and Famars) and Mont Rouge (about half a mile north-west of Gaumont Farm), then back to the Scheldt; and, secondly, to take Famars and Mont Houy (2,000yd south-west of Aulnoy, and 1,500yd south of le Poirier). To the right of the 51st Division, the 4th Division was initially to enter Quérénaing, and then advance to the railway beyond.

The 153rd Brigade, 51st (Highland) Division, of which the 6th Argyll and Sutherland Highlanders was a part, faced strong resistance during this advance and didn't reach its objective to the west of the railway until 2.30 p.m. Their sister brigade, the 152nd, had been driven back to the railway by a counter-attack, which was then repulsed by the 153rd Brigade. It was during this fighting that Lt W.D. Bissett of the 1/6th Argyll and Sutherland Highlanders won his VC, as a result of a spirited bayonet charge. His deed was gazetted on 6 January 1919 as follows:

> East of Maing, on 25 Oct., in command of the company, after a determined enemy counter-attack had turned his left flank, he withdrew to the railway. The enemy continued to advance in force after his men had exhausted their ammunition.

Under heavy fire he mounted the railway embankment and, calling upon his men to charge with the bayonet, drove back the enemy with heavy loss, and later, again charging forward, established his line.

To emphasise the cost of the fighting, Bissett was one of five officers and 120 men who were involved in counter-attacks east of Maing, of whom only ten remained alive. In addition, he was wounded and gassed the day after winning his VC, and spent three weeks in hospital before being posted to Italy.

Bissett was presented with his VC by the King in the Quadrangle of Buckingham Palace on 10 July 1919, and, on the following day, together with his wife, he received a civic reception from Paisley.

William Davidson Bissett was born at Bauchlands, St Martin's, Perthshire, on 7 August 1893, the son of John and Nellie Mime Bissett (née Davidson) of Ewing Cottage, Comrie Road, Crieff, Perthshire. John was a plumber by trade. William was educated at Taylor's Institution, Crieff, and at Morrison's Academy in the same town. On 29 April 1912 he gave his occupation as engineer when he enlisted as a private in the Argyll & Sutherland Highlanders (TF). On the outbreak of war, as a member of the 1/6th (Renfrewshire) Battalion, he sailed for France on 1 May 1915. On 25 July Bissett was promoted to lance corporal and, three months later on 24 October, to full corporal. On 1 May 1916 he became battery bombing sergeant. On 19 December he was commissioned and, after training in England, rejoined his battalion in France on 22 May 1917. In the following year he was made a full lieutenant.

A week before news of his VC was published in the *London Gazette*, Bissett was honoured in his hometown of Crieff. At an evening ceremony in Porteous Hall, he was presented with an inscribed gold watch, together with some war bonds. He was also presented with a silver cigarette holder from the choir of St Columba's Church, Crieff, together with a silver cigarette case from his officer colleagues. Bissett's parents also attended the ceremony, which was presided over by Provost Mungall.

Referring to the occasion when he won his VC, Bissett said:

> ... that the men of his company were absolutely confident. He was proud of his men, and he himself was as happy as a school-boy. His servant, Private M'Neill MM, an old soldier, was also confident of success, and when they had men like these the VC was easily won ...

Bissett was demobilised on 24 September 1919. He was friends with two other holders of the VC, who were also members of the Argyll and Sutherland Highlanders: Lt J. Buchan and Capt A. Henderson, whom he had known as a private.

Also in 1919 Bissett married Hilda Heywood, a nursing sister, at Emmanuel Parish Church, West Hampstead, and the couple lived in North London at the time. Over the years they seemed to move house an amazing number of times. Even in the following year, records show a link with Barnard Castle in County Durham and, in 1921, their address was 11 Library Street, Wigan. Later, Bissett was involved in an engineering business in London, for a time living in Walton-on-Thames, Surrey.

Bissett's service file at The National Archives includes correspondence between him and the War Office. In 1923, writing from Holly Cottage, Wadhurst, East Sussex, he asks whether he could be employed as a recruiting officer. He was given a negative response and informed that he wasn't eligible.

In November 1932 Bissett wrote an article on the war, which was published in the *Daily Sketch* under the heading 'Looking Back On All That'. The tone of the piece was quite bitter:

> Our one desire was to see how the country was faring. But one became disgusted to find two distinct sections of the people at home – one sacrificing their all to the needs of the country; the other regarding war as an ideal Garden of Eden for Self first, last and all the time, and exhibiting a hatred towards the enemy whom we of the front line had learned to regard as worthy of our steel and served by youths fired with like ambition to serve their country ...

Bissett also wrote that, by 1916, they had 'realised that the "Glory of War" had gone from modern warfare'. Of post-war life for members of the armed services, he said:

> Glad to escape from uniform, we found, as ex-Servicemen returning to civil life to earn a livelihood, that Service to Country in days of need was of little avail – indeed, more of a hindrance – in our quest. Even a roof over one's head was obtained only with difficulty ... The only bright spot for an ex-serviceman was to meet a pal, and thoughts and talk were of days of the Front Line, and we wondered what the position would have been if the enemy had succeeded in his aims ... Ex-servicemen did not expect the Garden of Eden or the keys of Utopia. But they did expect a straight deal. And time has proved how little likelihood there was of receiving it ...
>
> ... last, but not least, thousands who escaped death or disability only returned to a living hell in civilian life – jobless, destitute, well nigh hopeless. But never a regret among them that they answered their country's call. A generation sacrificed to the God of War ...

In 1939 Bissett visited France with the Old Contemptibles Association of the Argyll and Sutherland Highlanders. Whatever his views on post-Great War society, he still took up the challenge when the Second World War broke out. During the period from May 1939 to May 1940, he served briefly with the Royal Army Ordnance Corps with the rank of captain. He was then transferred to the Pioneer Corps. He served for the next five years in home postings, before he was demobilised in September 1945 with the rank of major.

In 1946 Bissett attended the Victory Parade on 8 June, and later the Hyde Park Review in June 1956. Also in 1946 his son, Donald, a corporal in the East Surrey Regiment, was gaoled for nine months for falsely signing cheques and defrauding his father of £45. In the 1950s Mr and Mrs Bissett moved to North Wales.

At the age of 77 William Bissett died at the War Memorial Hospital, Wrexham, Denbighshire, on 12 May 1971, leaving his wife, who also died in 1971, together with Donald. Bissett's home in North Wales had first been at Betws-Y-Coed, Caernarfonshire, and in the 1960s at Queen's Bridge Hall, Overton-on-Dee, Flintshire. His funeral service took place at Overton Church, and was followed by cremation at Pentrebychan Crematorium, Wrexham, on 17 May.

Hilda, Bissett's widow, was unable to attend her husband's funeral as she was in hospital at Ellesmere. Bissett's son, Donald, didn't show up either, although his daughter-in-law did. However, representatives from the Royal British Legion, with whom Bissett had been an active member, and from his former regiment and other associations, attended. Bissett's ashes were later taken to Aldershot Military Cemetery, where he is commemorated with a headstone. In addition to his VC, which is in the museum of the Argyll and Sutherland Highlanders at Stirling Castle, he won the 1914–15 Star, BWM, VM, Defence Medal (1939–45), War Medal (1939–45), French *Croix de Guerre* and Coronation Medals for King George VI (1937) and Queen Elizabeth II (1953).

N. HARVEY

Near Ingoyghem, Belgium, 25 October

On the same day that Lt Bissett won his VC to the east of Maing in France, Pte Norman Harvey won his VC in Belgium as a member of the 1st Royal Inniskilling Fusiliers 109th Infantry Brigade (36th (Ulster) Division) at Ingoyghem, east of Courtrai. The division had crossed the River Lys to the north-east of Courtrai eleven days before and had suffered heavy casualties. Despite these losses, the division continued to advance towards the ridge that was between the Lys and the Scheldt rivers. On 25 October the 9th (Scottish) Division was to the right of the Ulster Division and had taken the high ground between Ooteghem and Ingoyghem in order to take the ridge. The Ulster Division was then to capture Kleineberg to the north-east of Ingoyghem. The 1st and 2nd Royal Inniskilling Fusiliers, already depleted in numbers, were to be used in this operation.

Harvey's platoon sergeant, who witnessed the heroic action, wrote of it as follows:

> … Suddenly very heavy machine-gun fire opened on us from a farm about forty yards to my left front. It held my platoon up, and we all got down to fire. Five of my men were wounded, and I saw Private Harvey rush forward under heavy machine-gun fire and go round the left of the farm.
>
> Later, I heard a few rifle shots, and the machine stopped firing, and then I saw Private Harvey bring about a dozen Bosches from the farm. I went forward to the farm and found two dead

Bosches and one badly wounded, with the bayonet. There were two machine-guns there …

Harvey's citation was published in the *London Gazette* on 6 January 1919:

> For most conspicuous bravery and devotion to duty near Ingoyghem on 20 Oct. 1918 [*sic*], when his battalion was held up and suffered heavy casualties from enemy machine-guns. On his own initiative he rushed forward and engaged the enemy single-handed, disposing of 20 and capturing two guns. Later, when his company was checked by another enemy strongpoint, he again rushed forward alone and put the enemy to flight. Subsequently, after dark he voluntarily carried out single-handed an important reconnaissance and gained valuable information. Private Harvey throughout the day displayed the greatest valour, and his several actions enabled the line to advance, saved many casualties, and inspired all.

When the announcement of his VC reached Newton-le-Willows, his hometown in Lancashire, the press descended on Harvey's family, who at that time were living in a row of buildings called Parkside Old Station Buildings, adjacent to the main Manchester railway line.

Four months later he was presented with his VC by the King in the Quadrangle of Buckingham Palace on 15 May 1919. His sister, Honey Westcott, accompanied him to the ceremony.

Norman Harvey was born in Bull Cottages, Newton-le-Willows on 6 April 1899, the son of Mr Charles William and Mary Harvey. He was educated locally at St Peter's Church of England School and later worked briefly at Messrs Randall in the High Street, before taking up employment with Messrs Caulfields' at Newton. At the age of 15 he joined the South Lancashire Regiment in November 1914, and was slightly wounded in France when aged only 16. Two years later he was severely wounded. When at last his age was discovered by the authorities, he was kept back in England for a short time, even then being too young for overseas service. He was given a course of instruction in bayonet work and, finally, when he was still only 19 years old, he returned to France in the spring of 1918 when he was transferred to the 1st Battalion, Royal Inniskilling Fusiliers, with the service number 42954.

When Harvey returned to Newton-le-Willows, he was given a rousing reception by around 2,000 people, and at a special ceremony was presented with an illuminated address, together with £100 in war bonds. Also in 1919 he had been promoted to lance corporal and was later demobilised when he took up working with the railways. During the same year Norman Harvey married Norah Osmond in Duffryn Church; Norah had served in the Queen Mary Army Auxiliary Corps during the war. The couple later had two daughters and one son. In November 1929 Harvey attended the House of Lords VC Dinner and, nearly five years later, he was one of the guests invited to the opening of a new Mersey Tunnel, a ceremony performed by King George V.

In the Second World War Harvey returned to the Army when he was nearly 40 years old, re-enlisting with the Royal Engineers and becoming a member of No. 199 Workshop Company. In addition, the veteran soldier became a sort of father figure to the men in the company. On the occasion of full company parades, it was the practice for Harvey to reply on parades with 'Sgt Harvey VC, sir!', followed by the company presenting arms, after which the commanding officer would salute Harvey, and then the roll call would continue.

In April 1941 Harvey had reached the rank of company QMS. When serving near Haifa in Palestine, he sadly died as a result of a rifle shot, probably by his own hand, on 16 February 1942. He was later buried in Khayat Beach War Cemetery, Haifa, Plot A, Row A, Grave 4. The cemetery is 2 miles south-west of the town centre, in what is now part of Israel.

Harvey's decorations, which included the 1914–15 Star, BWM, VM, 1939–45 Star, Defence Medal (1939–45), War Medal (1939–45) and King George VI Coronation Medal, were offered for sale on 26 November 1980. They were accompanied by two photographs, a pay book and various documents, and the entire lot was sold at Sothebys for £9,000. They are now with the Royal Inniskilling Fusiliers Regimental Museum in Enniskillen, Northern Ireland.

Harvey's name is listed on a plaque in memory of winners of the VC in St Anne's Cathedral, Belfast, and on a memorial in the grounds of Ulster Tower, Thiepval.

T. CALDWELL

Near Audenaarde, Belgium, 31 October

Six days after Norman Harvey won his VC, Sgt T. Caldwell of the 12th (Ayr & Lanark Yeomanry) Battalion Royal Scots Fusiliers (TF) (94th Brigade, 31st Division) won his VC on 31 October, to the east of Ingoyghem, near Audenaarde in Belgium. It was close to the scene of one of the Duke of Marlborough's most famous victories. The NCO was in charge of a Lewis gun section whose dangerous task was to clear a farmhouse of the enemy, but while this was being accomplished his section came under intense fire from a neighbouring farm. However, as the citation shows, this presented little trouble to the heroic sergeant. The citation was published on 6 January 1919 as follows:

For most conspicuous bravery and initiative in attack near Audenaarde on the 31st Oct. 1918, when in command of a Lewis-gun section engaged in clearing a farmhouse. When his section came under intense fire at close range from another farm, Sergt. Caldwell rushed towards the farm, and, in spite of very heavy fire, reached the enemy position, which he captured single-handed, together with 18 prisoners. This gallant and determined exploit removed a serious obstacle from the line of advance, saved many casualties, and led to the capture by his section of about 70 prisoners, eight machine-guns and one trench mortar.

Thomas Caldwell was born in Carluke, Lanarkshire, Scotland, on 10 February 1894, and he was educated at Carluke Secondary School. He enlisted in the Royal Scots Fusiliers, with the service number 295536. After winning his VC in October 1918 he returned home to Carluke, where a special public reception had been arranged. He was presented with a clock, together with the sum of £1,000, as well as an illuminated address. Two other holders of the VC also came from Carluke: William Angus of the Highland Light Infantry, and Donald Cameron, a submariner. In June 1920 Caldwell attended the Buckingham Palace Garden Party, and in November he attended the Cenotaph and Westminster Abbey commemorations.

Having arrived in Australia with L. Cpl William Angus in November 1927, seeking employment, he managed to secure a job with the Electricity Trust of South Australia. He then sent for his wife, Jeannie Ker, whom he had married in 1921, and their five children to join him. For a time he was line foreman in the south-east. He retired in 1959, at the age of 65, and was living in Tipparra Avenue, Parkholme, South Australia. In 1968 he attended the biennial reunion of the VC/GC Association in London, having attended the June 1956 Centenary in Hyde Park twelve years before.

At the age of 75 Thomas Caldwell died in Adelaide on 6 June 1969, and he was cremated at Centennial Park Crematorium, Adelaide, on 12 June. His ashes were interred in Wall 104, Row E, Niche 12. There is also a wall plaque on display. Thomas was survived by his wife and three daughters.

In 1972 the Royal Highland Fusiliers (which was an amalgamation of the Royal Scots Fusiliers and the Highland Light Infantry) arranged for Caldwell's widow to fly from Australia to Scotland, as her late husband had bequeathed his VC to the Royal Scots Fusiliers. Mrs Caldwell personally presented the medal to Maj. Gen. Charles Dunbar, colonel of the Royal Highland Fusiliers. Both David Lauder VC and John Hamilton VC attended the ceremony.

Caldwell's VC was later put on permanent display at the museum in Sauchiehall Street, Glasgow. His other decorations include the 1914–15 Star, BWM, VM, King George VI Coronation Medal (1937) and Queen Elizabeth II Coronation Medal (1953).

Company Sergeant Major Caldwel has a road named after him in Carluke and his name is also included on a memorial arch to VC winners from Lanarkshire, which was was unveiled in Hamilton on 19 April 2002. Lieutenant John O'Neill, who had won his VC in mid-October 1918, also in Belgium, is another of the men whose name is commemorated on the arch.

H. Cairns

Valenciennes, France, 1 November

Sergeant H. Cairns of the 46th South Saskatchewan Battalion, CEF, won his VC on 1 November 1918 when the Canadian Corps reached the outskirts of the city of Valenciennes. It was the first day of what became a three-day battle to take the important city. The Canadian attack began in cold drizzling rain, headed by their 10th and 12th Brigades. On the left, the attack initially went well and Mont Houy, identified as the key to the city, was captured and many prisoners taken. However, on the right, the 46th Battalion was held up by heavy machine-gun fire from the steelworks at Marly, which was known to be full of enemy troops. They were also under fire from enemy positions in other suburbs to the southeast of the city. The Canadian advance was also severely hampered by enemy artillery based to the north of the city. The 46th Battalion managed to leapfrog the 44th as planned and the infantry entered the outskirts of the city, only to be held up on the right flank. It was then that Cairns seized his opportunity. Grabbing his Lewis gun and firing from the hip, he caused havoc among the enemy positions. His VC was gazetted on 31 January 1919 as follows:

> For most conspicuous bravery before Valenciennes on 1 Nov. 1918, when a machine-gun opened on his platoon. Without a moment's hesitation Sergt. Cairns seized a Lewis-gun and single-handed, in face of direct fire, rushed the post, killed the crew of five, and captured the gun. Later, when the line was held up by machine-gun fire, he again rushed forward, kill-

ing 12 enemy and capturing 18 and two guns. Subsequently, when the advance was held up by machine-guns and field-guns, although wounded he led a small party to outflank them, killing many and capturing all the guns. After consolidation he went with a battle patrol to exploit Marly, and forced 60 enemy to surrender. Whilst disarming this party he was severely wounded. Nevertheless, he opened fire and inflicted heavy losses. Finally he was rushed by about 20 enemy, and collapsed from weakness and loss of blood. Throughout the operation he showed the highest degree of valour, and his leadership greatly contributed to the success of the attack. He died on the 2nd Nov. from wounds.

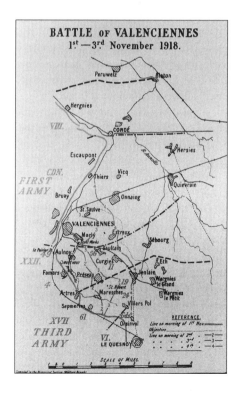

Lieutenant General Sir Arthur Currie, the Canadian Corps commander, wrote a more detailed account of Cairns' actions:

> Then, after consolidation, he ascertained that a battle patrol was pushing out to exploit Marly. Sergeant Cairns with his Lewis-gun broke open the door of a yard and came upon 60 Germans. They threw their hands up, but as their officer filed past he shot Cairns through the body. Cairns sank to his knees but continued firing. A moment later the butt of his gun was smashed and he collapsed from loss of blood.

Another eyewitness takes up the story:

> The sergeant fell to his knees but was able to swing his beloved Lewis-gun up and fire a burst. The German officer fell dead in front of [him], but by then the Germans had regained their weapons and a wild mêlée broke out in the courtyard. Cairns was hit once again and another round shattered the butt of his Lewis-gun. Still he fired, cutting down swathes of the enemy until he himself collapsed from loss of blood.
>
> Lieutenant Johnny MacLeod and two men provided a heavy covering fire as two others dragged Cairns out of the courtyard; incredibly [he] was still alive.
>
> By now more men had arrived to assist the beleaguered patrol outside the courtyard. Cairns was placed on a door which was to act as a makeshift stretcher. As two men began to carry the unconscious Cairns away the infuriated Germans opened fire on the stretcher-bearer who was killed. Moments later, what remained of the German garrison surrendered.

Sergeant Cairns was carried to a forward dressing station, but there was nothing that could be done. On 2 November, while low, grey clouds scudded overhead, the gallant sergeant succumbed to his wounds.

The operation was a very successful one for the Canadian Corps and had gone very much to plan. A total of 1,800 enemy prisoners were taken and 800 killed in the fighting. Sergeant Cairns was to be the last Canadian to be awarded a VC during the war. He was buried 10 miles north of Cambrai at Auberchicourt British Cemetery in

Plot I, Row A, Grave 8. Auberchicourt was formerly a mining village in the Department of the Nord, and is east of Douai on the road to Valenciennes. At the time it had also been the advance headquarters of Gen. Sir Henry Horne, who was in command of the British First Army. The cemetery can be found on the north side of the road to Erchin and was begun at the end of October 1918, and used until February 1919. Three Canadian casualty clearing stations used to be nearby, the 1st, 6th and 23rd.

Hugh Cairns, the son of George H. and Elizabeth Dotes Cairns (née Donkin) of 832 Avenue 'G' North, Saskatoon, Saskatchewan, was the third of a family of eleven children. He had been born in Ashington, Northumberland, on 4 December 1896 and the family emigrated to Canada in 1911. Hugh was a member of Christ Church choir and a keen footballer. He had already left school in Ashington and became an apprentice with the Northern Plumbing Company. In July 1915 Hugh enlisted with his brother Abbie (Albert) as members of the 65th Infantry Battalion, which was being raised in Saskatoon. His service number was 472168 and he was described as being 5ft 8in, chunky and with a ruddy complexion.

On reaching Bramshott, Surrey, on 29 June 1916, the battalion was broken up, with most of the men, including the two brothers, being transferred the following day to the 46th South Saskatchewan Battalion, which was to be part of the 4th Division of the CEF. Cairns won the DCM in June 1917, when he came to the notice of his colonel for the first time. The 46th Battalion had been ordered to provide a platoon to destroy a German machine-gun post, while at the same time two battalions of the 10th Brigade were to attack the enemy positions between the River Souchez and La Coulotte. The attack on 3 June began very well, but the success was short-lived and, by the end of the afternoon, men from the No. 13 Platoon of the 46th Battalion became isolated. In addition, they were running short of ammunition. It was at this point that Cairns, then still a private, took a hand. According to his DCM citation:

> ... he led a party forward at a critical moment and supplied covering fire to the flank of an attacking battalion. With great

initiative he recovered two guns which had been left behind, and posted them, repelling three enemy attacks, and successfully covering our subsequent withdrawal. Though wounded, he held on until his ammunition was expended, when he made his way back to our line ...

At one point Cairns lost his temper with one of the Canadian battalions and, in the hearing of their adjutant, roared out: 'The sons of bitches may be good in training, but they're not worth a damn in the line!'

Not surprisingly, the adjutant complained to the 46th Battalion's Col Dawson, and demanded that Cairns be court-martialled for insubordination. However, nothing more was said about the matter and Cairns was duly awarded his DCM. During the fighting he had been wounded in the back by shrapnel.

Cairns took part in most of the fighting that the CEF were involved in, including that at Hill 70 in August and, a few months later, at Passchendaele in November. In August 1918 he fought in the Amiens battle. He was promoted from lance corporal to sergeant during this period. Sadly, in early September, he received the tragic news that his elder brother, Abbie, with whom he had enlisted and had his initial training, had died of wounds in the fighting on the Drocourt–Quéant Line. According to colleagues, this grim news inspired Cairns to greater efforts, saying he wouldn't rest until he had accounted for at least fifty Germans.

After the war Hugh Cairns's VC, the last to be awarded to a Canadian, was posted on 20 February 1919 to the Colonial Office for presentation to Cairns' father, George. At the present time his decorations are in the care of the Canadian War Museum, Ottawa. Apart from the VC and DCM, they include the BWM, VM and French Knight of the *Légion d'Honneur*.

On 8 June 1921, a 12ft marble statue of the NCO, with a polished base, was dedicated as a central part of the Saskatoon Football Club's war memorial in Kiwanis Park on 25th Street Bridge. The memorial had been paid for by the club

Fifteen years later, on 25 July 1936, in the presence of his parents, Cairns was commmemorated again when he had an avenue renamed after him in Valenciennes, the city which he had helped to capture:

the 'Avenue Serjeant Hugh Cairns' . These ceremonies took place in front of the town's Hôtel de Ville, the day before the unveiling of the Vimy Memorial. A commemorative plaque is on display at the Hôtel de Ville. His parents' travelling expenses were paid for by an anonymous group of Canadian businessmen.

Other commemorations in his Canadian hometown include a school and armoury. In 1995, a plaque to his memory was erected on a house which was presumed to have been his home, but it was later relocated to 832 Avenue 'G' North on 7 July 2005.

J. CLARKE

Happegarbes, France, 2 November

Acting Company Sergeant Major James Clarke of the 15th (S) Battalion, Lancashire Fusiliers (1st Salford, 96th Brigade, 32nd Division) won his VC on 2 November 1918 at Happegarbes, near Landrecies. As attempts were being made to force the Sambre–Oise Canal, it was vital for the Allies to control the ground to the west of it. All the bridges had been destroyed or severely damaged and the enemy was still in position on the west bank. To the west of Landrecies, the most important feature was the Happegarbes spur, which would allow command of the canal as far as Catillon, 3 miles away.

The canal was approximately 75ft wide and 7ft deep, and the lower ground on either side had already been flooded by enemy troops, turning much of the area into a swamp. In addition, and to add to the difficulties, the higher ground on the west side of the canal was made up mostly of orchards and paddocks, and was enclosed by thick hedges. To the east, though, beyond the immediate area of the canal, the landscape was made up of valleys and ridges, with many hedges and much wire. The task of controlling the ground to the west of the canal was given to the 15th Lancashire Fusiliers and, on 30 October, the battalion moved into the line west of the spur, astride the Le Cateau–Landrecies road. At 6 a.m. on 2 November the battalion, assisted by two tanks, moved off under heavy artillery and machine-gun fire on a three-company front.

Sergeant Clarke's citation, published in the *London Gazette* on 6 January 1919, described his role in the operations as follows:

> For most conspicuous bravery and initiative during the attack at Happegarbes on 2 Nov. 1918, when in command of a platoon. He led his men forward with great determination, and on being held up by heavy machine-gun fire, rushed forward through a thick, strongly held ridge, captured in succession four machine-guns, and single-handed bayoneted the crews. Later he led the remnants of his platoon to the capture of three machine-guns and many prisoners. In the later stages of the attack on the same day, when his platoon was held up by enemy machine-guns, he successfully led a tank against them over very exposed ground. Continuing the attack on 3 Nov., after capturing many prisoners and gaining his objective, he organised his line most skillfully and held up the enemy. On 4 Nov., in the attack on the Oise–Sambre Canal, under heavy fire from the canal bank, he rushed forward with a Lewis-gun team in the face of an intense barrage, brought the gun into action, and effectively silenced the enemy's fire, thus enabling his company to advance and gain their objectives. Throughout the whole of these operations Sergt. Clarke acted with magnificent bravery and total disregard of personal safety, and by his gallantry and high sense of duty set an inspiring example to all ranks.

By 4 November the 15th Lancashire Fusiliers, together with two companies from the KOYLI, had achieved their objective as the Happegarbes spur had been cleared of Germans and the west bank of the canal secured.

Three months later the King presented Clarke with his VC at an investiture held at Buckingham Palace on 13 February 1919.

James Clarke was the second son of John and Hannah Clarke, and was born at Greenfield Cottage, High Street, Winsford, Cheshire, on 6 April 1894. He was educated at St John's School, Over Winsford. After leaving school at the age of 14, he took up work as an agricultural labourer, and in 1913 moved to Rochdale where he worked as a carter with a firm called Butterworth Brothers in Milne Row. Later he moved to William Tatham and Sons, who were also in Rochdale. In August 1915 he married a cardroom worker, then, two months later, on 10 October, he enlisted in the 1/6th Battalion (TF), Lancashire Fusiliers, who had been formed on the outbreak of war. He later transferred to the 15th Battalion, which arrived in Boulogne on 22 November 1915. He was promoted to sergeant and, later, was made acting CSM.

After Clarke won his VC, there was some rivalry between the towns of Winsford and Rochdale as to which one should claim him as their own. On 1 February 1919 he was given a public reception at Rochdale but, not to be outdone, Winsford also organised a reception on 14 February, when, accompanied by his wife, he was welcomed home. A procession began at his former school of St John's and continued to the Drill Hall in Weaver Street, where Clarke was given a civic reception. He was also presented with an illuminated address, £10 in cash and £50 in war savings certificates. Mrs Clarke was presented with a gold necklace, together with a pendant. The couple's home at this time was at 29 Clyde Street, Rochdale. On 31 March a correction to Clarke's citation in the *London Gazette* was made: he had originally been listed as Sgt John Clarke instead of A/CSM James Clarke. A few weeks later he was discharged from the Army on 13 May 1919. In the following year he attended the Garden Party in Buckingham Palace on 26 June 1920, and, nine years later, he attended the House of Lords VC Dinner on 9 November 1929.

James Clarke was never fully fit after the war and suffered from poor health. Nevertheless, he worked as a stoker for eight years in a gas works in Wilmslow. At some point, and only briefly, he and his wife moved south to Dagenham in Essex, but his life didn't improve and, mainly because of his continuing ill health, he was frequently unemployed. Those jobs that he did try his hand at included a stint as a temporary road worker in Manchester, and he also had a job at the Belle Vue greyhound stadium. His wife was able to earn some money working in a cotton mill.

In 1933, when he had been unemployed again for some ten months, he decided to try his hand at earning some money by operating a barrel-organ in central Manchester. He later tried doing the same in

Coventry Street, London, but this time he was arrested by the police on a charge of obstruction. The magistrate stated: 'I do not want to fine you – but I do want to impress upon you that you must not play in a street that is so crowded. You are discharged under the Probation Act.'

Clarke took part in the Victory Parade on 8 June 1946 in London, but died the following year of pneumonia in Birch Hill Hospital, Rochdale, on 16 June, at the age of 53. He left a widow and three children. After a full military funeral he was forgotten, as his grave in Rochdale Cemetery (Section O/P, Grave 14155) was left unmarked. If he had been a serving soldier at the time of his death, a proper headstone would have been erected. However, the Lancashire Fusiliers Regimental Association later arranged for a simple wooden cross to be placed on the grave. In 1993 it was decided to improve on this and £600 was raised to pay for a proper headstone for the grave of the local hero. This headstone was dedicated on 11 November 1994 in the presence of James Clarke's daughter, Mrs Elsie Kemp, and other members of his family. The 'Last Post' and 'Reveille' were sounded by a bugler of the Royal Regiment of Fusiliers, which had absorbed the Lancashire Fusiliers. On 24 July 1984, Clarke's VC was sold at Christies for £8,800, then again, some twelve years later at an auction at Spink, London, on 13 March 1996, for £22,000. At the present time the decorations are on display in the Ashcroft collection in the Imperial War Museum. Apart from the VC, they include the BWM, VM and King George VI Coronation Medal (1937).

On 14 November 2010 a special James Clarke VC memorial parade and service was held in his hometown of Winsford, to which many of his relatives had been officially invited. At the same time a special memorial rose garden was opened and can be found outside the Winsford Lifestyle Centre.

W. AMEY
Landrecies, France, 4 November

One week prior to the Armistice, no fewer than seven men gained the nation's highest military honour on 4 November 1918, and their lives will be dealt with in alphabetical order. Lance Corporal William Amey of the 1/8th Battalion, The Royal Warwickshire (TF) Regiment (75th Brigade 25th Division) won his VC at Landrecies The divisional attack began in misty conditions, from the south of the town, with the 75th Brigade in the centre. The battalions involved, from left to right across the battlefield, were the 1/8th Worcesters, the 1/8th Royal Warwicks, the 1/5th Gloucesters and the 15th Lancashire Fusiliers of the 32nd Division. The centre of the brigade was held up by fire from the direction of Faubourg Soyeres, to the north-west of the centre of Landrecies. During the 1/8th's attack, Amey lost contact with his own company and attached himself to another. After fighting at a farm, Amey single-handedly attacked a strongly fortified château in Faubourg Soyeres, which was holding up the advance. When assistance did arrive, the enemy was overcome and the Royal Warwicks were then able to reach the lock on the Sambre–Oise Canal. They then found the main bridge had been destroyed, but they were able to cross the water by using a wooden bridge to the north. Other troops crossed the canal using the lock gates. By early afternoon the enemy was in full retreat from the town. The very informative citation for Amey's VC was published in the *London Gazette* on 31 January 1919 as follows:

For most conspicuous bravery on 4 Nov. 1918 during the attack on Landrecies, when owing to fog many hostile machine-gun nests were missed by the leading troops. On his own initiative he led his section against a machine-gun nest, under heavy fire, drove the garrison into a neighbouring farm, and finally captured about 50 prisoners and several machine-guns. Later, single-handed, and under heavy fire, he attacked a machine-gun post in a farmhouse, killed two of the garrison and drove the remainder into a cellar until assistance arrived. Subsequently, single-handed, he rushed a strongly held post, capturing 20 prisoners. He displayed throughout the day the highest degree of valour and determination.

The 1/8th Royal Warwicks continued their advance over the following two days, but took no further part in the fighting. A Special Order of the day, dated 25 January 1919 and written by Lt Col P.H. Whitehouse DSO, tells of Amey's role in the attack on Landrecies:

Throughout the day the conduct of Lance-Corpl. Amey, in the face of such opposition and danger, was of the highest type and beyond all praise. The work done by him not only resulted in clearing up a critical situation, but was instrumental in the saving of many lives.

Amey was decorated with his VC by the King at an investiture in the ballroom of Buckingham Palace on 22 February. He was one of six VC winners honoured that day.

William Amey was born in 3 Osborne Buildings, Mount Street, Duddeston, in the Nechells ward of Birmingham, on 5 March 1881. After leaving school he worked for Messrs Verdy Ltd. In May 1915 the family address was probably still in the Nechells ward of the City, which was then part of an industrial area and south of Aston Station. After the Second World War the area was redeveloped and now forms part of Showells and Robertson Gardens.

When William Amey enlisted in the 1/8th Royal Warwickshire Regiment in Birmingham, his service number was 307817. He was soon promoted to lance corporal, and before gaining his VC he also won the MM. His battalion served mainly on the Western Front in France but was transferred to the Italian theatre for ten months between November 1917 and September 1918.

Amey was demobilised in 1919, with the rank of corporal, and moved to Leamington Spa, where he remained for the rest of his life, working in business as an agent. In June 1920 he attended the Garden Party at Buckingham Palace for holders of the VC, and in November 1929 attended the House of Lords VC Dinner. In Leamington Spa, Amey became a prominent member of the local British Legion branch.

At the early age of 59 William Amey died at Warneford Hospital, Leamington, on 28 May 1940, and he was given a full military funeral. He was buried in All Saint's Cemetery three days later. His coffin was covered with a Union Jack and six soldiers acted as pall-bearers. The 'Last Post' and 'Reveille' were sounded at the graveside. Apart from members of the Amey family, mourners included the Mayor of Leamington and two holders of the VC, Arthur Hutt and Henry Tandey. The British Legion was also represented, as was the Coventry Branch of the Old Contemptibles Association.

After Amey died his VC passed to his widow, who later remarried, becoming Mrs Evelyn Maycock, but after her second husband's death she was left short of money and her first husband's decorations were the only objects of potential value which she possessed. On 29 July 1963 the medals were sold at Sothebys for £600 to the Friends of the Warwickshire Regiment. A few weeks later the Friends handed them over to the Royal Warwickshires Museum at a special ceremony on 20 September in St John's House, Warwick. Apart from the VC and MM, they included the BWM, VM and King George VI Coronation Medal (1937).

Eighteen years later, in May 1981, an exhibition was held in the Art Gallery, Leamington Spa, which was to commemorate the lives of the four holders of the Victoria Cross who had links with the Warwickshire town. They included Maj. Gen. Charles Goodfellow, Col John Barrett, Pte Henry Tandey and, of course, L. Cpl William Amey.

A special service to the memory of holders of the VC who had links with the Midlands and, in particular with Coventry and Warwickshire, was held in Lichfield Cathedral, Staffordshire, on 10 June 2007.

A. ARCHIBALD

Sambre–Oise Canal, near Ors,
France, 4 November

Sapper (Spr) Adam Archibald was one of the four sappers who were to win the VC in the Sambre–Oise Canal crossings at the beginning of November 1918, when it was already known to the Allies that the end of the war was only likely to be a few days away. Though the enemy had been forced to give up its hold on the city of Valenciennes, it didn't deter the German Army from trying to impede Allied progress as much as possible and to make a last-ditch stand on the Sambre–Oise Canal, which was part of a near 40-mile front. In most places in the Ors sector the canal was 70ft wide from bank to bank and 6–8ft deep, and the low ground to the side was like a swamp.

Archibald was a member of A/Maj. Waters' 218 Field Company, which was acting in support of the 96th Brigade, 32nd Division. On 4 November, to the immediate north-east of the village of Ors, and after the Allied artillery began to shell the German positions across the Sambre–Oise Canal in the early hours, these two engineers worked desperately to construct a bridge across the canal for the 2nd Manchesters to use. On the left of the Manchesters were the 16th (S) Lancashire Fusiliers (2nd Salfords) and to the right were the 1st Dorsets.

The sappers were to put together two cork-float footbridges for the canal, which, at the point of assault, was 35–50ft wide. Archibald and Waters, who were both to win the VC, were two of the few survivors of the German machine-gun and rifle fire. The enemy also used gas to deter the advance. The two men continued with their work despite a continuing hail of bullets, eventually restoring one of the bridges, which allowed two platoons of infantry to cross the canal before the makeshift bridge was destroyed. The remaining infantry-men and sappers withdrew to defensive positions in order to regroup, and later crossed at Ors over bridges made by another field company.

For their extreme gallantry, A/Maj. Waters and Spr Archibald gained the VC, and Archibald's was gazetted six weeks before Waters', on 6 January 1919, as follows:

> For most conspicuous bravery and self-sacrifice on 4 Nov. 1918, near Ors, when with a party building a floating bridge across the canal. He was foremost in the work under a very heavy artillery barrage and machine-gun fire. The latter was directed at him from a few yards' distance while he was working on the cork floats; nevertheless, he persevered in his task, and his example and efforts were such that the bridge, which was essential to the success of the operations, was very quickly completed. The supreme devotion to duty of this gallant sapper, who collapsed from gas-poisoning on completion of his work, was beyond all praise.

After this action, Archibald was sent to hospital in Le Havre in order to recover from gas poisoning. He was presented with his VC by the King in the Quadrangle of Buckingham Palace on 31 May 1919.

Adam Archibald, son of Rennie and Christina Anderson Archibald, was born in 53 Balfour Street, Leith, Midlothian, Scotland, on 14 January 1879. He attended Leith Walk Public School, Edinburgh, and on leaving he became apprenticed to a Leith plastering firm, prior to taking up a position with Stuart's Granolithic, Edinburgh. He con-tinued with his education at a local technical school and gained several trade certificates. He was a successful amateur gardener and an enthusi-astic bowler, and was also previously well known as a junior footballer, having had a couple of trial games for St Bernard's FC. At the age of 23 he married Margaret Lander Sinclair in Edinburgh on 6 June 1902. In time they were to have four children: three girls and a boy.

Archibald later became outside foreman at Stuart's Granolithic Works in Duff Street, Edinburgh. The family home was at first in 53 Balfour Street, Leith, but later they moved to 39 Hillhouse Road, Blackhall, Edinburgh. Under the Derby Scheme Archibald joined the Army, with the service number 213078, on 4 November 1915, initially serving with the 7th Durham Light Infantry before transferring to the Royal Engineers as a sapper. He went to Chatham for training on 10 November 1916 and left for France in September 1917.

In January 1919 he was still recovering from gas poisoning, but was well enough to return home three months later, on 17 April, when he was given an enthusiastic welcome in his hometown of Leith. Although he had been badly gassed, he still managed to serve in the Allied expedition to Archangel during the Russian Civil War before being discharged from the Army later in the year. He returned to his former employer, Stuart's, and he was presented with a cheque for £50. He later became manager in their Duff Street premises. He was present at the VC Garden Party in June 1920 at Buckingham Palace, and at the House of Lords VC Dinner in November 1929. He retired in the early 1940s, and attended the Victory Parade in London on 8 June 1946.

On 1 July 1946 Archibald took part in a large British Legion parade in King's Park, an historic parade ground in Edinburgh. A photograph was taken of him shaking hands with Gen. Sir Ian Hamilton, the 93-year-old president of the British Legion. The parade was attended by the King and Queen, together with their two daughters. There was a turn-out of 100,000 people for the parade, with 10,000 members of the British Legion drawn up on the parade ground in close columns, together with their banners, forming three sides of a square and marching past the royal party. A wreath was laid by the British Legion on the same day at the Castle Shrine, Edinburgh.

Archibald retired in February 1949 and was awarded a pension of £15 a month. Seven years later he attended the Hyde Park VC Centenary in June 1956.

At the age of 78 Adam Archibald died at his home in Leith on 10 or 11 March 1957, and was cremated at Warriston Crematorium three days later; his were ashes scattered in the Garden of Remembrance. In 1998 the Royal Engineers Museum in Gillingham acquired his decorations, which were added to those of the late Maj. Sir Arnold Waters VC.

Apart from his VC, Archibald was also awarded the BWM, VM, the King George VI Coronation Medal (1937) and Queen Elizabeth II Coronation Medal (1953).

The advantage of following in the footsteps of the 'Sapper VCs' gained during the operations to cross the Sambre–Oise Canal is that the area has not changed very much since 1918. These sites can, with the assistance of a good map, be identified quite easily. When it comes to researching Spr Archibald, it is obviously best to research his senior officer, A/Maj. Waters, at the same time.

To reach the area, if one is travelling from the direction of Cambrai on the N43, it would be advisable to take the D959 leading from Le Cateau–Cambresis and, when travelling through Eveque Wood, take the right turn to the village of Ors. As the road leaves the wood, it crosses a level-crossing and, just south of the bend in the Sambre–Oise Canal, is the site of Archibald's and Waters' heroic actions.

G. DE C.E. FINDLAY
South of Catillon, France, 4 November

The Battle of the Sambre, south of the enemy held village of Catillon, began on 4 November 1918 and, on what turned out to be a day of very high drama, no fewer than seven men gained the Victoria Cross. Not only did the operations have to get infantry and equipment across the Sambre–Oise Canal, but had to clear the enemy from the near bank first.

The attack against the section of the Sambre–Oise Canal, nearly 2 miles to the south of Catillon, was made by the 2nd Brigade of the 1st Division of IX Corps. Initially, engineers were to prepare the way for the infantry to cross the canal and ready made bridges were to be placed across the canal at its narrowest point.

Acting Major George Findlay, who already had a considerable military reputation as well as two MCs, was in command of 409 Lowland Field Company RE, together with an Australian tunnelling company under Capt. O.H. Woodward. They had four days in which to get ready for the operation, which included the task of preparing thirty bridges. They arrived in the area from the south, via the village of Mazinghien, and, just before reaching Rejet-de-Beaulieu, had turned off the main road and used a track leading to a suitable point about 300yd from Lock One of the canal, where they would unload their bridging materials. Company HQ was to be established to the southeast of the lock, which was north of the reservoirs which doubled the width of the canal.

During the preparations, essential reconnaissance operations had been carried out in order to obtain as many details of the positions at the lock as possible. This information assisted the sappers in calculating the exact measurements of the special bridges needed. Lock One was found to have a 17ft gap, for which twenty-three lightweight bridges were specially designed. Four more bridges of differing lengths were also made for use in crossing the various streams which ran parallel to the canal. Finally, two pack bridges for transport were also made ready.

Owing to the area being regularly swept by enemy artillery fire, several sappers became casualties. Another problem was that, unlike with some other sections of the canal, the enemy still held a few positions on the near bank which had to be dealt with as soon as possible. In particular were three enemy held buildings or strong points close to the canal bank. One of them was captured prior to the operation and the other two during the operation itself.

The night of 3/4 November was not only very dark, but also damp. Zero hour on the 4th was 5.45 a.m., when the assaulting troops, led by A/Lt Col D.G. Johnson and the 2nd Royal Sussex, were ready with 409 Field Company carrying the bridges behind them. On a misty morning the attack began with an Allied barrage. Enemy artillery soon responded, causing problems for the leading troops. In addition, Allied machine-gun barrages began firstly from the south and then the from the north. There were also problems with the length of some of the planks to be used for the crossing; even so, by 6.10 a.m. two bridges had been laid across the canal under heavy enemy fire.

Findlay was in charge of the sappers and, as a result of his very successful leadership, earned a well-deserved VC, which was gazetted on 15 May 1919 as follows:

For most conspicuous bravery and devotion to duty during the forcing of the Sambre–Oise Canal at the lock, two miles south of Catillon, on 4 Nov. 1918, when in charge of the bridging operations at this crossing. Major Findlay was with the leading bridging and assaulting parties which came under heavy fire while trying to cross the dyke between the forming-up line and the lock. The casualties were severe, and the advance was stopped. Nevertheless, under heavy and incessant fire he collected what men he could and repaired the bridges, in spite of heavy casualties in officers and other ranks. Although wounded,

Major Findlay continued his task and after two unsuccessful efforts, owing to his men being swept down, he eventually placed the bridge in position across the lock, and was the first man across, subsequently remaining at this post of danger till further work was completed. His cool and gallant behaviour inspired volunteers from different units at a critical time when men became casualties almost as soon as they joined him in the fire-swept zone, and it was due to Major Findlay's gallantry and devotion to duty that this most important crossing was effected.

Captain Woodward was a witness to this canal crossing and, at Zero plus fifteen minutes, he saw Findlay leading his men across the lock by simply jumping across the partly open lock gates. Once across, he stormed a German machine-gun post located in a boiler-house. Woodward described what he saw as a magnificent sight, although the cost in sapper casualties was high. Woodward then offered his assistance, which Findlay gladly accepted. It was not until 7.30 a.m. that Findlay considered it might be safe enough for the Australian tunnelling company to begin its task of putting a tank-bridge over the canal. Although bombardment continued, many of the machine-gun posts had been dealt with. Once the first girder was in position, the job became easier and the bridge was ready four-and-a-half hours after Zero hour. At 11 a.m., having succeeded, they were ordered to retire, so they collected up their casualties and took the dead back to the village cemetery at Rejet-de-Beaulieu. The enemy artillery had ceased fire, indicating that they had had to withdraw their guns in order to avoid capture. Apart from twenty-three wounded, the company lost ten men, including one officer.

Over a year later, Maj. Findlay was presented with his VC, and MC and bar by the King at an investiture at Buckingham Palace on 27 November 1919. It should be pointed out that he had been first recommended for a DSO rather than a VC.

George de Cardonnel Elmsall Findlay was the third of four sons of Robert Elmsall Findlay and Jane Cecelia Louise Findlay, and was born in Boturich, Balloch, Dunbartonshire, on 20 August 1889.

His father was a director of Findlay, Richardson & Co. East India Merchants in Glasgow. From the age of 3 George lived in Boturich Castle, one of several homes owned by his family. He attended school at St Ninian's preparatory school, where he became captain of football, before moving to North London and attending Harrow School where, in 1908, he won the Spencer Cup at Bisley, and the Silver Arrow, generally excelling at sport. After leaving Harrow he decided on an Army career and became a student of the RMA in Woolwich. On 10 January 1910 he was commissioned into the Royal Engineers and trained in Chatham. He was 20 years of age, and by then had reached a height of 6ft – it seems that the Findlays were quite tall as a family. He served first with the 5th Field Troop, and at one point broke both his legs in a riding accident, which resulted in ten months' sick leave. He was later appointed Assistant Adjutant for Musketry at Chatham. He trained recruits in musketry after the war began, but from February 1915 he worked for the next fifteen months on lines of communication. He arrived in France in March 1915 and, a year later, became a staff officer to the Chief Engineer of V Corps, from May 1916 to June 1917, when he became OC of 409 Lowland Field Company (TF), a position he held until September 1919. This field company provided engineers for the 1st Division.

As a result of his war service, Findlay was Mentioned in Despatches twice, on 9 April 1917 and on 16 March 1919. He also received the MC for his work during the Passchendaele Offensive in November 1917. In October 1918 he was awarded a bar to his MC for work which culminated in the taking of the Hindenburg Line (*London Gazette*, January 1919).

In June 1920 he attended the Buckingham Palace Garden Party for VC holders, and in November he was at the Cenotaph and at Westminster Abbey for the burial of the Unknown Warrior.

His favourite recreational activities were game- and rifle-shooting, together with riding and other outdoor pursuits. On his father's death he inherited Boturich Castle, which he later sold to a relative. Together with his widowed mother, he moved into Drumfork House on the edge of Helensburgh. After his mother's death, George remained living in the house.

In 1921, at the age of 42, Findlay married Dorothy Gordon, but the marriage was annulled shortly after. He was later appointed captain and adjutant of the 52nd (Lowland) Division engineers and, on 23 February 1926, he was promoted to major. He served in India and was unable to attend the House of Lords VC Dinner in November 1929. On 1 December 1933 he was promoted to lieutenant colonel while still serving in India. In the following year he returned to England on sick leave and was later appointed Commander of the Royal Engineer (CRE) Highland Area, with his HQ in Perth. He retired in 1938.

In March 1936 Findlay was fined £5 for driving in Richmond Park when the gates were closed, and for having a lapsed driving licence. He told the court that the fine was an enormous sum. On 1 August 1939 Findlay retired from the Army, but a few weeks later he was called back to serve as a temporary colonel from 1939 until 1940 as Chief Engineer Northern Ireland District. In 1941 he retired again, only to be called back once more, in 1943, and this time he served for three more years until 1946. During this time he worked with the Allied Military Government in Italy.

Back at home in Scotland, Findlay had been first elected to Dunbartonshire County Council as member for Cardross and Craigendoran in 1941, and thus automatically became a member of the Helensburgh District Council. He was also a prominent member of the local British Legion. From 1957 he was Deputy Lieutenant of the County of Dunbarton. In June 1956 he attended the VC Centenary Review at Hyde Park, and two years later attended the first dinner of the VC/GC Association at the Café Royal, London. He always attended as many VC functions as he was able. On 3 June 1959, much to everyone's surprise, Findlay married again, at the age of 70, to Miss Nellie Constance Barclay Clark at St Bride's Episcopal Church, Kelvinside, Glasgow.

Findlay had been a member of Dunbartonshire County Council for twenty-three years before his retirement in 1964, and with his engineering skills he was always in demand when inspections and decisions needed to be made regarding new roads, dams and housing schemes.

Findlay died at Drumfork House, at the age of 77, on 26 June 1967, and at his own request was given a private funeral at Kilmaranoch, Balloch, near Gartocharn, and was buried beside his brother, Charles, and sister, Cis. Three rough granite-grey crosses mark their graves. His wife, Constance, outlived him by nearly twenty-four years. After his death the local British Legion presented a bench in his memory, which was given a prominent site in the Hermitage Park Garden of Remembrance. At one time he had been president of the local branch and, later, life president. He also served on the County War Pensions Committee and took a keen interest in the Army Cadet Force. In his will he left £63,183 net, with estates in England and Scotland, and his decorations are with the Royal Engineers in Gillingham. Apart from the VC, MC and bar, they include the 1914–15 Star, BWM, VM (1914–19), MiD Oakleaf, 1939–45 Star, War Medal (1939–45), King George V Silver Jubilee (1935), King George VI Coronation Medal (1937) and Queen Elizabeth II Coronation Medal (1953).

D.G. JOHNSON
South of Catillon, France, 4 November

Acting Lieutenant Colonel D.G. Johnson of the South Wales Borderers was attached to and in command of the 2nd Royal Sussex of the 1st Division, and won his VC in the same action as Maj. Findlay of the Royal Engineers. He greatly assisted the sappers under the command of Maj. Findlay in their attempts to lay bridges across the Sambre–Oise Canal at Lock One, on 4 November 1918, to the south of Catillon. In particular, he was responsible for the lock house, one of three enemy held positions on the near side of the canal. The citation for his VC was published in the *London Gazette* on 6 January 1919 as follows:

For most conspicuous bravery and leadership during the forcing of the Sambre Canal on the 4th Nov. 1918. The 2nd Infantry Brigade, of which the 2nd Battn. Royal Sussex Regt. formed part, was ordered to cross by the lock south of Catillon. The position was strong, and before the bridge could be thrown a steep bank leading up to the lock and a waterway about 100 yards short of the canal had to be crossed. The assaulting platoons and bridging parties, Royal Engineers, on their arrival at the waterway were thrown into confusion by a heavy barrage and machine-gun fire, and heavy casualties were caused. At this moment Lieut.-Colonel Johnson arrived, and, realising the situation, at once collected men to man the bridges and assist the Royal Engineers, and personally led the assault. In spite of his efforts heavy enemy fire again broke up the assaulting and bridging parties. Without any hesitation, he again reorganised the platoons and bridging parties, and led them at the lock, this time succeeding in effecting a crossing, after which all went well. During all this time Lieut.-Colonel Johnson was under a very heavy fire, which, though it nearly decimated the assaulting columns, left him untouched. His conduct was a fine example of great valour, coolness and intrepidity, which, added to his splendid leadership and the offensive spirit that he had inspired in his battalion, were entirely responsible for the successful crossing.

Johnson was presented with his VC, together with a bar to his DSO and the MC, in the Quadrangle of Buckingham Palace on 14 June 1919. At the same investiture, Lt Robert Gorle and Lt James Johnson were also presented with their VCs.

Dudley Graham Johnson was born at Rockcliffe, Bourton-on-the-Water, Gloucestershire, on 13 February 1884, one of seven sons of Capt. William and Mrs Rosina Johnson. The family later moved a few miles to Fern Bank, Oddington, Moreton-in-Marsh. Captain Johnson was a member of the 6th (Inniskilling) Dragoons, while Rosina's father was Sir John Arnott, owner of *The Irish Times*.

Dudley Johnson was educated at Bradfield College (Army House) for three years between 1898 and 1901, and later joined the 3rd (Militia) Battalion Wiltshire Regiment in 1901, serving on St Helena and guarding Boer POWs. He later joined the Regular Army as an officer in the 2nd South Wales Borderers in July 1903, when he was just 19 years old.

In 1907 Johnson was made a full lieutenant, and was adjutant of the 2nd Battalion for three years from 1909 to 1912. Also in 1912, Johnson married Marjorie Grisewood at Daylesford, Stow-on-the-Wold, on 12 June. The couple were to have a son, Peter John Dudley, who was born the day before the First World War began. A daughter, Patience Mary, was born nearly three years later, on 6 April 1917, and a second daughter was born after the war.

On the outbreak of war in 1914, Johnson was serving with the 2nd Battalion at Tsingtau in China, where he gained his first DSO

(*London Gazette*, 12 March 1915). According to the *Regimental History*'s account of events in November 1914: 'Captain Johnson, who had already won general admiration by dashing and fearless work on patrol, also assisted several of the wounded.' He also served in Mauritius and Hong Kong.

In 1915 he was with the same battalion on the Gallipoli Peninsula, where he was wounded on 25 April. In the autumn of 1915 he was attached to the 11th (S) Battalion (2nd Gwent) as second in command. He then returned to service at home until 1916, during which time he became a brigade major. He served in France with the 19th Division, and later with the 1st Division as Deputy Assistant Adjutant General from 1917 until 1918. For the first quarter of 1918 he took command of the 1st Battalion, South Wales Borderers, then transferred to command the 2nd Battalion, Royal Sussex, in April and May, and from August to December. On 27 May he had been wounded, which interrupted his service. In September 1918 he gained a bar to his DSO for services near Pontruet in France (*London Gazette*, 6 January 1919), and, in addition to his two DSOs and VC, he also won the MC (*London Gazette*, 1 January 1918). After the war he was again commander of the 2nd Battalion, Royal Sussex, as part of the Army of Occupation in Germany. From 1919 to 1923 he was the Chief Instructor, Small Arms School in Hythe, Kent. He was later transferred to Netheravon as Chief Instructor of the Machine Gun School for two years 1926–28. In 1920 he attended the Buckingham Palace Garden Party on 26 June and the Cenotaph Ceremony and burial of the Unknown Warrior on 11 November, when he was a member of the VC Honour Guard. Nine years later he attended the House of Lords VC Dinner on 9 November 1929.

Between 1928 and 1932 he commanded the 2nd Battalion, North Staffordshire Regiment, and from 1933–36 commanded the 12th (Secunderabad) Infantry Brigade. Johnson was appointed Companion of the Order of Bath (CB) and held the position of ADC to King George VI from 10 September 1936 until 6 January 1939. Between 1936 and 1938 he was Commandant and Officer in charge of Records, Small Arms Corps. In 1938 he was appointed GOC 4th Division, Eastern Command. He served in France and Belgium, being present at the evacuation of the BEF from Dunkirk in May 1940. Later in the year he became GOC Aldershot Command until 1941, and Inspector of Infantry, 1941. On retirement he became colonel of the South Wales Borderers from 1944 until 1949.

After the Second World War ended, Johnson retired as a general officer and became a borough councillor in Fleet, Hampshire. He was also President of the Hampshire British Legion and took part in county rallies of the association. In June 1956 he attended the Hyde Park Review, and the initial meetings of the VC/GC Association. In 1973 he unveiled a VC memorial display at the South Wales Borderers' Museum, a dedication to which families of the VC holders were invited to attend.

During his lifetime it had been a tradition at Church Crookham war memorial, during Remembrance Day services, for him to have the honour of reading out the names of those who had fallen in both world wars and whose names were listed on the memorial.

Johnson died at the age of 91 at 2 Heathfield Court, Fleet, Hampshire, on 21 December 1975; he had previously lived at Orchard House, Church Crookham, Hampshire. Appropriately he was buried in Church Crookham churchyard on 29 December, in the same grave as his wife, Marjorie (1887–1950). The bearers who carried his coffin were senior NCO from the Royal Regiment of Wales, the regiment which had succeeded the South Wales Borderers. The church was full and the service was relayed on loudspeakers to mourners outside. Apart from his family, many local organisations with whom he had been connected sent representatives to attend the service. His son, Peter, who had become a lieutenant colonel, attended and his son bore his grandfather's decorations on a black velvet cushion. The 'Last Post' was sounded by a bugler of the Royal Regiment of Wales. In his will he left £31,169 net and his military decorations to the Royal Regiment of Wales.

At the beginning of February 1976 a memorial service was held to commemorate the life of Maj. Gen. D. Johnson in Brecon Cathedral, Powys, where he is commemorated in Havard Chapel, due to its links with the South Wales Borderers. He is commemorated at Crookham Church with a plaque, and a Johnson Prize was initiated at Church Crookham School. In addition, the Royal British Legion's General Johnson Flatlets were built in his name in Guildford, Surrey.

Johnson's unique military life and career is also commemorated in the Royal Sussex Museum, and at Lock One on the Sambre–Oise

Canal, where there is a memorial to his memory and to the men of the 2nd Royal Sussex Regiment who fell storming the lock in November 1918. It was placed there in the mid-1990s.

Apart from his VC, CB, DSO and Bar, and MC, his other medals and decorations included the Queen's Mediterranean Medal (1899–1902), 1914–15 Star, BWM, VM and MiD Oakleaf, 1939–45 Star, Defence Medal (1939–45), King George V Silver Jubilee Medal (1935), King George VI Coronation Medal (1937) and Queen Elizabeth II Coronation Medal (1953).

J. KIRK
North of Ors, France, 4 November

Ors is a village between Le Cateau and Landrecies on the Sambre–Oise Canal. On 1 November the village was cleared by the 6th Division, and the 2nd Manchesters arrived in the line on the night of 30/31 October. During the next evening they tried to clear the west bank of any enemy pockets. Three days later, 2/Lt James Kirk, a member of the 10th Battalion, Manchester Regiment (TF), attached to the 2nd Battalion (96th Brigade, 32nd Division), gained a posthumous VC on 4 November 1918, just south of the elbow in the canal, north of the village. His VC was one of seven gained in the crossings of the Sambre–Oise Canal on that day, and was gazetted on 6 January 1919 as follows:

For most conspicuous bravery and devotion to duty north of Ors on 4 Nov. 1918, whilst attempting to bridge the Oise Canal. To cover the bridging of the canal he took a Lewis-gun, and under intense machine-gun fire paddled across the canal in a raft, and at a range of 10 yards expended all his ammunition. Further ammunition was paddled across to him, and he continuously maintained covering fire for the bridging party from a most exposed position till killed at his gun. The supreme contempt for danger and magnificent self-sacrifice displayed by this gallant officer prevented many casualties and enabled two platoons to cross the bridge before it was destroyed.

218 Field Company, Royal Engineers, in support of the 96th Brigade, were to provide crossings for the infantry, but the task was extremely hazardous and the sappers were unable to carry out the task without the active support of the infantry, whose aim was to reach the eastern side of the canal. Repeated efforts were made to repair a bridge which had been built by two Royal Engineers who won VCs in the same action (A/Maj. Arnold Waters and Spr Adam Archibald), but work had to be abandoned and the remainder of the battalion sheltered as best it could on the western bank. Later, the 1st Dorsets sent word that it was now possible to cross the canal further southwards in Ors itself. Additional material concerning this part of Kirk's action was published in *The Victoria Cross 1856–1920*:

> ... he continued firing, covering the Royal Engineers in their task. He was wounded in the arm and the face, but still fired continuously from a most exposed position until he was shot through the head and fell dead ... It was a conscious death to save the men of his platoon and to inspire all who saw him with an example of most magnificent devotion.

Major General Lambert, commander of the 32nd Division, wrote to Kirk's father: 'The great victory which ended the war was due to the spirit which he gave his life to encourage, and which his regiment and the nation will, I hope, ever be proud to remember.'

Writing on behalf of his battalion, the OC, Lt Col Robertson, said the following:

> If we may be allowed, we would like to share the grief you feel in that he did not live to wear the Victoria Cross, and tell you how proud we all are that we had the honour of serving as comrades with such a soldier, and respect the glory and honour which he has brought to the battalion, an honour for which, I know, he if anyone would have gladly died to obtain. My sincere respects, sir, always.

Kirk was buried north-west of the village in the British corner of Ors Communal Cemetery (A22), in the same row as A/Lt Col John Marshall, attached to the 16th Lancashire Fusiliers, who also won a posthumous VC, and the poet Wilfred Owen, a fellow member of the 2nd Manchesters. News of their son's death reached Kirk's parents on Armistice Day and, nearly four months later, they were presented with their son's posthumous VC by the King in the ballroom of Buckingham Palace on 1 March 1919.

James Kirk was born at Willow Bank, Ladybrige Road, Adswood, Cheadle Hulme, Stockport, Cheshire, on 27 January 1897, the third child and second son of James and Rachel Kirk. His father was a jouurneyman dyer or salesman by trade. Young James was educated at Miss Chadwick's, Cheadle Hulme, and Brentnall Street, Stockport. He was well known as a sportsman in the Ashton area and played cricket and football, in particular for Seymour Old Boys' Association FC. After he left school he became a clerk in a warehouse owned by Messrs Ogden & Madeley in Manchester.

Two months after the war began he enlisted in the 2/6th Battalion (TF), Manchester Regiment, on 10 October 1914, where he trained at Southport prior to moving to Crowborough in East Sussex. He left for the Dardanelles on 2 August 1915 as one of the 200 replacements for the 1/6th Battalion. These replacements were thrown into the action and Kirk was present at the storming of Achi Baba in September. Two months later, he was evacuated from the peninsula with frostbite and spent six weeks in a Cairo hospital. By now he was a lance corporal.

After finishing his convalescence he became a member of the 1st Camel Transport Corps, and in January 1916 was promoted to QMS. He was to remain with the corps for just over a year, but in January 1917 returned to the 1/6th Manchester Battalion and went with them to France. In April 1917 he was made a sergeant, then in December he was recommended for a commission. After cadet training with the 17th Officer Cadet Battalion in Kinmel Park, Rhyl, and officer training from 18 February, he was made a second lieutenant with the 10th Manchesters and returned to France in October as a reinforcement or replacement officer with the 2nd Manchesters. This battalion was part of the 96th Infantry Brigade, 32nd Division, and, after a long march, they arrived on the west side of the Sambre–Oise Canal on the night of 30/31 October.

Kirk's home was at 530 Edge Lane, Droylsden, Manchester, which now displays a brass plaque to his memory, unveiled in October 1996. Outside the Manchester Regimental Museum in Ashton-under-Lyne is a plaque to eight Tameside holders of the VC, including Kirk, which was unveiled on 20 April 1995. His name is also remembered in the Manchester Regimental Chapel in Manchester Cathedral and on the Droylsden War Memorial. Kirk's VC is part of the collection of the Military Medal Museum in San Jose, California.

J.N. Marshall

North of Catillon, France, 4 November

Acting Lieutenant Colonel J.N. Marshall of the Irish Guards (Special Reserve), attached to the 16th Lancashire Fusiliers (96th Infantry Brigade, 32nd Division), gained a posthumous VC at the crossing of the Sambre–Oise Canal, about 1,500yd north-east of Ors on 4 November 1918. The final objective was the Guise–Landrecies road, though the official citation says that the action took place 'near Catillon', which is misleading.

Zero hour for the assault was 5.45 a.m., and the Allied barrage came down on the enemy held east bank of the canal as the 32nd Division moved up to the west bank. The 16th Lancashire Fusiliers, in the centre of the brigade, were to cross the canal over a bridge specially prepared by the Royal Engineers. The sappers had built the bridge of duck-boards and petrol cans, and a few men, mainly officers, began to use it to cross the canal despite extremely heavy German machine-gun fire. The bridge then broke loose, but was repaired, only for shell fire to break it up again.

Lieutenant Colonel Marshall, with total disregard for his personal safety, organised parties of volunteers to help repair it under appalling conditions, but during the operations he was was shot through the head, dying instantly. The citation for his posthumous VC was published on 13 February 1919 as follows:

For most conspicuous bravery, determination and leadership in the attack on the Sambre–Oise Canal, near Catillon, on the

4th Nov. 1918, when a partly constructed bridge came under concentrated fire and was broken before the advanced troops of his battalion could cross. Lieut.-Colonel Marshall at once went forward and organised parties to repair the bridge. The first party were soon killed or wounded, but by personal example he inspired his command, and volunteers were instantly forthcoming. Under intense fire and with complete disregard of his own safety, he stood on the bank encouraging his men and assisting in the work, and when the bridge was repaired attempted to rush across at the head of his battalion, and was killed by so doing. The passage of the canal was of vital importance, and the gallantry displayed by all ranks was largely due to the inspiring example set by Lieut.-Colonel Marshall.

One observer described the crossing as a complete failure, resulting in at least 100 casualties, without any real progress being made.

Marshall was buried in Ors Communal Cemetery, in a grave which is in line with A22. The headstones in Row A also include the graves of the poet Wilfred Owen and James Kirk VC. The inscription on Marshall's headstone reads: 'Splendid is death when thou fallest courageous leading the onslaught'. The majority of men buried in the Ors Communal Cemetery are from the 2nd Manchesters or the 16th Lancashire Fusiliers, who fell in the period 4–6 November. This simply emphasises the number of casualties suffered by the 32nd Division in the fighting for the canal. After Marshall's death, his former second in command, Harold C. Pemberton, wrote to Marshall's widow as follows:

I have been with the battalion but a short time, but in all my military experience I have never seen such a marvellous effect of one personality on a body of men. He came to the Battn. when it was practically disorganised owing to heavy casualties and during the few weeks he was with it he created an atmosphere of confidence and a Battn. of smiling, well-disciplined, and contented men. We would have followed him anywhere. Once again on behalf of his subordinates and comrades let me convey our deeply rooted sympathy.

The King presented Marshall's VC to his widow in the ballroom of Buckingham Palace on 30 April 1919.

James Neville Marshall was born at 2 Crosby Place, Steven Street, Stretford, Manchester, on 12 June 1887. He was the first of two boys in a family of six. His father was James Henry Marshall, who came from Fermanagh in Northern Ireland, and his mother was Mary Marshall (née Walmsley). The family moved to Acock's Green, Birmingham, in 1891, an area which has since been redeveloped. James Marshall junior (usually known as Neville) attended a private school before winning a scholarship to King Edward VI Grammar School, Camp Hill, where he was known by the nickname 'Bogey'. He remained there until March 1902 when he left, probably for financial reasons, needing to get a job to help with the family finances. He became a clerk at the Midland Institute and later worked in the Medical Faculty of Birmingham University. However, there is a gap in available information about Marshall's movements between 1904 and 1910.

On 27 May 1910 a tragedy occurred in the family when James Henry Marshall hanged himself at the age of 63. In the following year James Neville Marshall probably moved to Harlow, Essex, and, although he was not qualified, he set up as a veterinary worker, mainly working with horses, and became well known in equine circles. At first he lodged in Harlow itself, but in 1912 his address was Bromleys Farm, Latton, Harlow. On 20 September 1911 he had married Edith Maud Taylor, a young woman who shared his interest in horses. Her address at the time of his death was Lascelles Lodge, Matching Green, Harlow

In mid-September 1914 Marshall, who had friends in Belgium, was serving in the 1st Division of the Belgian Army, where he was attached to the 1st Regiment of the Field Artillery. During this time he was wounded several times and was subsequently discharged as medically unfit. By the end of the war, judging by his wound stripes, he had been wounded on at least ten occasions and four of those can be verified. In January 1915 he was decorated for his services. His time in the Belgian Army was followed by a long convalescence in England

and, when he had recovered, he volunteered for Army service, being commissioned in the Special Reserve, Irish Guards. He was a member of the 3rd (Reserve) Battalion, Irish Guards, from 8 December until 12 May 1916, and trained at Warley Barracks.

He was posted to the 1st Battalion and arrived in Belgium on 15 June, joining the battalion in positions close to Ypres. He was soon wounded and spent ten days out of the line. He was seriously wounded again on 14 July. He was sent home and was not fit for active service for seven months. On 1 January 1917 his first MC was gazetted for his work in Belgium. On 30 March he was back in France with the 2nd Battalion, Irish Guards, during which time his battalion spent time in the 1916 Somme battle area. In mid May 1917, during a visit to British troops, Marshall was decorated by the King of the Belgians.

On 25 May he was transferred as second in command of the 1/6th Lancashire Fusiliers (125th Brigade, 42nd (East Lancashire) Division), serving with them until 12 February 1918, latterly with the rank of major. From 6 May he was back with the Irish Guards, rejoining the 3rd Battalion until 31 May. The next day he was transferred to the 2nd Manchester Regiment until 11 October, when he was moved to the 16th Lancashire Fusiliers, being now a lieutenant colonel (Special Reserve).

It appears from his letters home that Marshall was becoming considerably depressed at the prospect of the war dragging on. He was also suffering from haemorrhages from his wounds. Nevertheless, the reason why he served with so many different battalions was probably because he was a strict disciplinarian who was very successful in bringing a battered battalion back into shape. One observer said that Marshall was used for 'stiffening' purposes.

On 17 December 1970 Marshall's decorations were presented by his sister, Mrs Dorothy Stevens, to the Irish Guards at their regimental headquarters in Wellington Barracks, London. Apart from the VC, the MC and bar, these included the BWM (1914–1920), VM, MiD Oakleaf, Belgian *Croix de Guerre,* and French Knight of the *Légion d'Honneur.* His memorial plaque was also included, and he had been Mentioned in Despatches three times. In his will Marshall left £303 3s 7d net. In the early 1970s Marshall's former adjutant, Lt Col G.A. Potts, recorded the events of the three weeks which led up to Marshall's death on 4 November 1918. Potts himself had returned to

France on 12 October, having recovered from a wound sustained six months before. He was posted to the 16th Lancashire Fusiliers, where Marshall took him on as adjutant.

It is probable that James Neville Marshall was not always what he claimed to be. Possibly because of the sheer strength of his personality and self-confidence, he might well have given the impression that he was, say, a qualified doctor or vet. He seems at different times in his life to have assumed responsibilities that he was certainly not qualified for. Before the war he practised as a vet, his Belgian citation addressed him as 'Doctor', and there was even mention of him possessing a science degree at one point.

What is absolutely certain, though, is that he was a wonderful soldier in terms of leadership and sheer courage, and a man who was 'bravest of the brave' and never shirked from 'leading from the front'. His death surely robbed the British Army of a senior officer who, at the very least, would have made a first-class brigadier.

Marshall's name is commemorated on the Memorial Cross in the grounds of St Mary's Church, Old Harlow, and again included on the Roll of Honour held in the church. He is remembered on the memorial at Old Harlow Baptists' Church. His name also appears on the Potter Street, Laton and Surrounding District Memorial Cross. In the Harlow War Memorial Institute is a billiard table with a brass memorial plaque to Marshall fixed to it. His name is also mentioned on a tablet in King Edward VI's School, Vicarage Road, Kings Heath, Birmingham.

A.H.S. WATERS
Near Ors, France, 4 November

In the attempts to cross the Sambre–Oise Canal at Ors on 4 November 1918, the sappers worked very closely with the infantry. Within the 96th Brigade area of the 32nd Division, 218 Field Company, under the command of A/Maj. Waters, was involved in the job of bridging a section of the canal to the north of Ors. The engineers managed to get two of their cork-float footbridges across the canal, with considerable assistance from Lt J. Kirk of the 2nd Manchesters. However, almost immediately, the bridges were destroyed by German artillery. Waters, ably assisted by Spr Adam Archibald, managed to restore one of them while under fire at point-blank range. The fire was so intense that it seemed impossible that the two men could escape with their lives. Many of the rest of the company were killed, wounded or gassed and, indeed, Archibald collapsed from the effects of gas as soon as his work was complete. However, despite these extremely brave attempts, the enemy fire was so intense that the 96th Brigade had to break off the assault and move back into Ors itself, where 206 Field Company had managed to put bridges across the canal. For their efforts, both Waters and Archibald were to be awarded the VC and, during the day, 218 Field Company won three DCMs and two MMs. Waters' VC was gazetted on 13 February 1919 as follows:

For most conspicuous bravery and devotion to duty on the 4th Nov. 1918, near Ors, when bridging with his Field Company the Oise–Sambre Canal. From the outset the task was under artillery and machine-gun fire at close range, the bridge being damaged and the building party suffering severe casualties. Major Waters, hearing that all his officers had been killed or wounded, at once went forward and personally supervised the completion of the bridge, working on cork-floats while under fire at point-blank range. So intense was the fire that it seemed impossible that he could escape being killed. The success of the operation was due entirely to his valour and example.

Waters was presented with his VC, DSO and MC by the King at Buckingham Palace on 15 March 1919.

Arnold Horace Santo Waters was the son of the Revd Richard Waters and Abigail Waters, and was born in Plymouth on 23 September 1886. He was one of four children, two boys and two girls. His father was a minister of the United Methodist Free Church and the family left Plymouth in about 1905. Arnold attended the Hoe Grammar School in Plymouth and, after finishing his schooling, he trained as an engineer at University Tutorial College, London. His first position was being articled to the Plymouth Borough Surveyor. He qualified in engineering in 1905 and worked with a contractor for four years.

He became a member of the staff of a Birmingham firm of consulting engineers, Messrs Wilcox and Raikes, in 1910 and prior to the war he was involved in work in the Rhymney Valley and Eastern Valleys in South Wales.

At the age of 28 Arnold Waters enlisted in the Reserve with 90 Field Company. On 30 January 1915 he was commissioned as a second lieutenant into the Royal Engineers. He was a member of 90 Field Company and was promoted to full lieutenant in 1917. He then became temporary captain, after which he transferred to 206 Field Company. When he became an acting major he transferred to 218 Field Company and then became honorary colonel with 127 Construction Regiment. He won an MC on 30 June 1917 for his work in destroying enemy wire near Nieuport, which was gazetted on 8 January 1918. He was transferred to 218 Field Company in the summer of 1917.

His DSO was gazetted in the Birthday Honours on 3 June 1918, and he was also Mentioned in Despatches in the same month. On receiving the news of Waters winning the VC, the Mayor of Plymouth moved that an illuminated address should be presented to the local hero. Waters had been recommended for a bar to his DSO, but the King, on seeing his record, cancelled the DSO and substituted the VC. After the war, Waters returned to engineering and, from the 1920s, was in business under the name of AHS Waters & Partners. The firm specialised in providing advice and guidance to local authorities in England and Wales on water supply and sewage disposal. Later, two of his sons also worked in the business. As an expert in his field, he was regularly called in as an expert witness at public inquiries.

In June 1920 he attended the Buckingham Palace VC Garden Party, and nine years later the House of Lords VC Dinner in November 1929.

In April 1922 he published an article in a British Legion journal under the title 'Why am I a Member of the Legion?' with the subtitle 'Rank Carries No Privilege or Distinction':

I am a member of the Legion because:

(1) It is the natural postwar organisation of men who went through the mill together, and whose comradeship now can still be useful as it then was indispensable.
(2) It helps to remind us, when we need the reminder, of those whose memory must live for ever.
(3) It is our own show, where every one of us can find plenty of opportunities for doing some useful service to another less fortunate than himself.
(4) It will be what we make it, and it is up to us together to make it the best thing possible.

Apart from his involvement with the British Legion, Waters, who was a very Christian man and a staunch Methodist, also worked hard throughout his life on behalf of people who had been disabled during the war. One of his posts, which he held for many years, was chairman of the Birmingham and Sutton Coldfield War Pensions Committee. In addition, he was president of the Birmingham and Midland Limbless Ex-Servicemen's Association and treasurer of the Boys' Brigade (Birmingham Battalion).

In 1924 Waters married Gladys E. Barriball, daughter of a Methodist minister. Another sapper VC holder, Cecil Knox, was his best man, the bridal car at the wedding was drawn by members of the British Legion. The couple were to have three sons.

In 1933–34 Waters was president of the Institute of Structural Engineers and, uniquely, held the position again from 1943–44. During the Second World War he was Divisional Food Officer for the West Midlands (1939–45). At the end of the war he prepared a report on the problem of restoration of the Midlands ironstone industry. He was chairman of the Planning Ministry's advisory committee on sand and gravel for seven years. In addition, he was chairman of the South Staffordshire Waterworks Co. (1946–59), deputy lieutenant for the County of Warwick and, in 1929, a Justice of the Peace (JP) and chairman of the magistrates for Sutton Coldfield. He was also a life governor of Birmingham University. In 1949 he was made a CBE, and he was knighted in 1954. In 1952 he was appointed honorary colonel of 127 Construction Regiment TA (later 48th Divisional Engineers) Volunteers until 1958. In June 1956 he attended the VC Centenary Review in Hyde Park.

Waters lived with his wife at St Winnow, Ladywood, Four Oaks, Sutton Coldfield, and, even in his nineties, although he had poor sight, was still tall and upright. On being questioned about his VC action on the banks of the Sambre–Oise Canal, he revealed to a friend that he was protected from the machine-gun fire by the bodies of the sapper and infantry casualties all around him. He died at his home in Four Oaks on 22 January 1981, leaving a widow and three sons. He was cremated in Sutton Coldfield Crematorium; his name is listed in the Book of Remembrance and his ashes are in the Garden of Remembrance, All Saint's Church, Streetly, Warwickshire. A memorial service was held to commemorate his life at Four Oaks Methodist Church, Sutton Coldfield, on 17 February. As can be seen from the above, Arnold Waters was a man of considerable public spirit, who throughout his life took his responsibilities very seriously.

Waters' awards were presented to the Royal Engineers Museum at Gillingham by his widow, Lady Waters, in the early 1980s. Apart from his VC, CBE, and DSO, they include his MC, 1914–15 Star, BWM, VM, MiD Oakleaf, King George VI Coronation Medal (1937), Queen Elizabeth II Coronation Medal (1953) and Queen Elizabeth II Silver Jubilee Medal (1977). A painting that depicts Archibald's and Waters' action on the Sambre–Oise Canal hangs in the same museum and prints of it are for sale. In 2018, a VC commemorative paving stone will be laid in Plymouth, the city of his birth. Other VCs linked with the city are John Crowe (1918) and Alfred Richards (1915).

B.M. CLOUTMAN
Quartes Bridge, France, 6 November

To the north of Ors, A/Maj. Brett Mackay Cloutman of 59 Field Company, Royal Engineers, won the last VC of the First World War on the Western Front during the crossing of the River Sambre, on 6 November, at Quartes Bridge, Pont-sur-Sambre. The single-span bridge on stone abutments stood in rural surroundings; close by was a cottage, a lock and another building. The aim was to save the bridge from being destroyed, so that it could be used by Allied infantry. The enemy had placed charges on their side of the bridge and the cottage contained several machine-gun posts. The enemy was also concealed along the riverbanks. Cloutman's VC was gazetted on 31 January 1919 as follows:

> After reconnoitring the river crossings, [he] found the Quartes Bridge almost intact, but prepared for demolition. Leaving his party under cover, he went forward alone, swam across the river, and having cut the 'leads' from the charges, returned the same way, despite the fact that the bridge and all approaches thereto were swept by enemy shells and machine-gun fire at close range. Although the bridge was blown up later in the day by other means, the abutments remained intact.

When Cloutman swam across the river he was seen from the cottage windows, and the enemy fired at the section of riverbank which they knew he had to return to. However, Cloutman still managed to get back without being hit.

Visiting Quartes Bridge today, it is hard to imagine anything of the fighting of nealry 100 years ago. The bridge has been repaired and re-sited, and now boasts a set of blue-painted railings, although the original stone abutments can be seen under the replacement bridge. Today's structure is probably several feet higher than the original one, and the building which gave shelter to the German snipers still exists. To reach the site it is best to use the minor road which leads eastwards out of the town.

Brett Mackay Cloutman was born in Marsden House, Colney Hatch Lane, Muswell Hill, North London, on 7 November 1891. He was the youngest of three sons of Alfred Benjamin Cloutman (a governor of Maple & Co.), and stepsons of Alicia Mary Cloutman of the Old Hall, Highgate. Their home was in the parish of St Pancras. Prior to living at this house, the Cloutman family resided at Hill Crest, Waverley Road, Crouch End, North London. Cloutman was educated at Berkhamsted School and Stanley House School, Margate. Later he went to Bishop's Stortford College and graduated from London University in 1912 with Honours (Modern Languages). He was made a BA in the following year. Between 1909 and 1912 he had been a member of the London University OTC (Royal Engineers' Contingent). Cloutman later worked for his father's furnishing company, Maple & Co.

Four weeks after the war began, 20-year-old Brett Cloutman joined the Army on 2 September 1914, enlisting in the 12th Battalion, County of London Regiment (The Rangers). Owing to weak eyesight he failed to obtain a commission. However, in March 1915 he was fortunate enough to be granted one in the Kent (Fortress) Royal Engineers, Gillingham. A few weeks later, on 2 July 1915, he was made acting captain and first went into action at Vimy Ridge in April–May 1917. From October to November in the same year, he was stationed in the Ypres Salient and was involved in the fighting for Passchendaele Ridge. At the end of 1917 he was sent to Italy with 59 Field Company, part of 5th Division, where he spent the winter serving with the Italian Army on the River Piave. However, in the spring of 1918 he returned to Nieppe Forest in Belgium and, in August and after the Battle of Amiens, took part in the advance of the Third Army to the Sambre. Five weeks before he won the VC in the last week of the war, Cloutman had also earned the MC for his bravery and leadership on 30 September on the former Cambrai battlefield. The citation read:

> For conspicuous gallantry and devotion to duty at Banteux on the morning of 30 Sept. 1918. He made a personal reconnaissance under heavy machine-gun fire to ascertain the possibility of bridging the Canal de l'Escaut.

Cloutman had an elder brother, Lt Wolfred Reeve Cloutman of 178 Tunnelling Company, Royal Engineers, who died as a result of poisonous fumes when he was attempting to rescue a sergeant trapped in some old trench workings near Albert on 21 August 1915. He managed to carry the NCO 45ft up the ladder, but was then so overcome by the fumes he fell back into the bottom of the shaft and died from gas poisoning.

Halfway through the war, Brett Cloutman married Margaret Hunter (always known as Peggy) at Chiswick on 17 February 1916. She was the daughter of Mr and Mrs Walter Hunter of Bedford Park, West London. The couple were to have two daughters, Mary and Jill.

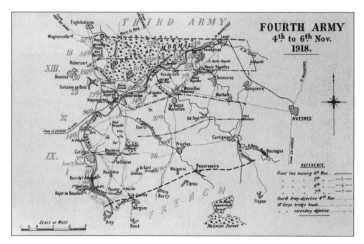

After his VC had been announced at the end of January 1919, Cloutman was presented with a handsome writing table from the directors and staff of Maples as a gift in recognition of his courage and bravery. He was presented with his VC at Buckingham Palace on 13 February 1919. Following demobilisation, he was placed on the Territorial Reserve of Officers.

After the Armistice he returned to the managerial staff of Maples, working in London and South America. In June 1920 he attended the Garden Party at Buckingham Palace, and in November 1929 the House of Lords VC Dinner. He decided to leave Maples in order to pursue a career in law, and, after he entered Gray's Inn as a student, was called to the Bar in 1926 when he joined the Western Circuit and built up a considerable practice. He frequently appeared in the North London Sessions. He was fluent in Spanish, French and German, the languages which he had studied at London University.

Cloutman served in the Second World War, when he was sent to Aldershot. Soon he was appointed second in command of 26 Field Company, which was reforming in Dumfries. He then served in Syria and later commanded the RE training depot in Egypt, before being appointed to serve as Chief Royal Engineer (CRE) in the Levant Engineer Battalion.

After the Second World War was over, Cloutman attended the Victory Parade in London in June 1946, and kept in close contact with the corps, especially with the 59th Field Squadron, later the 59th Independent Commando Squadron RE. At some point he set up a trust to provide funds for an engraved tankard to be presented to the most promising lance corporal of the squadron. It was to be presented every year on 6 November to commemorate Cloutman's VC. Should the trust be dissolved, then the funds would then pass to the RE Association (Corps Benevolence).

In 1946 he not only became a QC, but became a divorce commissioner. In 1947 he was Senior Chairman, War Pensions (Special Review) Tribunals, and Senior Official Referee of Supreme Court of Judicature from 1954–63. In June 1956 he attended the Hyde Park VC Centenary, and in 1957 he was knighted. In 1958 he attended the inaugural meeting of the VC/GC Association. He was also chairman of the Metropolitan Union of YMCAs and had been Master of the Glass-Sellers' Company. In addition, he was chairman of the Brotherhood of the Ferme Park Baptist Church and a governor of Eltham College. In 1970, a year before his death, he gifted his decorations and medals from both wars to the Royal Engineers. Also included in the gift were the war medals of his brother, Lt W.R. Cloutman. Apart from the VC and MC, Brett's decorations included the BWM, VM, 1939–45 Star, Africa Star, Italy Star, Defence Medal (1939–45), War Medal (1939–45), MiD Oakleaf, King George VI Coronation Medal (1937) and Queen Elizabeth II Coronation Medal (1953).

At the age of 79 Brett Cloutman died at his home at 2 Old Hall, Highgate Village, London, on 15 August 1971. After cremation at Golders Green, Hoop Lane, Barnet, on 17 August, his ashes were taken to France and placed on his brother's grave at Norfolk Cemetery, Albert, Plot I, Row A, Grave 14. His brother, Wolfred, had died on 17 August 1915 and Norfolk Cemetery had been established earlier that month.

Brett Cloutman is also remembered through his name being used by a troop of the Royal Engineers, and also with the name of a Barrack block in Gibraltar Barracks, Minley. On 7 April 2013, a plaque to the memory of the fourteen VC holders cremated in Golders Green Crematorium was unveiled, which included the name of Brett Cloutman.

SOURCES

The main sources used in the preparation of this book include the archives listed below, followed by additional material from other places, individuals, archives or obituaries:

The Lummis VC files at the National Army Museum, London
The Victoria Cross files at the Imperial War Museum, London
The National Archives (TNA), Kew, Surrey
Regimental Museums and Archives
The *London Gazette* 1914–1920 (HMSO)

Stand To! and *Bulletin* are journals published by the Western Front Association. The Victoria Cross Society also publishes a regular journal.

C.H. Frisby
Bailey, Roderick, *Forgotten Voices of the Victoria Cross* (Ebury Press, 2010)
James Brazier
Pearce, Sergeant L., *A History of the Coldstream Guards Victoria and George Cross Holders* (Regimental Headquarters Coldstream Guards, 1995)

Viscount Gort
'How Gort Won His VC' (*Sunday Graphic*, no date)
Sunday Dispatch (12 November 1939)
Victoria Cross Society Vol 19, October 2011, Field Marshal Gort VC, DSO, MC. Part 1: J.P. Lethbridge, pp. 36–40
Victoria Cross Society Vol 20, March 2012, Field Marshal Gort VC, DSO, MC. Part 2: War Looms, pp. 46–50

S.L. Honey
Canadian War Museum, Ontario
Department of Tourism & Information (Historical Branch, 15 July 1964)
Dictionary of Canadian Biography (online edition)
'First World War Hero Won the Victoria Cross' (no source, no date)

T.N. Jackson
Pearce, Sergeant L., *A History of the Coldstream Guards Victoria and George Cross Holders* (Regimental Headquarters Coldstream Guards, 1995)

G.F. Kerr
Canadian War Museum, Ontario

Dictionary of Canadian Biography (online edition)
Historical and Museums Branch (Ontario, 2 November 1973)

G.T. Lyall
'English Heroes' (*This England*, no date)
'A Strange Story Of The Desert' (*Eastern Daily Press*, 1 January 1973)
Victoria Cross Society, vol. 6, March 2005, pp. 36–8
Victoria Cross Society vol. 20, March 2012, pp. 35–40

T. Neely
Lindsay, Sidney, 'Merseyside Heroes' (unpublished manuscript)
Daily Post and *Mercury* (27 February 1920)

M.F. Gregg
Canadian War Museum, Ontario
Dictionary of Canadian Biography (online edition)
Hundevad, J., 'The Inspiring Career of Milton Gregg, V.C.' (*The Legionary*,
    October 1968)
Hundevad, J., *Veterans' Champion: The Inspiring Career of Canada's New
    Minister of Veterans' Affairs*
Melville, G., 'Atlantic gallantry – the Victoria Cross' (*The Atlantic Soldier*, April
    1996)
The Regimental Rogue
'Soldier, Statesman, Politician, VC Winner Milton Gregg Dies' (Robert England
    papers)

H. Tandey
'A legend under fire – Hero "couldn't have had Hitler in his sights"' (*Daily
    Mail*, 27 October 1997)
Chapman, Roger, *Beyond Their Duty: Heroes of the Green Howards* (The
    Green Howards Museum, Richmond, Yorkshire 2001), pp. 54–6
Hendry, A., 'Regrets of a British soldier just too kind to shoot Hitler' (*Express*,
    29 July 1997)
Ministry of Defence (Service Record)
Obituary of Mr H. Tandey VC, DCM, MM, in *The Iron Duke* (no date)
'V.C. Going To Trenches For Beer And Songs – Green Howards Reunion' (*Daily
    Telegraph*, 27 September 1963)
The Victoria Cross Society, vol. 2, March 2003, pp. 24–6

E. Seaman
J. Bevan

B.W. Vann
Mr J. Chilton
'Coates V.C. Hero Remembered By The Few' (*Gloucestershire Echo*, 18
    November 1975)
TNA WO 374/70397 Vann's service file
This England (winter 1992)
Stand To! No. 45, Jan 1996, 'War Memorials to Local Regiments in
    Nottinghamshire Churches' (Louis Ackroyd)
Mrs B.Vann

B.A. Wark
Dictionary of Australian Biography (online edition)
For Valour (no date)
Staunton, A., *Victoria Cross: Australia's Finest and The Battles They Fought* (Hardie Grant Books, Australia, 2005)

J. MacGregor
Spink Catalogue (6 November 1996)
Canadian War Museum, Ontario
Dictionary of Canadian Biography (online edition)

J. Crichton
Bryant, G., 'Private Defied Death To Help Platoon' (*Review*, November 1960)
National Archives, Wellington
The 79th News (January 1957)

R.V. Gorle
National Archives of Zimbabwe

W. Merrifield
Dictionary of Canadian Biography (online edition)
Canadian War Museum, Ontario

F.C. Riggs
Bournemouth Development Services
The Tiger & Rose (York and Lancaster Regiment, May 1953)

W.H. Johnson
Bulletin 94, November 2012, p. 23
'Worksop hero at last is honoured' (*Worksop Guardian*, 21 June 1991)
Robert Ilett

J. Maxwell
Victoria Cross Society Vol 16, March 2010, Page 40-41 Harry Willey-Joseph Maxwell VC, MC & Bar, DCM
'V.C. Paints Awesome Picture of War – Warns Youth of Propaganda' (no source, no date)

W.H. Coltman
'Joy B. Cave – A peaceable VC' (*Coin & Medal News*, no date)
'John Devonport – William Coltman' (*Gallery*, November 1991)
Victoria Cross Society, vol. 8, March 2006, pp 33–4

G.M. Ingram
'Queen Dedicates Shrine Before Silent 250,000 Crowd' (no source, end February 1954)
J. Towers
The Covenanter (Summer 1977)

J.H. Williams
'Mike Graham: Ebbw Vale remembers "Williams VC"'

C.N. Mitchell

Canadian War Museum, Ontario
Dictionary of Canadian Biography (online edition)
F.C. Swinnard, *Lt Col Coulson Norman Mitchell, V.C., M.C., R.C.E. (1899–1978)*

W.L. Algie

Dictionary of Canadian Biography (online edition)
Canadian War Museum, Ontario
Glendinings Catalogue (22 March 1995)

F. Lester

Lindsay, Sidney, 'Merseyside Heroes' (unpublished manuscript)
Graham Maddocks
Murphy, J., *Liverpool VCs* (Pen & Sword, Barnsley, 2008)

H.B. Wood

Gun Fire, no. 28: 'Reluctant Hero, Harry Blanshard Wood of York (and Bristol), a great War VC'

J. Johnson

Foulkes, Edward: *The Victoria Cross episode of 2nd Lieutenant James Johnson, 36th Bn., Northumberland Fusiliers on October 14 1918, opposite Lille* (typescript)
Stand To! No. 21, winter 1987, Edward Foulkes MBE, DCM, MM: 'A VC Episode'

J. McPhie

'Veterans see V.C. given to museum' (*Daily Telegraph*, 31 August 1966)
Bulletin 55, October 1999, pp. 28–31 'Peter Simkins: My Thirty-Five Years at the Imperial War Museum'
Napier, Gerald, *The Sapper VCs* (Stationery Office, 1998)

M. Moffatt

'5 V.C.s at Lourdes – Centenary recalls Peace Pilgrimage' (*Catholic Herald*, September 1934)
'Sad End of Sligo V.C.' (*British Legion Victory Souvenir*, Dublin, 1946)

J. O'Neill

'Interview With Walter Fliess, interned alien on *Dunera*, 1940' (IWM Department of Sound Records)

T. Ricketts

Canadian War Museum, Ontario
Dictionary of Canadian Biography (online edition)
Joy Cave
'Sergeant Thomas Ricketts, V.C.' (*Evening Telegram*, St John's, 13 February 1967)
'War heroes and their war-torn families' (*Evening Telegram*, St John's, 6 November 1989)
'V.C.s won by Newfoundlanders: Where are they now?' (*Sunday Telegram*, St John's, 6 August 1989)

The Victoria Cross Society, no. 4, March 2004, Terry Hissey: 'Sergeant Thomas Ricketts VC, 1901–67', pp. 3–4

H.A.Curtis
Cooper, Bryan, *The Tenth (Irish) Division in Gallipoli* (Herbert Jenkins Ltd, 1918)
Royal Dublin Fusiliers

R.E. Elcock
Geoffrey Noon
This England (no date)

J.B. Daykins
The Tiger & Rose (The York & Lancaster Regiment, no date)

A.R. Wilkinson
The Military Historical Society (November 1975)
Victoria Cross Society Vol 14, March 2009, pp. 32–6.

D.S. McGregor
Middleton-Heriot, D., *Heriot's! A Centenary History of George Heriot's School Former Pupils, Rugby Club* (Sportsprint Publishing, Edinburgh, 1990)

F.G. Miles
Victoria Cross Society, vol. 5, October 2004, p. 3
Victoria Cross Society, vol. 8, March 2006, p. 17

H. Greenwood
Express (30 April 1998)
Derek Hunt
The Military Historical Society (November 1975)
Observer (11 April 1997 and 16 January 1998)
Victoria Cross Society, vol. 2, March 2003, p. 23
Victoria Cross Society, vol. 4, March 2004, p. 61
'The Windsor Victoria Cross Exhibition: The Story of the Windsor VCs, 16th–31st May 1998' (souvenir programme)

F.W. Hedges
WO 95 2044 (TNA)
WO 339/32788 (TNA)

W.D. Bissett
Campbell, Revd A., *Crieff in the Great War* (T & A Constable, 1925)

N. Harvey
Lindsay, Sidney, 'Merseyside Heroes' (unpublished manuscript)

T. Caldwell
Hamilton, David, 'The hidden heroes of Carluke' (*Sunday Express*, 1 January 1995)
Victoria Cross Society, vol. 3, October 2003, p. 11

H. Cairns
Canadian War Museum, Ontario
Dictionary of Canadian Biography (online edition)
Esprit de Corps (November 1991, vol. 1, issue 6)
The Legionary (June 1936)
'The V.C. From Ashington' (*Newcastle Evening Chronicle*, November 1967)

J. Clarke
'V.C. Who Had Had No Breakfast' (no source, 30 March 1933)
John Byrne, John, 'VC winner is remembered with permanent memorial'
    (*Rochdale Observer*, 19 November 1994)

W. Amey
Monty Said: 'VC Priced Too Highly' (*Daily Mail*, 10 June 1963)

A. Archibald
B. Donald
Napier, Gerald, *The Sapper VCs* (The Stationery Office, 1998)
The Scotsman (1 July 1946)

G de C.E. Findlay
A.D. Blewett
Napier, Gerald, *The Sapper VCs* (The Stationery Office, 1998)
'O.H. Woodward – With the Tunnellers: An Officer's Narrative' (*Reveille*, 1 July
    1935)
R. Findlay

J. Kirk
Napier, Gerald, *The Sapper VCs* (The Stationery Office 1998)
Victoria Cross Society Vol. 19, October 2011, pp. 40–41

J. N. Marshall
Bailey, Roderick, *Forgotten Voices of the Victoria Cross* (Ebury Press, 2010)
'English Heroes' (*This England*, no date)
Graham, Arthur S., *James Neville Marshall VC, MC and Bar* (privately pub-
    lished 1998, corrections 1999)
Napier, Gerald, *The Sapper VCs* (The Stationery Office, 1998)
Tape recording made by Lt Col G.A. Potts IWM

A.H.S. Waters
Dr E.J. McCabe
G.U. Houghton, *Passing of an Era. Colonel Sir Arnold Waters, VC* (nd)
Napier, Gerald, *The Sapper VCs* (The Stationery Office, 1998)

B.M. Cloutman
Napier, Gerald, *The Sapper VCs* (The Stationery Office, 1998)
Royal Engineers Journal (no date)
Victoria Cross Society, vol. 12, March 2008, pp 38–42
Parker, Laurence V., 'A Bridge Over Troubled Water: Sir Brett Cloutman VC,
    MC, QC, KBE'

BIBLIOGRAPHY

The following list of published sources used in the preparation of this book does not include the many unit histories which were consulted.

Arthur, M., *Symbol of Courage: Men Behind the Medal*, (Pan, 2005)

Ashcroft, M., *Victoria Cross Heroes* (Revised edition, Headline/Review, 2007)

Australian Dictionary of Biography

Bailey, Roderick, *Forgotten Voices of the Victoria Cross* (Ebury Press, 2010)

Bancroft, J. W., *Devotion to Duty: Tributes to a Region's VC* (Aim High Publications, Manchester, 1990)

Bancroft, J.W., *The Victoria Cross Roll of Honour* (Aim High Productions, Manchester, 1989)

Bean, C. E. W., *The Official History of Australia in the War of 1914–1918*, Vol. 6, *The A. I. F. in France During the Allied Offensive 1918* (University of Queensland Press, 1983)

Brazier, K., *The Complete Victoria Cross: A Full Chronological Record of all Holders of Britain's Highest Award for Gallantry* (Pen & Sword, Barnsley, 20100

Canadian War Records, *Thirty Canadian VCs, 1918* (Skeffington, Canada, 1919)

Chapman, R., *Beyond Their Duty: Heroes of the Green Howards* (The Green Howards Museum, Richmond, Yorkshire 2001)

Clark, B., *The Victoria Cross: A Register of Awards to Irish-born Officers and Men* (The Irish Sword, 1986)

— *Deeds that Thrilled the Empire: True Stories of the Most Glorious Acts of Heroism of the Empire's Soldiers and Sailors during the Great War* (Hutchinson, London, no date)

De la Billiere, P., *Supreme Courage: Heroic Stories from 150 Years of the VC* (Abacus, 2005)

Denman, T., *Ireland's Unknown Soldiers: The 16th (Irish) Division in the Great War, 1914–1918* (Irish Academic Press, Dublin, 1992)

Doherty, R. & Truesdale, D., *Irish Winners of the Victoria Cross* (Four Courts Press, Dublin, 2000)

Edmonds, Sir J. E.(ed.) - *Military Operations France and Belgium.* Macmillan/ HMSO 1922- 1949

Gliddon, G. (ed), *VCs Handbook: The Western Front, 1914–1918* (Sutton Publishing, Stroud, 2005)

Harvey, D., *Monuments to Courage: Victoria Cross Headstones & Memorials* (D. Harvey, 1999)

James, E. A., *British Regiments, 1914–1918* (Samson Books, 1978)

Kelleher, J.P. (comp.), *'Elegant Extracts :The Royal Fusiliers Recipients of The Victoria Cross 'For Valour'* (The Royal Fusiliers Association, London, 2010)

The King' s Regiment 8th, 63rd, 96th: For Valour (Fleur de Lys Publishing, Cheshire, no date)

Lindsay, Sidney, *Merseyside Heroes* (unpublished manuscript)

The London Gazette, 1916–1920

McCrery, N., *For Conspicuous Gallantry: A Brief History of the Recipients of the Victoria Cross from Nottinghamshire and Derbyshire* (J. H. Hall & Sons, Derby, 1990)

Montgomery, Sir A., *The Story of the Fourth Army in the Battles of the Hundred Days, August 8th to November 11th 1918* (Hodder & Staughton, 1920)

Murphy, James, *Liverpool VCs* (Pen & Sword Military, Barnsley, 2008)

Napier, G., *The Sapper VCs: The Story of Valour in the Royal Engineers and its Associated Corps* (The Stationery Office, London, 1998)

Nicholson, G. W. L. N., *Canadian Expeditionary Force, 1914–1919* (Queen's Printer, Ottawa, 1962)

O'Moore Creagh, General Sir, Humphris E.M., & Miss, E., *The VC and DSO,* Vol. 1 (1924)

Pillinger, D. & Staunton, A., *Victoria Cross Presentations and Locations* (D. Pillinger & A. Staunton, Maidenhead, 2000)

The Register of the Victoria Cross (This England Books, 1988)

Ross, Graham, *Scotland's Forgotten Valour* (Maclean Press, 1995)

Shannon, S. D., *Beyond Praise: The Durham Light Infantrymen who were Awarded the Victoria Cross* (County Durham Books, Durham, 1998)

Smith, M., *Award for Valour: A History of the Victoria Cross and the Evolution of British Heroism* (Palgrave Macmillan, 2008)

Smyth, Sir John VC, *The Story of the Victoria Cross* (Frederick Muller, 1963)

Staunton, A., *Victoria Cross: Australia's Finest and the Battles they fought.* (Hardie Grant Books, Victoria, 2005)

Wigmore, L. & Harding, B., *They Dared Mightily* (Second Edition revised by Williams, J. & Staunton, S., Australian War Memorial, Canberra, 1986)

Williams, W. Alister, *Heart of a Dragon: The VCs of Wales and the Welsh Regiments, 1914–1982* (New Edition Bridge Books, Wrexham, 2008)

INDEX